Tiefer, originally trained as a physiological psychologist, has written "A Feminist Perspective on Sexology and Sexuality." The work includes European writers such as John Shotter of Nottingham University, Joan Meyer of the University of Amsterdam, and Verena Aebischer of the University of Paris, Nanterre.

These essays offer challenging new ways to do scholarly work, approaches that rely less on power, domination, and right, and more on open dialogue. With enthusiasm, wit, and courage, these writers present an exciting new understanding of the structure of knowledge and feminist scholarship.

MARY McCANNEY GERGEN is a feminist scholar who teaches psychology at Pennsylvania State University on Philadelphia's Delaware County campus. She is coauthor of *Social Psychology* and coeditor of *Historical Social Psychology* (both with Kenneth Gergen).

FEMINIST THOUGHT
AND THE STRUCTURE OF KNOWLEDGE

FEMINIST THOUGHT AND THE STRUCTURE OF KNOWLEDGE

EDITED BY
MARY McCANNEY GERGEN

NEW YORK UNIVERSITY PRESS
NEW YORK AND LONDON

© 1988 by New York University
All rights reserved
Manufactured in the United States of America

Library of Congress Cataloging-in-Publication Data

Feminist thought and the structure of knowledge / edited by Mary
McCanney Gergen.
p.   cm.
Includes bibliographies and index.
ISBN 0–8147–3013–2 (alk. paper)
1. Feminism—Philosophy.   2. Women scholars.   3. Knowledge, Theory
of.   I. Gergen, Mary M.
HQ1154.F448 1988
305.4′2′01—dc19   87–33980
                                                                CIP

New York University Press books are Smyth-sewn
and printed on permanent and durable acid-free paper.

To Ken with love

Contents

THROUGHOUT the twentieth century, feminist ideas have been primarily associated with political action in everyday life. The seminal ideals of feminism have traditionally focused on ways to affect conditions in society so that the mantle of oppression may be cast off and women may become free and equal agents. As a result of probing into existing social orders, construing what is and what might be, feminists have created a growing body of challenging ideas. As these ideas have become elaborated and assessed there has emerged a formidable assemblage of feminist scholarship. It is a corpus of writing that now encompasses virtually every domain of academic inquiry. From its beginnings in political action, feminist pursuits have now begun to enrich and alter the structure of knowledge.

Despite the creation of new metatheories, theories, and methods, the impact of feminism in scholarly circles has yet to realize its full potential. In many cases, established academicians have given little notice to such developments. Feminists have described the many difficulties in formulating critical and constructive accounts, chief among them that the means of formal communication are shaped by patriarchal systems for patriarchal purposes.

I have been deeply impressed and encouraged by the work of those feminists who have persisted in the creation of new languages, perspectives, and solutions to the problems raised by the domination of patriarchal systems. I have also become enthralled by the potential inherent in

drawing the various threads of feminist thought together and making
them available to practitioners in various disciplines. I have imagined the
impact on various institutions, especially academic ones, if the voices of
feminism might be raised in unison. I have envisioned the power for
transformation that one clear song of feminism might some day hold.

The image of feminist revisions of social forms, especially within the
academy, has been shared by many feminists. A thriving literature attests
to the involvement of feminists in transforming scholarly fields. But each
approach is shaped by orienting goals. As the editor of this book my goal
was to draw attention to the ways in which existing and emerging feminist ideas could be applied to contemporary disciplines of learning. Within
this context, I invited a number of feminist scholars to address this issue.
An immediate goal of this project was to encourage those active within
various disciplines to present ways in which their colleagues and peers
might alter their processes of scholarship along feminist lines. A long-
term goal is the implementation of paradigmatic shifts congenial to feminist thought within the community of scholars.

Many barriers stand between this vision of transformation and the
alteration of actual practices. Feminists would be the first to acknowledge
that social change does not occur simply because an idea for change is a
good one. But many lines of influence may create multiple reverberations
in social systems, and small changes in one system may create larger ones
elsewhere. There seemed ample reason to proceed.

In keeping with this spirit, an adventuresome group of feminist scholars
agreed to share, with each other and a community of interested people,
their views on how their feminist perspectives and practices might challenge and change their disciplines. The conference that ensued, entitled
"Feminist Thought and the Structure of Knowledge," was held in April
1986 at the Delaware County campus of Penn State University. Con-
jointly with this conference a book was planned to focus on the central
theme of the meetings. All invited speakers were asked to contribute to
this volume. Following this invitation, twelve chapters were created. The
range of subject matter is fairly broad, as the authors' disciplines of origin
include anthropology, biology, philosophy, psychology, sexology, and
sociology. European perspectives are offered in chapters by authors from
England, France, and the Netherlands. The chapters stand as a powerful
tribute to the rich and challenging character of feminist thought. Yet most

of these statements are personal as well as professional and political. It is clear that for most participants, feminist thought goes far beyond the academy in its implications. Its goals demand large scale social transformation.

The opening chapter is Ruth Hubbard's contribution, "Some Thoughts about the Masculinity of the Natural Sciences." The natural sciences may be considered the final sanctuary of male-dominated scholarship, and few observers dare to tread heavily in these hallowed halls. Hubbard's long association with other members of the inner sanctum has enlightened her and perhaps encouraged her shrewd analysis. She discusses how the natural sciences have been shielded from outsider opinions and have become a resource exclusively produced and shared among the elite of society. She clarifies the problems associated with so-called objectivity in the natural sciences and calls for an opening of these sciences to others now excluded.

Leonore Tiefer's chapter, "A Feminist Perspective on Sexology and Sexuality," shares Hubbard's concerns with the ideological influences over so-called objective knowledge. Sexology is an ideal discipline to analyze if one wishes to expose the politics of scholarship. The allocations of resources, the censorship of subject matter and methods, and the imposition of paternalistic values and social goals have all fostered a science that is deeply constrained by male-dominated forces. Tiefer proposes a new version of the science that emphasizes the social construction of sexuality and uses methods of research appropriate to this conceptualization. She asserts that women should become beneficiaries of the research enterprise, not victims to professionalism within the field.

Kenneth Gergen's chapter, "Feminist Critique of Science and the Challenge of Social Epistemology," looks at the relationship of various feminist critiques of science to developments in recent philosophical inquiry. He summarizes the thrust of the arguments against empiricist philosophy and scientific practices. In addition, he examines the epistemological bases for various feminist perspectives and questions whether these "successor science projects" are not still incorporating features of the rejected empiricist models. Along with Hubbard and Tiefer, Kenneth Gergen supports a postmodernist feminism that emphasizes the centrality of discourse communities in the social construction of reality.

In her chapter, "The Reproduction of Patriarchy in Feminist Anthropology," Peggy Sanday explores feminist issues within the practices of anthropology. Sanday contrasts anthropological work that emphasizes the dominance of patriarchy in world cultures with that of investigators, like herself, who question this as a universal principle. Using as a contrast to her views the work of Michelle Rosaldo and Simone de Beauvoir, she analyzes the social and intellectual origins of the thought structures that give rise to these two positions regarding the status of women in society. She struggles with questions of how one might transcend these social and intellectual limitations. Sanday concludes with an illustration of how anthropological fieldwork might be altered through a process of dialogue wherein the anthropologist and the subjects of inquiry meet and are mutually changed by the encounter.

Concern with patriarchal structure is also emphasized in John Shotter and Josephine Logan's chapter, "The Pervasiveness of Patriarchy: On Finding a Different Voice." The authors stress a dominant theme within the volume more generally: the difficulty of developing a feminist perspective that is not tainted by androcentric influences. They stress how difficult it is for any scholar to speak in a voice that has not been modulated by male supremacy. They argue that feminist practices do not yet exist as a distinctive and comprehensive mode of thought and action. They encourage a rejection of the Cartesian model of mastery and possession and the development of a model that stresses joint actions, nurturance, and communal ties to those around us and to those who have preceded us.

Attempts to transcend the boundaries of androcentric procedure are widely extant. In my own chapter, "Toward a Feminist Metatheory and Methodology in the Social Sciences," I first detail how traditional research methods have violated many tenets of feminist belief. A major focus of the critique is on the status of "objectivity" in social science research methodology. In addition, I illustrate how a methodology formulated within a feminist framework might be used within the social science arena. Using a study developed around the concerns of women in their forties, I show how one might carry out "emancipatory" research, inquiry that is contextualized, participatory, and action-oriented.

Joan Meyer's contribution, "Feminist Thought and Social Psychology," also criticizes socio-psychological research for its narrow scope and artificial methods. She illustrates how using quantitative means to express relations between the sexes, for example, disguises rather than clarifies the complexity of the issues. Her views emphasize the necessity for accepting the ambiguities and multiplicities of people's psychological states. Meyer describes studies by her colleagues and herself that derive from feminist metatheory. She especially emphasizes the importance of: the material and normative contexts of the research; the subjective responses of research participants; and the social consequences of the research.

The tension between traditional empiricist and feminist research strategies is confronted headlong in Rhoda Unger's chapter, "Psychological, Feminist, and Personal Epistemology: Transcending Contradiction." Here she shares her ambivalent feelings about traditional psychological methods and her burgeoning beliefs in social constructionism. While her paper begins with a critique of empirical investigations, it ends with an effort at reconciliation. Unger also expands on the problems of the "double-bind" experienced by women who get trapped in social situations, particularly in the "man's world," where role violations lead to punishment regardless of conduct. Her chapter demonstrates a version of this dilemma in her own efforts to combine social constructionism and empiricism.

In her chapter, "Knowledge as a Result of Conflicting Intergroup Relations," Verena Aebischer emphasizes the recent reevaluation that feminist issues have undergone in French intellectual circles. Evolving from interest only in abstract political issues to concern with personal aspects of people's lives, French intellectuals have become increasingly involved with topics once considered too personal, private, and inconsequential for scholarly concern. "Women's talk" is a prime example. Aebischer argues that feminists have played a major role in liberating knowledge from its previous captivity. She also illustrates with examples from her own work how research procedures also have been changed by feminist views.

Aebischer's emphasis on research domains that are uniquely feminine is echoed in the chapter by Polly Young-Eisendrath, "The Female Person and How We Talk about Her." This chapter is chiefly concerned with the ways in which women's views of themselves are limited by existing cultural assumptions. Young-Eisendrath's interest in the development of women's self-concepts is an outgrowth of her experiences as a psychotherapist and educator. She argues that because one's experience of self is dependent on the culture for its creation, one is vulnerable to implicit cultural evaluations. She contends that women must assert themselves in order to overcome the model of inadequacy developed within a male-dominated society. She stresses the need to reevaluate the meaning of various "feminine" qualities such as dependency and concern with physi-

cal appearance beyond the confines of androcentric language and evaluation.

In her chapter, "Women, History, and Practical Deliberation," Emily
Grosholz employs a feminist perspective to examine historical scholarship.
She emphasizes the need to use practical deliberation as the chief method
for structuring the past. Grosholz defines practical deliberation as the
"dialectical assessment of the moral significance of actions as we try to
decide what to do next." Grosholz believes that deliberations "have the
power to change the meaning of past events, and so how they bear upon
the present and the future." She also acknowledges the need to maintain
"open negotiations" concerning the construction of reality and to avoid
"murderous" encounters, since the opponents in the construction of his-
tories are often men and women who love each other and live together.

In the concluding chapter, "Impasse in Feminist Thought?"
J. G. Morawski celebrates the new enthusiasm for feminist scholarship.
At the same time she issues a warning that many difficult problems lie
barely beneath the surface of triumph. Particularly problematic are issues
related to political repression, reliance on personal experience to validate
feminist views, theory construction, disciplinary boundary rules, and linguistic practices. Morawski sees a dual process of deconstruction and
reconstruction as necessary for solving these various problems. The feminist imagination, which is central to feminist thought, will be the source
of an envisioned new world.

How far have we traveled along the path to a new world transformed
by feminist ideals? Not far enough surely, but definitely in the right
direction. While perhaps we should be wary of celebrating our new
successes, as Morawski suggests, we might still rejoice that much has been
accomplished. I find many harmonious tones in the chapters that have
been collected here. Certainly these provide a common base for the
ongoing phase of transformation: altering the nature of existing disciplines. Overall, these chapters stress the need to relinquish "objectivity"
as practiced today, especially in the sciences. They also generally agree
that the knowledge of any phenomena depends on interpretation, as
contextualized in a social and material world. Attention to the ways that
power is distributed and the ways that hierarchies of authority determine
social reality is central to most authors. Each chapter also acknowledges
that values are inevitably incorporated into the procedures of any discipline. The importance of viewing reality as socially constructed is explicit

in most chapters. Often the themes of ambiguity and multiplicity of views are also expressed. The dichotomy of truth versus falsehoods is not seen as a feminist idea. Overall the chapters seem effervescent with enthusiasm for new ways of doing scholarly work, ways that rely less on power, domination, and right, and more on open dialogue, imbued with expression of values and feelings and with self-reflexivity.

While none of these chapters gives a blueprint of how the next several decades should proceed within academic communities, each one provides a stimulus for the reconstruction of many scholarly endeavors. How this view is translated into practice is open to question. It will require the development of inspired activities, which will also provide guidelines for others who wish to travel this path. There are no definitive signposts that clearly point the way, but with many actors jointly endeavoring to create new vistas, new forms of knowledge, creation may well emerge. What is required of feminist scholars is perseverance, courage, and wit.

This book is based on a collaborative effort of those who spoke and those who listened at the conference, those participating in the broader dialogue of which this conference is but a manifestation, and those who specifically planned and developed the event. I especially want to recognize campus executive officers John Vairo, who created the Faculty Colloquium series, and Edward Tomeszko, who continues to give it support, and those staff members of Penn State University who helped me to organize and run the 1986 colloquium. I hope the readers of this volume will be as appreciative of these efforts as I have been. Financial support from various departments of Penn State University, Pennsylvania Humanities Council, Boeing Corporation, and Wawa Dairies also enabled this project to proceed. My special thanks go to my editor, Kitty Moore of New York University Press, whose enthusiasm for the work has been inspirational. She helped at every turn to make this book a reality. I wish to thank Despina Gimbel of New York University Press for her dedication as well.

Lastly I wish to thank Kenneth Gergen for his involvement and support, especially during the process of making this book. His intellectual perspective has been a vital force in the development of our feminist views.

Contributors

VERENA AEBISCHER is an assistant professor at the Paris-X University, Nanterre. She also works with the European Community in Brussels on a research project on equal opportunities for girls and boys. She is coeditor of several books on language and sex and the author of *Les femmes et le langage: Representations sociales d'une différence*. (Women and Language: Social Representations of a Difference).

KENNETH J. GERGEN is professor of psychology at Swarthmore College. He is the author of several books, including *Toward Transformation in Social Knowledge*. After receiving his Ph.D. from Duke University, Dr. Gergen taught at Harvard University.

MARY M. GERGEN is an assistant professor at Penn State University, Delaware County campus. She received her Ph.D. from Temple University in psychology, with a special concentration in social psychology. Previously she has worked in research capacities at Swarthmore College and Harvard University. She is the coauthor of *Historical Social Psychology* with Kenneth Gergen.

EMILY GROSHOLZ teaches philosophy at Penn State University. Her essays and reviews have appeared in various scholarly and literary journals. An advisory editor for *The Hudson Review*, she was recently a Fellow at the National Humanities Center.

RUTH HUBBARD is a professor of biology at Harvard University and teaches courses on the interactions of science and society, particularly as they affect women. She has written articles for professional and general publications and has edited several books.

JOSEPHINE LOGAN graduated from Trent Polytechnic in Nottingham, England in 1985 with a first class honors degree in communication studies. She is currently doing research into privatism for a Ph.D. at the University of Nottingham. She has already published a number of papers on female insecurity, the mass media, discourse analysis, the therapeutic relationship, and privatism.

JOAN MEYER, an active feminist in the Netherlands for nearly twenty years, was a member of the National Advisory Council for Emancipation and wrote the first national report on the situation of women in the Netherlands in 1977. She is currently employed by the departments of social psychology and psychology of labor and organizations of the University of Amsterdam.

J. G. MORAWSKI is associate professor of psychology at Wesleyan University, Middletown, Conn. Her contribution to this volume is one facet of a larger ongoing exploration into how knowledge is organized, warranted, and shared. Her research involves historical, social, and philosophical analyses of our "legitimated" knowledge of the social world.

PEGGY REEVES SANDAY is professor of anthropology at the University of Pennsylvania. She is the author of several books and articles and has edited others. At present she is completing a book on sexual meanings and sexual expression on an American college campus. For the past several years she has been conducting a study of gender meanings and world view in West Sumatra, Indonesia.

JOHN SHOTTER has published papers on the computer simulation of language acquisition, mother-infant interaction, and social psychology theory. He is the author of several books. He currently holds a chair in general social science at the University of Utrecht, the Netherlands. He was previously a reader in social psychology at the University of Nottingham, England.

LEONORE TIEFER originally trained as a physiological psychologist at the University of California, Berkeley, has in recent years taken a more clinical and social approach. Actively involved in sexology research and practice, she uses feminist analysis for critique and the generation of alternate models.

RHODA K. UNGER is a professor of psychology and director of the honors program at Montclair State College. She is the author and/or editor of five books on various aspects of women and gender as well as numerous research publications. She is past president of the division of the psychology of women of the APA, the recipient of the first Carolyn Wood Sherif Award from that organization, and has been twice the recipient of a distinguished publication award from the Association for Women in Psychology.

POLLY YOUNG-EISENDRATH is a Jungian analyst, Chief Psychologist at Clinical Associates West in Bala Cynwyd, Pa., where she practices psychotherapy and analysis, and guest lecturer in human development at Bryn Mawr College. Previously, she was on the faculty of the Graduate School of Social Work and Social Research at Bryn Mawr. She is the author and coauthor of several books, has written numerous journal articles, and lectures extensively on feminism, developmental psychology, and Jung's psychology.

FEMINIST THOUGHT
AND THE STRUCTURE OF KNOWLEDGE

ONE

Some Thoughts about the Masculinity
of the Natural Sciences

Ruth Hubbard

THE FACTS OF SCIENCE

THE BRAZILIAN educator Paulo Freire has pointed out that people who want to understand the role of politics in shaping education must "see the reasons behind the facts" (Freire 1985, p. 2). I want to begin by exploring some of the reasons behind a particular kind of facts, the facts of natural science.

Ever since I began to think critically about science and about my own activities as a scientist, I have been fascinated by "facts," what they are, and how they get to be. After all, facts aren't just out there. Every fact has a factor, a maker. The interesting question is: as people move through the world, how do we sort those aspects of it that we permit to become facts from those that we relegate to being fiction—untrue, imagined, or imaginary, so-called figments of the imagination—and from those that, worse yet, we do not even notice and that therefore do not become fact, fiction, or figment? In other words, what criteria and mechanisms of selection do people use in the making of facts?

One thing is clear: making facts is a social enterprise. Individuals cannot just go off by themselves and come up with their own brand of facts.

When people do that and the rest of us do not agree to accept or share the facts they offer us as descriptions of the world, they are considered schizophrenic, crazy. If we do agree, either because their facts sufficiently resemble ours or because they have the power to force us to accept their facts as real and true—to make us see the emperor's new clothes—then the new facts become part of our shared reality and their making, part of the fact-making enterprise.

Making science is such an enterprise. As scientists, we must follow certain rules of membership and go about our task of fact making in professionally sanctioned ways. We must submit new facts to review by our colleagues; we must be willing to share them with strangers by writing and speaking about them (unless we work for private companies with proprietary interests, in which case we must still be willing to share our facts, but only with particular people). If we follow proper procedure, we become accredited fact makers. In that case our facts come to be accepted on faith and large numbers of people believe them even though they are in no position to say why what we put out are facts rather than fiction. After all, a lot of scientific facts are counterintuitive, such as that the earth moves around the sun, or that if you drop a pound of feathers and a pound of rocks they will fall at the same rate.

What are the social or group characteristics of people who are permitted to make scientific facts? Above all else they must have a particular kind of education that includes college, graduate, and postgraduate training. That means that in addition to whatever subject matter they learn, they have been socialized to think in particular ways and have familiarized themselves with a narrow slice of human history and culture that deals primarily with the experiences of western European and North American upper-class men during the past century to two. They also have learned to obey certain rules of individual and social behavior and to talk and think in ways that let them earn the academic degrees required of a scientist.

But who has access to that education? Until the last decade or so, predominantly upper middle- and upper-class youngsters, most of them male and white. Lately, a slightly larger number of white women and a few more people of color (women and men) have gained access, but the class composition has not changed appreciably: the scientific profession still draws its membership overwhelmingly from the upper middle and upper classes.

How about other kinds of people? Have they no role in the making of science? Quite the contrary. In the ivory, that is white and male, towers in which science gets made, people from working-class and lower middle-class backgrounds are numerically well represented. But they are the technicians, secretaries, clean-up personnel. Decisions about who gains the status of fact maker are made by professors, deans, and university presidents who call on scientists from other similar institutions to vouch-safe the quality of a particular candidate and to guarantee that he or she conforms to the standards prescribed by the university and the scientific profession. At the larger, systemic level, decisions are made by govern-ment and private funding agencies that operate by what is called peer review. What that means is that like-minded people from similar personal and academic backgrounds get together to decide whether a particular fact-making proposal has enough merit to be financed. It is a club in which people mutually sit on each other's decision-making panels. The criteria for access are supposed to be objective and meritocratic, but in practice orthodoxy and conformity count for a lot. Someone whose ideas or personality are out of line is less likely to succeed than "one of the boys"—and these days some of us girls are allowed to be one of the boys, particularly if we have learned the rules by which the game is played.

Thus, science is made, by and large, by a self-perpetuating, self-reflexive group: by the chosen for the chosen. The assumption is that if the science is "good" it will somehow, in the long run, "serve the people." But no one, no group is responsible for seeing that it does. Public accountability is not built into the system.

What are the alternatives? How could we have a science *for* the people and to what extent could—or should—it be a science *by* the people? After all, divisions of labor are not necessarily bad. There is no possibility that in a complicated society like ours, everyone is able to do everything. Inequalities that are bad come not from the fact that different people do different things, but from the fact that different tasks are valued differently and carry with them different amounts of prestige and power.

For example, American and European societies assign different values to mental and manual labor. We value mental labor more highly than manual labor. We often pay more for it and think it is more significant, somehow better. This is a mistake, especially so in the context of a scientific laboratory, because it means that the laboratory chief—the per-son "with the ideas"—often gets the credit, whereas in reality the laboratory workers—the people who work with their hands—are the ones who perform the operations and make the observations that generate new hypotheses and that permit hypotheses and ideas to become facts.

But it is not only because of the way natural science is done that head and hand, mental and manual work, are often closely linked. Natural science requires a conjunction of head and hand because it is an understanding of nature *for use*. To understand nature is not enough. Natural science and technology are inextricable; natural science is true only to the extent that it works. Its laws are relevant only to the extent that they can be applied and used as technology. The science/technology distinction is an ideological device of relatively recent historical origin and one that does not hold up in the real world of economic, political, and social practices.

Woman's Nature: Realities versus Scientific Myths

Let us look at some examples of the kinds of self-serving facts that I am talking about. Since we are exploring male bias in science, I will take my examples from research into sex differences, but similar examples exist in many areas of research. At times of tension and upheaval, such as the past decade, some researchers always try to "prove" that differences in the political, social, and economic status of women and men, blacks and whites, or poor people and rich people, derive from inborn qualities and traits. They try to "prove" that blacks are innately less intelligent than whites, or that women are innately weaker, more nurturing, less good at math than men.

The *ideology* of woman's nature can differ drastically from the *realities* of women's lives and can indeed be antithetical to them. In fact, the ideology often draws a smokescreen that obscures the ways women live and makes people look away from the realities or ask misleading questions about them.

What are some of the realities? One is that women, with few exceptions, work and have always worked, though the term "work" over the centuries has been increasingly defined by what men do. Women's work is often trivialized, ignored, and undervalued, both in economic and political terms. It is not called work when women "only" care for their households and children. Much of the work women do does not appear in the Gross National Product (GNP) and hence has neither reality nor value in standard descriptions of the economy. Women work considerably more than men if *all* the work women do is counted—on average, about seventy to eighty hours per week as against men's fifty or sixty—since in addition to working for pay, most women also do most or all housework, as well as most volunteer work in schools, hospitals, and other parts of the community. Women earn fifty-seven cents for every dollar men earn, not because we do not work as much or are less effective than men, but because women usually are paid less than men in workplaces and are not paid anything for much of the work we do. If women stopped doing all work for which we are not paid this society would grind to a halt, for much of the productive work men do depends on women's unacknowledged and unpaid labor.

The ideology that labels women as the natural reproducers of the species and men as producers of goods has not been used to exempt women from also producing goods and services; rather, it has shunted us out of higher-paying jobs, professional work, and other kinds of paid work that require continuity and provide a measure of power over one's own and, at times, other people's lives. Most women who work for pay do so in job categories such as secretary or nurse, which often involve a great deal of concealed responsibility but are underpaid. This is one reason why insisting on equal pay *within* job categories cannot remedy women's economic disadvantage. Women will continue to be underpaid as long as access to better-paying job categories is limited by social pressures, career counseling, training and hiring practices, trade union policies, and various other subtle and not so subtle societal mechanisms, such as research that "proves" that girls are not as good as boys in mathematics and scientific subjects. An entire range of discriminatory practices is justified by the claim that they follow from the limits that biology places on women's capacity to work. Though exceptions are made during wars and other emergencies, these are forgotten as soon as life resumes its normal course. Then women are expected to return to their subordinate roles not because the quality of their work during the emergencies has been inferior, but because these roles are seen as natural.

Recently a number of women employees in the American chemical and automotive industries actually have been forced to choose between working at relatively well-paying jobs or remaining fertile. In one instance, five women were required to submit to sterilization by hysterectomy in order to avoid being transferred from work in the lead pigment department at the American Cyanamid plant in Willow Island, West Virginia to janitorial work at considerably lower wages and benefits (Stellman and Henifin 1982). Even though none of these women was pregnant or planning a pregnancy in the near future (indeed, the husband of one had had a vasectomy), they were considered pregnant or "potentially pregnant" unless they could prove that they were sterile. This goes on despite the fact that exposure to lead can damage sperm as well as eggs and can affect the health of workers (male and female) as well as a "potential fetus." But it is important to notice that this vicious choice has been forced only on women who have recently entered relatively well-paid male jobs. Women whose work routinely involves exposure to chemical or radiation hazards in traditionally female jobs, like nurses, X-ray technologists, cleaning women in surgical operating rooms, beauticians, secretaries, workers in the ceramics industry, and domestic workers are not warned about the chemical or physical hazards of their work to their health or to that of a fetus, should they be pregnant. In other words, scientific knowledge about fetal susceptibility to noxious chemicals and radiation is being used to keep women out of better-paid job categories from which they had previously been excluded by discriminatory employment practices, but in general women (or, indeed, men) are not protected against health-endangering work.

The ideology of women's nature that is invoked at these times would have us believe that a woman's capacity to become pregnant leaves her always physically disabled by comparison with men. The scientific underpinnings for these ideas were elaborated in the nineteenth century by the white, university-educated, mainly upper-class men who made up the bulk of the new professions of obstetrics and gynecology, biology, psychology, sociology, and anthropology. These professionals used their theories of women's innate frailty to disqualify the girls and women of their own race and class who would have competed with them for education and professional status. They also realized, and protested openly, that they did not want to lose the kinds of personal attention and services they were accustomed to receive from their mothers, wives, and sisters and that they were likely to lose if these women gained access to the professions. They did not invoke women's weakness to argue against the exploitation of poor women made to work long hours in the homes and factories belonging to members of the upper classes; nor did they protest the ways black slave women were forced to work in the plantations and homes of their masters and mistresses.

Nineteenth-century biologists and physicians claimed that women's brains were smaller than men's and that women's ovaries and uteruses required much energy and rest in order to function properly. They "proved" that therefore young girls must be kept away from schools and colleges once they had begun to menstruate, and they warned that without this kind of care women's uteruses and ovaries would shrivel and the human race would die out. Yet again, this analysis was not extended to poor women, who were not only required to work hard, but often were said to reproduce *too* much. Indeed, scientists interpreted the fact that poor women could work hard and yet bear many children as a sign that they were more animal-like and less highly evolved than upper-class women.

During the past decade, feminist scholars have described this history. We have analyzed these self-serving theories and documented the absurdity of the claims as well as their class and race biases and their glaringly political intent (Hubbard and Lowe 1979; Lowe and Hubbard 1983; Bleier 1984; Fausto-Sterling 1985). But this kind of scientific myth making is not past history. Medical men and biologists in the nineteenth century fought women's political organizing for equality by claiming that our reproductive organs made us unfit for anything but childbearing and childrearing, while somewhat later Freud declared women to be intrinsically less stable and intellectually less inventive and productive than men. Beginning in the 1970s, there has been a renaissance in sex differences research claiming to prove scientifically that women are innately better than men at home care and mothering while men are innately better fitted than women for the competitive life of the market place.

Questionable experimental results obtained with animals (primarily that prototypic human, the white laboratory rat) are treated as though they can be applied equally well to people. On this basis, some scientists are now claiming that the secretion of different amounts of so-called male hormones (androgens) by male and female fetuses produces life-long differences in women's and men's brains. They claim not only that these (unproved) differences in fetal hormone levels exist, but imply (without evidence) that they predispose women and men *as groups* to exhibit innate differences in our abilities to localize objects in space, in our verbal and mathematical aptitudes, in aggressiveness and competitiveness, nurturing ability, and so on (Money and Ehrhardt 1972; Goy and McEwen 1980; *Science* 1981, pp. 1263–1324). Sociobiologists claim that some of the sex differences in social behavior that exist in our society (for example, aggressiveness, competitiveness, and dominance among men; coyness, nurturance, and submissiveness among women) are human universals that have existed in all times and cultures. Because they claim that these traits are ever-present, they deduce that the traits must be adaptive (that is, promote human survival) and have evolved through Darwinian natural selection, so that they have become part of our genetic inheritance (Wilson 1975).

In recent years, sociobiologists have tried to prove that women have a greater biological investment in our children than men, and that women's disproportionate contributions to child and home care are biologically programmed to help us ensure that our "investments" mature—in other words, that our children live long enough to have children themselves. The offered rationale is that an organisms's biological fitness, in the Darwinian sense, depends on producing the greatest possible number of offspring, who themselves survive long enough to reproduce. This is what determines the frequency of occurrence of an individual's genes in successive generations. Following this logic a step further, sociobiologists argue that women and men must adopt basically different strategies to maximize the spreading of their genes over future generations. The calculus goes as follows: because women cannot produce as many eggs as men can sperm and, in addition, must "invest" at least the nine months of pregnancy (whereas it takes a man only the few minutes of heterosexual intercourse to send a sperm on its way to personhood), each egg that becomes a child represents a much larger fraction of the total reproductive fitness a woman can achieve in her lifetime than a sperm that becomes a child does in a man's life. From this biological asymmetry, they claim, follow female fidelity, male promiscuity, and the unequal division and valuing of labor by sex. As sociobiologist David Barash presents it, "mother nature is sexist," so don't blame her human sons (Dawkins 1976; Barash 1979, esp. pp. 46–90).

In devising these explanations, sociobiologists ignore the fact that human societies do not operate with a few superstuds; nor do stronger or more powerful men usually have more children than weaker ones. Men, in theory, could have many more children than women can, but in most societies equal numbers of men and women engage in *producing* children, though not in caring for them. Yet these kinds of theories are useful to people who have a stake in maintaining present inequalities. They have a superficial ring of plausibility and offer naturalistic justifications for discriminatory practices.

As the new scholarship on women has grown, a few anthropologists and biologists have tried to mitigate the male bias that underlies these kinds of theories; they describe how females contribute to social life and species survival in important ways that are overlooked by scientists who think of females only in relation to reproduction and look to males for everything else (Lancaster 1975; Hrdy 1981; Kevles 1986). However, unless scientists also challenge the basic premises that underlie the standard (male-centered) descriptions and analyses, such revisions do not offer radically different formulations and insights. (For examples of more fundamental criticisms of evolutionary thinking and sociobiology, see Lowe and Hubbard 1979; Hubbard 1982; Lewontin, Rose, and Kamin, 1984).

Subjectivity and Objectivity

There is another issue that gets into the masculine nature of science, and here I come back to Paulo Freire, who said: "Reality is never just simply the objective datum, the concrete fact, but is also people's [and I would say, certain people's] perception of it." And he spoke of "the indispensable unity between subjectivity and objectivity in the act of knowing" (Freire 1985, p. 51).

The recognition of the "indisputable unity" between subject and object is what feminist methodology is about, but it is especially necessary for a feminist methodology in science because the scientific method rests on a particular definition of objectivity, one that feminists must challenge and call into question. Feminists and others who draw attention to the devices that the dominant group uses to deny other people access to power—be it political power or the power to make facts—must come to understand how that definition of objectivity functions in the processes of exclusion that I have discussed above.

Natural scientists attain their objectivity by looking upon nature and natural phenomena (including other people) as isolated objects. To do this they usually deny, or at least do not acknowledge, their relationship to the "objects" of their study. In other words, natural scientists describe their activities as though they and their activities existed in a vacuum. In that vacuum they then make facts and formulate laws. For example, take the "ideal gas laws." These laws are said to describe the behavior of particles (gas molecules) that bear no relation to each other or to other substances—particles that are not real, but "ideal." Look at that word: it derives from "idea," imaginary, in your head. But whereas something that's "just in your head" may be bad in everyday life, it is good, "ideal," in scientific parlance. The head and hand again. Clearly, the ways mind and matter, or head and hand, are valued are different in the two social milieus of daily life and the scientific laboratory, but let us not make the mistake of thinking that they are different but equal. In terms of its power to name, describe, and structure reality and experience, the world of the scientific, white, male ("ivory") tower has it all over our everyday lives in their many colors, shapes, and sizes.

A pertinent example of the kind of context stripping that is commonly called objectivity is the way E. O. Wilson opened the final chapter of his *Sociobiology: The New Synthesis* (Wilson 1975, p. 547). He wrote: "Let us now consider man in the free spirit of natural history, as though we were zoologists from another planet completing a catalog of social species on earth." That statement epitomizes the fallacy we need to get rid of. There is no "free spirit of natural history," only a set of descriptions put forward by the mostly white, educated, Euro-American men who have been practicing a particular kind of science during the past two hundred years. Nor do we have any idea what "zoologists from another planet" would have to say about "man" (which, I guess is supposed to mean "people") or about other "social species on earth," since that would depend on how these "zoologists" were used to living on their own planet and by what experiences they would therefore judge us.

What feminists have to contribute is the insistence that subjectivity and context *cannot* be stripped away, that they must be acknowledged if we want to understand nature and use the knowledge we gain without abusing it. Natural scientists must try to understand our position in nature and in society as subjects as well as objects. We must let our natural and social contexts be subjects as well as objects, if we want to learn about nature and society without damaging them.

Another example of the absurdity of pretended objectivity is a study described in the fall of 1984 in the *New York Times,* in which scientists suggested that they had identified eight characteristics in young children predictive of the likelihood that they would later develop schizophrenia. The scientists were proposing a longitudinal study of such children as they grow up to assess the accuracy of these predictions. This is absurd because such experiments cannot be done. How do you find a "control" group for parents who have been told that their child exhibits five out of the eight characteristics, or worse yet, all eight characteristics thought to be predictive of schizophrenia? Do you tell some parents that this is so although it isn't? Do you *not* tell some parents whose children have been so identified? Even if there were universal agreement among psychiatrists in the diagnosis of schizophrenia—which there is not—this kind of research cannot be done objectively and certainly not ethically.

The problem is that the context stripping that worked reasonably well for the classical physics of falling bodies (that experience no friction) and "ideal" particles (that don't interact) has become the model for how to do every kind of science; this is so even though physicists early in this century recognized that the experimenter is part of the experiment and influences its outcome. That insight produced Heisenberg's uncertainty principle in physics: the recognition that the operations the experimenter performs disturb the system so that it is impossible to specify simultaneously the position *and* momentum of atoms and elementary particles.

Therefore, how about standing the situation on its head and using the social sciences, where context stripping is clearly impossible, as a model; treat all science in a way that acknowledges the experimenter as a self-conscious subject who lives, and does science, within the context in which the phenomena she or he observes occur. Anthropologists often try to describe a new culture and take field notes about it as quickly as possible after they enter it, before they incorporate the perspective and expectations of that culture; they realize that once they come to know the foreign culture well and feel at home in it, they will begin to take what are perhaps its most significant aspects for granted and stop seeing them. Yet they realize at the same time that they must also acknowledge the limitations that their own personal and social backgrounds impose on the way they perceive the foreign society. Awareness of subjectivity and context must be part of doing science because our subjectivity and our context are part of being human.

The social structure of the laboratory in which scientists work and the community and interpersonal relationships in which they live also must be acknowledged as part of the subjective reality and context of doing science. Yet they are usually ignored when we speak of a scientist's scientific work, despite the fact that natural scientists work in highly organized social systems. Obviously, the sociology of laboratory life is structured by class, sex, and race, as is the rest of society. We saw before that to understand what goes on in the laboratory we must ask questions about who does what kinds of work. What does the lab chief—the person whose name appears on the stationary or on the door—contribute? How are decisions made about what work gets done and in what order? What role do women, whatever our class and race, or men of color and men from working-class backgrounds play in this performance?

Note that women have played a very large role in the production of science—as wives, sisters, secretaries, technicians, and students of "great men"—though usually not as accredited scientists. It is one of our jobs as feminists to acknowledge that role. If feminists are to make a difference in the ways science is done and understood, we must not try to become scientists who occupy the traditional structures, follow the established patterns of behavior, and accept the prevailing systems of explanation. We must understand and describe accurately the roles women have played all along in the process of making science. And we must question why certain ways of systematically interacting with nature and of using the knowledge gained from that interaction are acknowledged as science whereas others are not.

I am talking of the distinction between the laboratory and that other, quite differently structured, place of discovery and fact making, the household, where women explore and use our brands of botany, chemistry, and hygiene in our gardens, kitchens, nurseries, and sick rooms. The fact is that much of the knowledge women have acquired in those places is systematic, communicated, and effective. But just as our society downgrades manual labor, it also downgrades the practical knowledge that is produced away from professional settings, however systematic it may be. It downgrades the orally transmitted knowledge and the unpaid observations, experimentation, and teaching that happen in the household. Yet here is an entire spectrum of systematic, empirical knowledge that has gone unnoticed and unvalidated (in fact, devalued and invalidated) by the institutions that catalog and describe, and thus define, what is to be called knowledge.

What I propose here is the opposite of the project put forward by the domestic science movement at the turn of the century. That movement tried to make women's domestic work more "scientific" in the traditional sense of the word (Newman 1985, pp. 156–191). I am suggesting that we acknowledge the scientific value of much of the knowledge that women have traditionally accumulated and passed on in the home and in volunteer organizations.

I doubt that women as gendered beings have something new or different to contribute to science, but women as political beings do. One of the most important things is to insist on the political content of science and on its political role. The pretense that science is objective, apolitical, and value-neutral is profoundly political because it obscures the political role that science and technology play in underwriting the existing distribution of power in society. No active component of society—and science and technology are that—can be politically neutral. By claiming to be objective and neutral, scientists align themselves with the powerful against the powerless. Feminist science—by which I mean that done by scientists who consciously integrate feminist politics into their science—must insist on the political nature and content of scientific work and of the way science is taught or otherwise communicated to the public; it must expose the errors and dishonesty of the claim of scientific objectivity and neutrality. Science and technology always operate in somebody's interest and serve someone or some group of people. To the extent that scientists pretend to be neutral they support the existing distribution of interests and power. The male-dominated science we have is just as political and value-laden as a feminist science would be.

A feminist science would have to start by acknowledging our values and our subjectivity as human observers with particular personal and social backgrounds and with inevitable interests. Once we do that, we can try to understand the world, so to speak, from inside instead of pretending to be objective outsiders looking in. A feminist science and a more just science would have to give access to a wider spectrum of people and to provide kinds of understanding that are useful and useable by a broad range of people. For this, it would have to differ from the science we now have in that its important questions would have to be generated by a social process that is not dominated by experts in scientific fact making. A wider range of people would have to have access to the making of scientific facts. Also, the process of validation would have to be under more public scrutiny, so that research topics and facts that benefit only a small elite while oppressing large segments of the population would not be acceptable. Accountability would have to be built into all stages of the fact-making process. That kind of science would be very different from the science we now have, and necessarily more respectful of people and nature.

SUMMARY

MAKING science is a social process. The content of science depends on who the scientists are and on the society in which they operate. Because the science we now have has been produced predominantly by white, university-educated, upper middle- and upper-class men accustomed to working in hierarchical institutions, its "facts" reflect these origins.

Feminist inquiry takes cognizance of the societal position of the inquirers and examines how that position affects their interaction with the subject matter of their research. It stresses the dialectical interplay of subjectivity and objectivity in the construction of knowledge and reality. But feminist scientists need to go beyond that to acknowledge the insights women have produced in the course of growing and preparing food, nurturing children, and caring for the ill of all ages so that women's "domestic" contributions are credited as part of our knowledge about nature.

REFERENCES

Barash, D. (1979). *The whispering within*. New York: Harper and Row.
Bleier, R. (1984). *Science and gender*. New York: Pergamon.

Dawkins, R. (1976). *The selfish gene*. New York: Oxford University Press.

Fausto-Sterling, A. (1985). *Myths of gender*. New York: Basic Books.

Freire, P. (1985). *The politics of education*. South Hadley, Mass.: Bergin and Garvey.

Goy, R. W., and McEwen, B. S. (1980). *Sexual differentiation of the brain*. Cambridge: MIT Press.

Hrdy, S. B. (1981). *The woman that never evolved*. Cambridge: Harvard University Press.

Hubbard, R. (1982). "Have only men evolved?" In Hubbard, R., Henifin, M. S., and Fried, B. (Eds.). *Biological woman: The convenient myth*. Cambridge, Mass.: Schenkman, pp. 17–46.

——— and Lowe, M. (Eds.). (1979). *Genes and gender II: Pitfalls in research on sex and gender*. Staten Island, N.Y.: Gordian Press.

Kevles, B. (1986). *Females of the species*. Cambridge: Harvard University Press.

Lancaster, J. B. (1975). *Primate behavior and the emergence of human culture*. New York: Holt, Rinehart, and Winston.

Lewontin, R. C., Rose, S., and Kamin, L. J. (1984). *Not in our genes*. New York: Pantheon.

Lowe, M., and Hubbard, R. (1979). "Sociobiology and biosociology: Can science prove the biological basis of sex differences in behavior?" In Hubbard, R. and Lowe, M. (Eds.). *Genes and gender II: Pitfalls in research on sex and gender*. Staten Island, N.Y.: Gordian Press, pp. 91–112.

——— and Hubbard R. (Eds.). (1983). *Woman's nature: Rationalizations of inequality*. New York: Pergamon.

Money, J., and Ehrhardt, A. A. (1972). *Man and woman, boy and girl*. Baltimore: Johns Hopkins University Press.

Newman, L. M. (Ed). (1985). *Men's ideas/women's realities: Popular science, 1870–1915*. New York: Pergamon.

(1981). *Science* 211:1263–1324.

Stellman, J. M., and Henifin, M. S. (1982). "No fertile women need apply: Employment discrimination and reproductive hazards in the workplace." In Hubbard, R., Henifin, M. S., and Fried, B. (Eds.). *Biological woman—The convenient myth*. Cambridge, Mass.: Schenkman, pp. 117–45.

Wilson, E. O. (1975). *Sociobiology: The new synthesis*. Cambridge: Harvard University Press.

TWO

A Feminist Perspective on Sexology and Sexuality

Leonore Tiefer

PROLOGUE: FEMINISTS HAVE WRITTEN MUCH ABOUT SEXUALITY, BUT CONTRIBUTED LITTLE TO SEXOLOGY

FEMINISM is fundamentally a political movement and a political analysis that aims to understand and change the subordinate situation of women throughout the world. Sexuality, whatever it is (and just what it is persists as one of the central problems), is a prominent locus of women's oppression.

Feminists have been meticulous in their efforts to examine, identify, expose, and redefine the numerous points of contact between the ideology and practice of patriarchy, on the one hand, and sexual assumptions, practices, and beliefs on the other. From Simone de Beauvoir (1953) to Susan Brownmiller (1975), from Shulamith Firestone (1970) to Dana Densmore (1973) and Anne Koedt (1973) and Ingrid Bengis (1972), from Germaine Greer (1971) to Shere Hite (1976), from Andrea Dworkin (1974) to Gayle Rubin (1984), from Sidney Abbott and Barbara Love (1971) and Adrienne Rich (1976) to Linda Gordon (1976) and Kathleen Barry (1979), from Karen and Jeffrey Paige (1981) to Nawal el Saadawi, from Barbara Ehrenreich (1983) to Judith Walkowitz (1980), just to name a few, feminists have analyzed sexuality. They have written about sexual acts and sexual experiences, to be sure, but also about sexuality of pregnancy and motherhood, sexual behavior categories and hierarchies of normalcy, sexual violence against women such as rape and clitoridectomy, sexual representations and their varying impacts, prostitutes and other women in the sex industry, the material realities of sexuality including abortion and contraception, and so forth. In the process, feminist analysis has split into cultural feminist, liberal feminist, radical feminist, and socialist feminist subsets (Echols 1984; Jaggar 1983), each with its own set of assumptions and conclusions on sexuality.

Amazingly, very little of the ferment stimulated by these names, topics, or political differences has made much difference to or in sexology, the academic discipline whose subject is sexuality. I want to explore this phenomenon: 1) why has feminist scholarship on the subject of sexuality had so little impact on sexology, and 2) what would such impact look like if it were achieved?

WHAT IS SEXOLOGY?

IS SEXOLOGY a discipline or is it an area of study? Is it like religion, health or work, a subject that is examined through the varying lenses of psychology, sociology, anthropology, history, literature, biology, philosophy, art, and so on? Or is it a discipline, like psychology, with its own traditions, methods, values, and scholarly community? Asking this question directs our attention to hidden and confusing processes of professionalization, disciplinary development and legitimation, and boundary setting. These processes, political processes, are rarely addressed by scholars, and sexologists are no exception. Let me discuss something of the history of modern sexology, and then return to the question of the impact of feminist writings.

As yet there is no written history of modern sexology, but there are bits and pieces of scholarship here and there. Erwin Haeberle, a historian at the Institute for the Advanced Study of Human Sexuality, has recently championed a group of early twentieth-century German scholars as "the" founders of modern sexology, in contrast to the more familiar British group of John Addington Symonds, Edward Carpenter, and Havelock Ellis. Haeberle called a Berlin dermatologist, Iwan Bloch (1872–1922), "the father of sexology," and cited Bloch's "monumental" study, *The Sexual Life of Our Time* (1912), to provide an early definition of the field:

The purely medical consideration of the sexual life, although it must always constitute the nucleus of sexual science, is yet incapable of doing full justice to the many-sided relationships between the sexual and all the other provinces of human life. . . . [Sexuality] must be *treated in its proper subordination as part of the general science of mankind,* which is constituted by a union of all other sciences—of general biology, anthropology and ethnology, philosophy and psychology, the history of literature and the entire history of civilization. (Bloch, in Haeberle 1982, pp. 307–308, emphasis added)

Haeberle claimed that this movement away from a medical (i.e. pathology and treatment-oriented) point of view was the first step in creating a true science of sexuality. He credited Magnus Hirschfeld, another Berlin physician, with founding, in 1908, "the first journal devoted to sexology as a science," spelling out its scope and goals in three articles.

The first article explains the new scientific, as opposed to the traditional ethical or artistic, approach to sex. . . . The second article then lists 14 main areas of sexological study from anatomy, physiology, psychology, and comparative biology to legislature, politics, ethnology and ethics. The last article describes the various research tools and methods of the sexologist from the knife and microscope to literary sources, personal interviews, questionnaires, and statistical studies. (Haeberle 1982, pp. 308–310)

Haeberle did not anoint Hirschfeld "the father" of sexology possibly for the same reason that Hirschfeld was not popular with many of his contemporaries. In addition to his scholarly activities, Hirschfeld was outspokenly political on behalf of the decriminalization of homosexuality. Despite his dominance as a scholar (for example, he authored a five-volume encyclopedia titled *Sexual Knowledge* and a three-volume textbook on sexual pathology), he was not invited to the first meeting of the International Congress for Sex Research (1926, Berlin) organized by another physician, Albert Moll, because, Moll wrote to a colleague, "many serious researchers do not consider him an objective seeker of truth . . . he confuses science with propaganda" (Haeberle 1981, p. 272). Moll

pursued a "disinterested" approach to sexology, avoiding social and political resolutions at his congress. Hirschfeld's World League for Sexual
Reform (founded in 1928), by contrast, was clearly designed to influence
world opinion and national policies.

Hirschfeld was forced to leave Germany in 1930. The Berlin Institute
he had founded (1919) in the first flush of Weimar Republic freedom, by
the late '20s filled with documents and artifacts, films and files, was raided
by the Nazis in May 1933. It contents were stolen or publicly burned.
Hirschfeld died in 1935, Moll in 1938. Sexology was denounced as
"Jewish science," and sexologists scattered to the four corners of the
world. Their work was untranslated and for the most part unread and
forgotten until very recently. Haeberle's effort not only to revive their
story but to frame it and designate their roles in "the" history of sexology
should be seen as part of a complex process in the development of a
professional identity for current studies of human sexuality.

Let us take a look at another set of people and events in twentieth
century sexology. In the United States, interest in research on sexuality
was in considerable part stimulated and underwritten by John D. Rockefeller (Bullough 1985). Following his experience investigating prostitution while on a New York City grand jury, Rockefeller facilitated the
organizing of the American Social Hygiene Association (1913), with its
own arm for sociological research into prostitution. Over the next thirty
years, he provided over six million dollars to that organization.

As a result of this beginning, Rockefeller was prevailed upon to provide
money to the National Research Council (an agency of the National
Academy of Science) for a conference in 1921 to evaluate the advantages
and disadvantages of embarking on a program of sex research. The conference report advocated sex research to combat the

ignorance due to the enshrouding of sex relations in a shroud of mystery, reticence
and shame [through the use of] methods employed in physiology, psychology,
anthropology and related sciences. [It cautioned that] in order to eliminate any
suggestion that such inquiry is undertaken for the purposes of propaganda, it
should be sponsored by a body of investigators whose disinterested devotion to
science is well recognized. (Bullough 1985, p. 117)

The result was the establishment of the committee for Research in Problems of Sex, *but* the decision to "keep it clean" resulted in a focus on

nonhuman sexual activity, hardly what Rockefeller initially had intended. Nevertheless the money came in.

The Apolitical Stance

These decisions established a group dominant in sex research— in large part because of ongoing funding—biologically oriented researchers of animal sexual behavior. Bullough (1985) told the story of a human sexuality survey conducted by Gilbert Hamilton that was not funded by the Committee and had to obtain support from the Bureau of Social Hygiene. When the study was published in 1929, even the Bureau refused to have its name appear in any publicity except for the indication that a "group of scientific men" had acted as advisors to the project. This is particularly interesting when we recall that Hamilton's study reported the existence of multiple orgasm in women and also supported Kinsey's later finding that a wider range of sexual actvities was commonly practiced than was publicly acknowledge or condoned.

The first human sexuality research supported by the Committee was in fact Kinsey's, and he was apparently approved because he was a zoologist by training. His other qualifications—married with no whiff of homosexuality history, working at a rural institution—would make his work additionally proper. Kinsey received a great deal of Rockefeller money in the late '40s and early '50s, but after the publication of the female volume in 1953 (Kinsey et al. 1953), the Rockefeller Foundation withdrew its support. According to Bullough (1985), a conservative Tennessee Congressman, Carroll Reece, outraged by the revelations of widespread male experience with homosexuality reported in Kinsey's first volume (Kinsey, Pomeroy, and Martin 1948), had formed a congressional committee to investigate tax exempt organizations and made Kinsey's group the first on its list for investigation.

The upshot of these experiences—both the mostly forgotten German one (forgotten except that students of sex research hear vague worrying allegations that sex research ought never get politicized because "look what happened in Germany"—as if the Nazis would have left "really" scientific sexual research alone) and the more recent Kinsey one—is that sex research has developed a profoundly neutral, studiously apolitical, and what I would term ultrascientific stance. Even those substantially ignorant of history have their worries fed by recent examples of political intrusion into sex research—the current attorney general's use and abuse of research on erotica/pornography leaps to mind. (Attorney General's Commission on Pornography 1986). Thus the paranoia about any "nonobjective" taint to the field persists.

What is the evidence for the impact of this more-scientific-than-thou attitude? In his 1981 presidential address to the Society for the Scientific Study of Sexuality, sociologist Ira Reiss reviewed "The Current Status of Sexual Science" and said

. . . One reason it is crucial to have a sharp image of what is primary scientific research and theory is that such a conception can help in keeping out personal ideologies which may pose as scientific conclusions . . . Such private values can enter in on the side of positive support for sexual variety as well as opposing such behavior. In both cases, the entry of such values transforms sexual science into an ideology and hinders those who wish to improve our scientific understanding. (Reiss 1982, pp. 104–105)

It seems the current stance of sex researchers is that they have no axe to grind, no basic assumptions, no politics or ideology—that they, like police detectives, just collect the facts ma'am, just the facts and nothing else.

The Implicit Ideology

In fact, contemporary sex research *has* become focused on an ideology that is so implicit and unexamined as to be invisible. I have elsewhere written about how contemporary sexual discourse and research are dominated by health language and imagery and have become "medicalized" (Tiefer 1986, 1987). Because there is so little academic support for "controversial" sex research, which more or less means *any* sex research, sexual health workers have filled the vacuum with a reductionist account of human sexuality. They construe the subject as a universal, inherent, biologically driven essence expressed in numerous direct and indirect ways, influenced by social values and individual psychology. The publication of Masters and Johnson's (1966) physiological observations legitimated the belief that a particular sequence of physical changes constitutes a normal, inherent, universal pattern. This paved the way for the creation of an industry of health workers, both researchers and service providers, devoted to a system that takes Masters and Johnson's "human sexual response cycle" as a health norm and measures, studies, and treats deviations from it.

We can see now why contemporary sexology would not be receptive to the insights of feminists. Coming from a political critique of society and its institutions, any feminist description of or hypothesis about sexual relations would be suspect as an attempt to "transform sexual science into an ideology," to use Reiss' phrase. The historic domination of sex research by biologically oriented theorists (studying, for the most part, animal subjects) has blinded sexologists to the bias such domination has imposed on the field. Sexuality has been constructed as the sort of thing both animals and people have and do: behavior, orgasm, hormones, brain-behavior relationships. It seems quite "natural" to accept and adopt the Masters and Johnson contribution and just continue the discussion of the physiology and mechanics of sexuality as though they were the central elements.

Feminists have not yet clearly recognized the creation of this contemporary medicalized sexuality discourse. Rather, feminists applauded Masters and Johnson's "discovery" that women are capable of orgasmic sexual response, that the clitoris is the most sensitive genital structure, and that male and female sexuality are more similar than different. They felt these findings liberated women from the tyranny of the Freudian "vaginal orgasm" and paved the way for greater female sexual self-determination. They felt comforted by the biological "proof" offered of their demands for equality. Masters and Johnson expressed this view explicitly: "With orgasmic physiology established, the human female now has an undeniable opportunity to develop realistically her own sexual response levels" (1966, p. 138).

This naive belief that the shortest way to political equality is empirical equality echoes Magnus Hirschfeld's favorite dictum, "per scientiam ad justitiam," no less extraordinary a post-Enlightenment belief in the power of scientific progress in the 1960s than in the 1930s (Weeks 1985, p. 71). Feminists, while not forgetting that there can be no equality in bed without equality in the relationship, physiology to the contrary notwithstanding, seemed to have overlooked the fact that merely substituting one

set of physiological standards and expectations for another is not liberation in any sense of the word. Certainly the absence of interest by the
sexological community in other elements of feminist sexual analysis ought
to have suggested that the endorsement of the Masters and Johnson
physiological approach was more the result of its coherence with the
prevailing (implicit) ideology than a sign of hope for future rapprochement.

ELEMENTS OF A FEMINIST CRITIQUE

Anti-Essentialist. A feminist critique of sexology would have to focus
heavily on its essentialist assumptions. That is, a major elment of the
feminist agenda would be to insist that sexuality is *not* a biological given,
not an inherent human quality, *not* any sort of instinct or imperative, but
rather a fundamentally social construction, a way of being and of relating
that is created by social arrangements. Of course, biology is a precondi-
tion for sexuality, as it is for every other aspect of human functioning, but
to put more emphasis on the biology of sex than, say, on the biology of
piano playing (rather than the art, the culture, the gender relations) would
be rejected. Any sort of fixed, eternal human nature is anathema to
feminist thinking, and this holds true for sexuality.

This antiessentialist critique places sexuality within the domain of interpersonal relations, rather than as solely an individual matter, as the discourse of medicalization would have it. It also makes of sexuality an
historical not an ahistorical matter, with concepts and categories, metaphors and values a matter of historical time and place (Tiefer, 1987).

Usable Research. A second element of a feminist critique of sexology
would involve the selection of topics and methods for research. Currently,
sex research often depends on arbitrary questions of theory or exploitable
commercial potential. Frequently, the questions asked have to do with
the superiority of one sort of professional service over another in the
treatment of sexual problems. Small differences between groups are examined over and over again, while large ones (impact of gender role
training and powerlessness, effects of limited options and education, pressure of media images) are ignored. Methods typically involve question-

naire or laboratory studies of "subjects" who neither collaborate nor benefit. Most methods, assuming certain essentialist underpinnings, do not utilize a longitudinal approach.

Feminist research on sexuality would begin by adopting a collaborative stance, using participants' subjective perceptions to enrich objective measurements, and planning research to benefit the participants as well as the researchers. Research would be contextualized to as great a degree as possible, since no understanding of sexuality can emerge from any study that ignores the social, demographic, and cultural features of participants' lives. Such features would not be "controlled for," since that is not really desirable (and in fact impossible), but would rather be dealt with by multivariate statistics and qualitative methods. The assumption would be made that we are studying *sexualities,* and looking for ways that all women are alike would play no part.

Research for Women. To return to the original point, feminism is about improving the situation of women in the world. Sex research from a feminist perspective would keep that goal in mind in every phase of research from the choice of question and of participants to the choice of publication where the results will appear. For those of us socialized in the conventional professions, that will be a tall order, but a fair one.

EPILOGUE: FEMINIST ANALYSIS WILL BE EXCLUDED FROM SEXOLOGY UNLESS THE PARADIGM FOR RESEARCH SHIFTS

FEMINIST writings about sexuality such as the ones cited in the Prologue have taught more about how sex is really lived than sexological texts and journals. That's true for me, and I suspect it is true for many other "professional" sex researchers as well. These insights don't fit into textbooks and journal articles, however, because they seem taboo—political, subjective, polemical, speculative, unscientific. I believe it was and is a mistake to define sexology, the study of human sexualities, as a certain kind of positivistic-model science. Feminism must press sexology to study its subject matter in ways that really count, rather than just in ways that perpetuate its professionalism.

REFERENCES

Abbott, S. and Love, B. (1971). "Is women's liberation a lesbian plot?" In V. Gornick, and B. K. Moran, (Eds.). *Woman in sexist society*. New York: Basic Books.

Attorney General's Commission on Pornography. (1986). *Final Report*, Vols. I and II. Washington, D.C.: U.S. Department of Justice.

Barry, K. (1979). *Female sexual slavery*. New York: Avon Books.

Bengis, I. (1972). *Combat in the erogenous zone*. New York: Knopf.

Brownmiller, S. (1975) *Against our will: Men, women and rape*. New York: Simon and Schuster.

Bullough, V. L. (1985). "The Rockefellers and sex research." *Journal of Sex Research* 21:113–25.

de Beauvoir, S. (1953). *The second sex*. New York: Knopf.

Densmore, D. (1973). "Independence from the sexual revolution." In A. Koedt, E. Levine, and A. Rapone (Eds.). *Radical feminism*. New York: Quadrangle Books.

Dworkin, A. (1974). *Woman hating*. New York: Dutton.

Echols, A. (1984). "The taming of the Id: Feminist sexual politics, 1968–1983." In C. Vance (Ed.). *Pleasure and danger: Exploring female sexuality*. Boston: Routledge and Kegan Paul.

Ehrenreich, B. (1983). *The hearts of men*. Garden City, N.Y.: Doubleday.

el Saadawi, N. (1982). *The hidden face of Eve: Women in the Arab world*. Boston: Beacon Press.

Firestone, S. (1970). *The dialectic of sex: The case for feminist revolution*. New York: Morrow.

Gordon, L. (1976). *Woman's body, woman's right: A social history of birth control in America*. New York: Grossman.

Greer, G. (1971). *The female eunuch*. New York: McGraw-Hill.

Haeberle, E. J. (1981). Swastika, pink triangle and yellow star—The destruction of sexology and the persecution of homosexuals in Nazi Germany. *Journal of Sex Research* 17:270–87.

———. (1982). The Jewish contribution to the development of sexology. *Journal of Sex Research* 18:305–23.

Hite, S. (1976). *The Hite report*. New York: Macmillan.

Jaggar, A. M. (1983). *Feminist politics and human nature*. Totowa, N.J.: Rowman and Allanheld.

Kinsey, A. C., Pomeroy, W. B., and Martin, C. E. (1948). *Sexual behavior in the human male*. Philadelphia: Saunders

——— et al. *Sexual behavior in the human female*. (1953). Philadelphia: Saunders.

Koedt, A. (1973). "The myth of the vaginal orgasm." In A. Koedt, A., E. Levine, and A. Rapone (Eds.). *Radical feminism*. New York: Quadrangle.

Masters, W. H., and Johnson, V. E. (1966). *Human sexual response*. Boston: Little, Brown.

Paige, K. E., and Paige, J. M. (1981). *The politics of reproductive ritual*. Berkeley: University of California Press.

Reiss, I. L. (1982). Trouble in paradise: The current status of sexual science. *Journal of Sex Research* 18:97–113.

Rich, A. (1976). *Of woman born*. New York: Norton.

Rubin, G. (1984). "Thinking sex: Notes for a radical theory of the politics of sexuality." In C. Vance (Ed.). *Pleasure and danger: Exploring female sexuality*. Boston: Routledge and Kegan Paul.

Tiefer, L. (1986). "In pursuit of the perfect penis." *American Behavioral Scientist* 29:579–99.

———. (1987). "Social constructionism and the study of human sexuality." In P. Shaver, and C. Hendrick (Eds.). *Review of personality and social psychology, vol 7: Sex and gender*. Beverly Hills: Sage, pp. 70–94.

Walkowitz, J. R. (1980). *Prostitution and Victorian society: Women, class and the state*. Cambridge: Cambridge University Press.

Weeks, J. (1985). *Sexuality and its discontents*. London: Routledge and Kegan Paul.

THREE

Feminist Critique of Science and the Challenge of Social Epistemology

Kenneth J. Gergen

IN SCANNING contemporary feminist scholarship one is struck by the extent to which critique prevails. Regardless of domain, the dominant posture is one of attack. One of the chief targets of this assault is the edifice of traditional, taken-for-granted knowledge—largely viewed by feminists as saturated with male perspectives and values, and frequently as a self-serving vehicle for sustaining male domination. For example, critical analyses have been directed against traditional biological accounts of women's nature (Hubbard 1983; Hubbard, this volume); the view of women in psychological research findings (Weisstein 1971); the assumption of bifurcated gender differences (Kessler and McKenna 1978); theories of moral development (Gilligan 1982); the image of women in gynecological treatises (Scully and Bart 1973); the pervasiveness of male metaphors in biophysical theorizing (Keller 1984); the invisibility of women in sociological analysis (Smith 1979); the image of patriarchy sustained by anthropological writing (Sanday, this volume); the under-representation of women in social science research (Johnson and Freize 1978); androcentric views of sexuality (Tiefer, this volume) and aggression (Macaulay 1985); the exclusion of the feminist voice from political theory (Evans 1986); the male monopoly on historical representation

(Janssen-Jurreit 1982), and male bias in sex role and marital adjustment research (Long Laws 1971).

The fruits of these various endeavors more than amply justify the extensive reliance on critique. The emancipatory potential of this form of scholarship seems enormous: once immersed in its lines of argumentation, one can scarcely comprehend the world again in the familiar ways of old. As its implications are increasingly elaborated, feminist scholarship becomes increasingly dislocating. It furnishes a radical challenge to one's sense of identity, one's view of human relationships, and one's conception of society and its relation to nature.

As Harding (1986) pointed out, such critiques have led some feminists to advocate a stricter adherence to the empiricist rules of method. The inadequacies of the traditional structures of knowledge might be overcome, it is maintained, if increasing numbers of variables (including gender) are taken into account, a systematically expanded array of hypotheses is subjected to test, value biases are obliterated, and so on. Yet, as evident to Harding and others, these feminist empiricist avenues of amelioration are in the end inadequate. They appear to question only the way in which empirical science is conducted, but in their critiques open the door to a profound questioning of the very foundations of empirical science itself. Let us briefly explore this.

Within the past century most institutions engaged in the generation of what is commonly accepted as knowledge have been wedded to some form of empiricist philosophy. From the empiricist standpoint, propositions about the world should be judged primarily with respect to their adequacy in mapping the actualities of the world itself. To this end, procedural or methodological rules have been articulated that, with proper application, are said to yield objectively grounded propositions. Depending on disciplinary context, such rules typically demand that an investigator specify a range of observables to be explored, employ rigorous sampling procedures, develop standardized mensurational devices, control relevant variables, place hypotheses at risk through deductive test, deploy statistical analyses, and so on. Traditionally, criticism within the sciences attempts to demonstrate the inadequacies of knowledge claims in properly applying one or more of the procedural rules.

In striking contrast, little of the feminist criticism has proceeded on conventional, empiricist grounds. In its selection of alternative discrediting devices, feminist critique has served indirectly to call into question the traditional empiricst perspective itself. For, as it is demonstrated, even when empiricist rules of method are assiduously employed, the resulting forms of knowledge are deeply problematic. In this sense, feminists have called into question the assumptions that frame the very logic of empirical investigation (Unger, 1983). Let us consider two of these forms of criticism.

First, feminist critics have revealed numerous instances in which scientists' orienting assumptions have circumscribed the kinds of results (or realities) that research can derive. And, because these orienting assumptions represent prevailing masculine perspectives, scientific realities typically suppress the feminine voice. If, for example, an investigator presumes there are two distinct genders, each indexed by physical features of the body, any differences found between the indexed groups will subsequently be used to reinforce the assumption of bifurcated gender. The research is essentially designed in a way that results can only yield support for a position that is adopted a priori. To the extent that orienting assumptions frame the categories of subsequent understanding, the kinds of questions toward which research can be directed, and the kinds of answers that can be derived, rules of empirical procedure furnish no corrective. Or to put it another way, once an investigator has adopted a given ontology, this system of orientation determines what is counted as an event; data cannot correct or falsify the ontology because all data collected within the perspective can be understood only in its terms. In this sense social scientists do not generally theorize about the part played in human affairs by the holy spirit or the spirit of evil, not because there are no social patterns amenable to interpretation in such terms, but because such terms do not fall within the ontological givens of contemporary science.[1] Thus, to attack scientific process for its biasing forestructure of understanding is not merely to question the traditional use of scientific method, but the basic adequacy of scientific method itself.

Consider a second case. Many feminists critics have located cases in which scientific theories appear to justify either an androcentric ideology or a self-serving structure of power. However, in spite of the early attempts of empiricist foundationalists to separate clearly between fact and value, there would appear to be no means by which value neutrality can be achieved. To the extent that any set of observables is subject to multiple interpretations, rules of empirical procedure furnish no barrier against the free play of values in selecting one interpretation over another. For example, psychological research once yielded numerous cases in which women exposed to the opinions of a group majority shifted their opinions in the majority direction to a greater extent than men. Investigators in such situations also confront a variety of possible interpretations of such actions. For example, the women's actions may be described as conforming, indecisive, integrative, cooperative, and so on. Yet the data themselves fail to inform the investigator which, if any of these characterizations, is "the correct" or "objective" one. Should the investigator chose to call the actions "conforming" (which most did), or would one of the alternative descriptions be more appropriate? The data are uninformative on the matter. In effect, the feminist critique undermines the very thesis of value neutrality traditionally used to valorize scientific procedure.

THE PROBLEMATICS OF PRIVILEGED PERSPECTIVE

AS WE see, once the grounds of feminist critique are extended they begin to furnish an indictment of the empiricist orientation to knowledge more generally. The empiricist promise of objective, cumulative knowledge through systematized methods of inquiry is found wanting. For many feminists such an indictment is directly on target. For, as it is reasoned, the empiricist conception of knowledge is itself a projection of masculine ideology or values. In its separation of subject and object, reason from emotion, and knowledge from its socio-historical context, the empiricist orientation is inimical to human welfare (cf. Bleier 1984; Keller 1984).

Yet, once empiricist foundationalism has been exposed, the feminist critic is placed in a vulnerable position. Critiques of the kind we have described satisfactorily demystify both androcentric claims to knowledge as well as the foundations for this knowledge itself. They demonstrate the nonobjective character of established "fact" as well as the grounds for establishing fact. However, the effects of this two-pronged attack are simultaneously suffused with irony. For as this line of argument becomes increasingly compelling, it simultaneously erodes the very grounds for its own legitimacy. Most of the attacks on traditional knowledge call attention to its biases, errors, and misleading conclusions. Such criticism implies the possibility of an alternative set of propositions that would correctly portray the world—including gender variations. Yet, if the criticism succeeds in impugning the very concept of objective science, then how is it possible to speak of propositions as "mystifying" at all? On what grounds could feminists establish correct or unbiased readings of nature?

It is out of this perplexing context that *feminist standpoint epistemologies,* as Harding (1986) called them, have grown to fruition. As proposed by a number of feminist scholars, the concepts of accurate and objectively grounded knowledge need not be cast aside. Rather, there are many reasons to believe that the male orientation to knowledge is systematically distorted in ways that the female standpoint is not. The female orientation toward understanding has greater potential to yield valid knowledge than the male's. Thus, not only are the critiques of male knowledge structures salvaged, but so is the possibility for some form of science, and in particular, a uniquely feminist science.

Several rationales have been used to privilege the female perspective. For example, Hilary Rose (1983) proposed that women's mode of inquiry has remained a form of "craft labor." As such, it contrasts favorably with the "industrialized labor" orientation of the male. In craft labor the person's manual, mental, and emotional activities are unified, as opposed to fragmented. In contrast, the industrialized labor of contemporary male-dominated science is one in which the three components of labor are either fragmented or suppressed altogether. In their more unified orientation, argued Rose, feminine scientists will abandon the misleading Cartesian dualisms of mind versus body and reason versus emotion and will replace the masculine preoccupation with reductionism and linearity with views emphasizing holism and complex interdependencies. In a roughly similar way Nancy Hartsock (1984) proposed that it is the gendered division of labor that furnishes women with a superior vantage point. Women's relationships with the world are more sensuous, concrete, and direct than men's; they reveal a more natural relationship with nature. They are not abstracted and alienated from nature, as are the male's, but in harmony with it.

Although less willing to credit the female experience with special powers, other feminists also locate infirmities in the male perspective. As Jane Flax (1983) proposed, when child care is predominantly the task of women, the male child realizes his identity by alienating himself from the social world. He needs to dominate and/or repress others in order to develop and sustain his identity. When the core self is defined as exclusively against women, the male will come to develop and employ categories of understanding that recapitulate the infantile dilemma. Again, the dualism between subject and object, mind and body, reason and emotion are found problematic. They are seen as projections of the peculiarities of the male developmental experience. For Dorothy Smith (1979), women's work in the culture relieves men of the need to take care of their bodies and the local places where they live; men are thus freed to engage in the world of abstract concepts and administrative ruling. They have little direct experience in many of the activities of the day-to-day world, and their abstractions are ill-suited to comprehending the world that women know by direct experience.

Although these various theses are in many ways compelling, in her review of this work Harding (1986) expressed considerable reserve. Harding's particular concern is not the attempt to demonstrate the superiority of the feminine over the masculine perspective. Rather, she reasoned, there are other groups whose rights to epistemological advantage may, by the same criteria as those developed by the standpoint theorists, exceed those of the feminists who appear to be favored by the existing analyses—namely Western, educated women of substantial economic means. After all, Western women have systematically participated in the colonialization practices that have subjugated large sectors of the African world—both men and women. Would not the experiences of these people—and most especially the black African woman—"provide the starting point for 'truer paths' toward belief and social relations undistorted by race and gender loyalties?" (p. 191). What right or privilege do white, Western feminists have to voice? Added to this problem is one of locating a common perspective on knowledge and relationships generalizable across the spectrum of women. The feminist sphere is fractionated—socialist, secular humanist, radical, lesbian, black, existentialist, Marxist, and so on. Is any of these groups to be granted special epistemological privilege? On what grounds?

Harding's questions are indeed significant and penetrating, and no immediate solutions are in sight. Yet, in the end Harding is willing to endorse these "successor science projects" for pragmatic reasons: "they are central to transferring the power to change social relations from the 'haves' to the 'have nots' " (p. 195). Although the "one true story" cannot be told from the feminist perspective, many partial stories are needed if social transformation is to be achieved. I am inclined to agree with Harding on pragmatic grounds. However, there are more profoundly disturbing aspects of feminist standpoint epistemologies—even when liberalized by a dash of postmodernism. In particular, such successor science projects seem to retain problematic features of the very sciences they seek to replace.

At the outset there is little challenge to the traditional empiricist presumptions that knowledge is a state of individual minds, that this state involves the accurate representation of the world, that people vary in the degree to which they possess this state, and that special privilege should be granted to those in possession of such states. All of these assumptions are constituents of the Enlightenment matrix out of which the concept of modern science has been fashioned. They have also served as justifications for the elaborate hierarchies of power and privilege that have so effectively suppressed the feminist voice thus far. Are the feminist attempts at successor science not in danger of recapitulating much the same form of justification, and thereby favoring the establishment of alternative hierarchies? And what is to prevent these alternative hierarchies from engaging in the same exclusionary tactics that will diminish the voice of all those who do not accede to the newly favored concept of knowledge? In what sense do such assumptions not lend themselves to just those kind of alienating and defensive strategies that have been viewed as typically male? Was Keller (1985) not correct in drawing a parallel between the concept of knowledge, social power, and domination? To grant the first is to invite the second and third.

In addition to this valuational problem, feminist projects for a successor science seem vulnerable to many of the same kinds of arguments that have brought empiricist foundationalism into its currently deteriorated condition. During the past several decades, for example, we have confronted stinging arguments against inductivism (Hanson 1958); the logic of verification (Popper 1968); operationism (Koch 1959); word-object correspondence (Quine 1960); the separation of analytic from synthetic propositions (Quine 1951); the supposed interdependence of theoretical understanding and prediction (Toulmin 1961); the commensurability of competing theories (Feyerabend 1976); the separation of fact and value (MacIntyre 1973); the possibility of theoretically unsaturated or brute facts (Hanson 1958); the logic of deduction (Barrett 1979); the possibility of falsifying theory (Quine 1953); the nonpartisan character of scientific knowledge (Habermas 1971); the possibility of historical accumulation in behavioral knowledge (Gergen 1973); and the applicability of the covering law and mechanistic models of human action (White 1978), to name but a few. It is one thing to speak of women's experience as tied more closely than men's to the grit of daily relations, to the emotions, nature, generativity, and so on. However, it is quite another to mold from that congenial clay an idol of knowledge that would not be subject to many of these same criticisms. What would feminist knowledge claims look like that were not subject to contextual alteration in meaning; how would such propositions develop if perspective precedes perception; how would such propositions be put to test if deductive logic is but cultural artifact, and so on?

And perhaps most important, on what grounds are the feminist warrants for knowledge themselves to be justified? For example, how do we know that sound knowledge must be closely entwined with passion, that reductionism is false, or that linear thinking distorts reality? Are these propositions simply self-evident? Does their justification also depend on the special sensitivity of women, or on some other foundation? And if they depend on female experience, how would women escape the criticism leveled against their male counterparts, that their orientations are self-serving? The range of challenges to a feminist foundationalism seems formidable.

TOWARD A SOCIAL EPISTEMOLOGY

AT THIS juncture one is inclined to search for some alternative to positions that grant to one group of people some specialized or rare gift of insight rendering their perceptions of the world uniquely superior. It also seems that intimations for such an alternative are already contained within much existing feminist writing. As Harding (1986) saw it this movement may be termed postmodern. To appreciate its emergence let us return for a moment to the unfolding line of argument. As we saw, feminist criticism of traditional knowledge claims within the sciences has done much to expose problems with the empiricist view of knowledge more generally. Yet as we also saw, these criticisms of empirical knowledge themselves seemed to rest on knowledge claims. With the concept of objective knowledge impugned, the very grounds for the feminist claims were jeopardized. At this juncture, two alternatives were opened: first, one could respond by developing an alternative view of knowledge that would render the critique immune from its own implications, or second, one could forgo the very concept of objective knowledge itself. As we have seen, much feminist standpoint epistemology has gone in the former direction, and this direction now proves problematic. Remaining for serious consideration is the second alternative: the abandonment of the concept of objective knowledge.

Indeed the possibility for this latter view can be located in various feminist writings. For example, Flax's recent work (1986) proposes that there is no "feminist standpoint which is more true than previous (male) ones" (p. 37). She linked feminist criticism with postmodern thought more generally, in which uncertainty prevails concerning the appropriate grounding for scientific propositions. The possibility for abandoning the presumption of objective knowledge is also evident in Smith's (1979) argument that because men possess different categories of experience, they cannot adequately describe or explain the world of women. To extend this view is to say that women cannot properly account for the world of men, adults cannot adequately portray the world of children, practicing social scientists cannot penetrate the life of the society, and ultimately, there are no generalizable standards of accuracy for comparing diverse perspectives. (See also discussions by Stanley and Wise 1983; Spender 1985.)

If objectivity is abandoned, how are we to account for the array of existing knowledge claims? As is evident from many of the critiques of androcentric science, there is an emerging alternative. In particular, it becomes increasingly compelling to trace knowledge claims to social process. To the extent that feminist thinkers move in this direction, they also find wide-ranging support in other postmodern enclaves. Such a shift is evident not only in much postmodern literary criticism. It is also reflected in hermeneutic and interpretive studies; certain lines of agreement within the history and the sociology of science; strong currents within social constructionist analysis, ethnomethodology, historiography, and rhetorical study; and current reassessments of validity in ethnographic reporting. Throughout these enterprises one detects overtures for the emergence of a thoroughgoing social epistemology, or an epistemological standpoint from which knowledge claims are viewed as quintessential constituents of social interchange. This is hardly to say that there is broadly articulated agreement concerning the contours of a social epistemology. Controversy can be located at every turn. However, it does prove useful to attempt a preliminary articulation of a social epistemological standpoint around which significant accord might be achieved across the postmodern domain, both feminist and otherwise. In this way both elaboration and/or critique may be facilitated. Let us consider, then, four suppositions that many would consider critical to the development of a social epistemology:

1) *Knowledge claims may properly be viewed as forms of discourse.* Rather than adopting the traditional assumption that knowledge claims are reports on states of experience (typically privileged), we may usefully shift our concern to the level of discourse. As a number of feminist thinkers have argued, the traditional Cartesian distinctions between mind and body and subject and object are problematic. Although from different vantage points, similar conclusions have been reached by philosophers extending lines of late Wittgensteinian philosophy (Austin 1962; Ryle 1949; Rorty 1979), and by deconstructionist literary analysts concerned with the logocentric bias in literary interpretation (Derrida 1977). As these various lines of thinking are extended, we find that the traditional conception of knowledge as some form of mental representation ceases to be compelling. If we do not presume that there are minds that serve as mirrors of an independent world, then traditional questions of epistemology fall by the wayside. We need not ask how sense data are converted to perceptual categories, how the mental world could be built up from incoming stimuli, whether there could be identifiable objects of experience without preceding mental categories, and other perennially insoluble questions of philosophic and psychological import. Further, we need not develop hierarchies based on variation in experiential acuity; no class of people, including scientists armed with sophisticated technology and statistical procedures, may claim the right to superior perceptions of the world. Finally, with dualism abandoned, we need no longer view dis-

course about the world as an expression of private experience. We may properly turn our attention away from knowledge as mental representation, to knowledge claims. The latter claims may be viewed as moves in the process of discourse.

2) *What there is does not in itself dictate the properties of the discourse by which intelligibility is rendered.* As we see, the problems for the epistemologist are considerably altered by the foregoing line of argument. Rather than asking how some particular form of experience comes to be privileged, we shift attention to the problem of warranting discourse. On what grounds are particular forms of discourse to be justified or rendered superior? By posing the question in this manner, it first becomes apparent that mimesis is an inadequate grounds of privilege. That is, whatever the nature of what is the case, it places no intrinsic constraints over the discourse used in making an account of it. (Even the admission that there is an "it" to be accounted for is inappropriate in this regard, as such phrasing again suggests a world independent of the observer, and that the function of language is to provide pictures of this world. However, given the constraints over the Western tradition of letters, it is difficult to locate terms that are more appropriate to the epistemic position being developed here.) What I take to be this array before me can be described as a simple figure before a receding ground, a spectrum of colors, a mosaic of isolated geometric forms, an array of light reflections, assorted bundles of atomic particles, a desk and a bookcase, or the artifactual productions of an irresolute mentality. I could go on to generate words for each "perceptually discriminable atom" of my experiences, or I could describe all as one meaningless void. Whatever there is places no inherent constraints over the language by which I make it intelligible.

To furnish teeth to this emerging line of reasoning, we may venture that the validity of theoretical propositions in the sciences is in no way affected by factual evidence. How does this follow? First, we find that the concept of "validity" itself is problematic. If by this term one is invoking a traditional metaphysics of subject-object independence, privileged experience, and theoretical propositions as expressions of that experience, then the presumption of validity ceases to be of interest. But for the sake of moving understanding forward, let us define validity in terms of the match between theoretical discourse and a world independent of that discourse. Would validity in this sense not be enhanced by recourse to objective evidence? If what there is places no inherent constraints over how it is described, the answer would appear to be negative. For facts themselves must be "described" in order to count as facts, and if what there is does not constrain such descriptions, then whether the description corroborates the theoretical proposition primarily depends on one's choice of factual discourse. Each attempt to furnish a fact or an objective datum in support of a given theory is, in effect, a discursive move. It is an attempt to render support for one objectively unwarranted account with additional accounts of equal character. When facts are invoked in support of a given proposition, they are invariably not events (or things) in themselves but descriptive renderings of event. Because events in themselves place no essential demands over the renderings, they provide not objective but rhetorical support for relevant theoretical proposition. Let us consider an illustration and then deal with a possible objection.

Consider again the research attempting to explore gender difference in social conformity. What facts could be mustered that would bear on the validity of the proposition that females demonstrate a greater degree of social conformity than males? At the outset we realize that the proposition itself is uninformative as to what particulars would count toward its confirmation or disconfirmation. In our attempt to locate males and females, should we consider nonhumans, human fetuses, infants, the crippled, the schizophrenic, and the like? As ethnomethodological inquiry suggests, what counts as male and female also differs as one moves from one spectrum of the society to another. Children's definitions of sex differences differ from those of adults, and adults differ depending on whether they are from a Western culture, are trained in the medical professon, or are transsexuals (Kessler and McKenna 1978). Whose definition are we to accept? And what constitutes an act of conformity? Is not all coordinated social action "conforming" in a certain manner of speaking; is not all behavior independent in yet another frame of discourse? Whose definition of conformity are we to honor in this regard? As we see, no objective answer can be provided to the initial question of how we can go about locating facts relevant to the theoretical proposition.

But what if we bracket this problem and ask how facts generated by systematic inquiry could properly bear on the matter? Many psychologists establish controlled laboratory settings in which "males" and females" are exposed to the opinions of other research participants. At times these opinions seem erroneous; others agree, for example that the shorter of several lines is the longer, or that the number of items in an array is much larger or smaller than it actually is. Comparisons are then made in the extent to which males as opposed to females will alter their judgments so as to agree with the erroneous group judgment. Should the results of such work not bear on the validity of the general proposition? Consider the laboratory procedure: what if it were described in terms of shifting patterns of figure and ground, movements of bodies, bundles of atomic particles, colored patterns—all reasonable descriptions of the same set of events. Yet, should any of these intelligibilities be selected one has said nothing bearing on social conformity. To account fully for each movement through time and space of each laboratory subject, or each momentary state of the neurons, is to say nothing of interest to the theoretical proposition. In effect, the actual events serve as evidence only if one selects a particular discursive practice. There is nothing about the events in themselves that prescribes which practice must be selected. Thus, what counts as fact in this case is determined not by what there is but by the particular line of interpretive discourse to which one is committed.

In reply to this line of reasoning one might ask whether it is not a form of misleading linguistic realism that denies altogether a factual or objective world. Even if one agrees that when attempting to describe the facts relevant to a proposition one is indeed engaging in a discursive practice, and agrees that possibly these practices are not determined by what is the case, how can we deny the palpable certainty that *something* is the case, and that this something bears upon the legitimacy of the discursive practices? In reply, there is nothing within a social epistomology that necessarily grants or denies ontological status. That is, the attempt is neither to state that something is or is not the case. Rather, the account leaves questions of ontology in suspension; to state that something is the case is already to engage in a discursive practice that cannot itself be warranted by what is. Whatever is, simply is; to presume that it is independent of ourselves, that it is composed of separate entities, that it endures across time, and so on, are all discursive moves. Such statements move within a sphere of linguistic controls, distinctions, and variations that are not themselves determined by what is the case. To be sure, in both science and daily life we do often confront a sense of validity. Directions to the nearest druggist seem to be proved either correct or incorrect; one can seem to validate estimates of one's weight through observation, and so on. However, as we shall see in the next section, this sense of validity is more properly viewed as a social achievement. Such "proofs" are simply irrelevant to what is the case.

3) *Because discourse is inherently social we may look to social process for an understanding of how knowledge claims are justified.* Thus far it has been proposed that knowledge claims are neither mirrors of mental states nor ontological conditions. Rather, it is proposed, knowledge claims are forms of discourse. If these positions are defensible, then in our search for justification of knowledge claims we find ourselves confronting characteristics of discourse formation and sustenance. And as we do so, it is initially apparent that discourse is not the possession of single individuals—isolated social atoms—but a property of social interchange. My words are simply nonsense until you accord them status as meaningful; your utterances are transformed into language as I coordinate myself to them. In effect, the generation of meaning in language is in John Shotter's (1980) terms a *joint-action;* it requires the mutual coordination of actions among two or more persons. Such a conclusion would appear to be favored as well by much feminist writing (cf. Scheman 1983; Unger, 1983; Chodorow 1978; Frye 1983). It rejects the logocentric bias of language and calls attention instead to the interdependent character of human actions; the generation of knowledge is thus the fruit of social connection rather than separation. It is through harmony in human relatedness that reality, as a linguistic rendering, comes into being at all.

In this context we are again invited to reconsider the process of knowledge justification in terms of social process. Science becomes an inherently social enterprise, with the valorization of knowledge claims depending on communal processes rather than verisimilitude. It is in this arena that both historians and sociologists of knowledge have already made major contributions. Kuhn's (1970) classic work effectively replaced empiricist justificationism with social process as the basis of scientific revolutions. Although later weakening his thesis (Kuhn 1977) by falling back on arguments for "epistemic values" (empiricist justification in disguise), the force of the argument was then amplified by Feyerabend (1976, 1982). Since that time many historians of science (cf. Mendelsohn 1977) have gone on to detail the influence of social process on the formulation, perpetuation, and alteration of scientific accounts. At the same time, a

number of sociologists of science have begun to explore the social processes underlying the generation of what passes as scientific knowledge in the present. In the hands of analysts such as Barnes (1974), Latour and Woolgar (1979), Knorr-Cetina and Mulkay (1983), and others, principles of logic and observation play little role in the production of knowledge; communal processes are essential.

To be sure, these various reconceptualizations of science leave open the problem of advances in technology—or the capabilities of humans for generating new implements for solving pressing problems. They undermine the traditional view that such advances are the results of rigorous induction, deduction, and hypothesis testing. However, they do not furnish an adequate explanation of the increments in pragmatic skills that have accrued over the centuries. What account is to be furnished of our enhanced ability to cure disease, generate heat and light, fly through the air, and so on? This is not a viable setting for a full treatment of this problem, but we can begin to discern in the preceding account critical elements for an appropriate account. To draw from feminist concerns with the practical and the concrete, on the one hand, and with the organic connection of humans to their environment on the other, it may be ventured that pragmatic gains are made as we increasingly coordinate ourselves with nature. The generation of advanced technologies and predictive capability are the results of what Hilary Rose (1983) might call "craft labor"; they depend on a direct immersion in nature, a working with or a coordination of actions with one's surroundings. Thus, to the extent that laboratory sciences succeed in generating "advances" they do so in terms of practical activity.

The place of theory in this enterprise is thus moved to a secondary status. Scientific theory, on this account, does not serve the putative functions of description, nor is it theory that enables one to predict. Rather, theories enter the picture as means of coordinating the communities of scientists working together on various problems of practice. In effect, scientific theories possess practical utility in the communal activity of science. As we coordinate ourselves simultaneously with nature and with others, discourse takes on increasing utility. In Wittgenstein's (1963) sense we may view language as woven into various "language games." Words and phrases gain their meaning according to their utility in playing the game. In this sense terms such as protons, polymer, plenum, polity, and persuasion are essential not as descriptions of what there is, but as implements enabling scientific laborers to accomplish their more organically embedded tasks of prediction and control. Theoretical terms may all be viewed as critical constituents in a complex set of social interdependencies. While not approximations to the truth, they are nevertheless vital to carrying out the scientific enterprise.

4) *Because knowledge claims are constitutive of social life they should properly be opened to evaluation by the full range of discursive communities.* This latter emphasis on the pragmatic utility of language within the communal activity that we call science has further implications of significance. The pragmatic features of discourse are hardly limited to the scientific sphere; on the contrary, the scientific usage is undoubtedly derivative of the more general utility of language in carrying out daily affairs. At least within the modern Western world it would be difficult to participate in most organized patterns of relationship without a verbal language. It is not that language is essential to the expression of our states of mind; as we have seen from the preceding analysis, this view of language commits one to an unnecessary and obfuscating dualism. Rather, we may view verbal language as a vital constituent of many complex patterns of interrelationship. (See also Packer, in press; Shweder and Miller 1985.) To carry out a friendship, a business transaction, a romance, or a classroom exercise typically requires that participants coordinate movements of their limbs, eyes, facial expressions, and so on, along with the sounds emitted from their mouths. To do language in these settings is to enter into coordinated patterns of relatedness.

This preamble is essential to understanding the fuller implications of carrying out scholarly work—particularly inquiry in the social sciences and humanities. For, although developed within scholarly communities, scholarly discourse seldom remains at home. That is, such discourse is injected (often systematically) into the surrounding culture. As scholars undertake the tasks of description, explanation, logical analysis, and critique, they are essentially offering to the world forms of discursive practice. To all who would (or must) listen, these forms of practice may subsequently be utilized in carrying out local relationships. (See also chapters by Grosholz and by Shotter and Logan, this volume.)

This insinuation of scholarly language into the society is of no small consequence, for as we have seen, the linguistic practices of the community are integrally woven into more general patterns of cultural life. Thus, as the linguistic potential of the culture is extended, modified, or expanded by the scholarly community, the social patterns of the culture are diminished, transformed, or enriched. On this view scientists do not serve as passionless automatons steeped in the rigors of holding mirrors to reality. Rather, in the very formulation of problems, the choice of possible solutions, and the attempt to evaluate one solution against the other, they are already entering into the life of the culture. To view the world as a Humean mechanist, a Cartesian dualist, a Hobbesian, a Freudian, or a Marxist has vital implications for the kinds of relationships in which we are engaged. Each frame of discourse favors certain actions and inhibits others; each sustains or alters the culture for good or ill according to some standard (See also Henriques et al. 1984; Mitchell 1983).

We thus see that to abandon the search for truth in science or other scholarly pursuits is not to undermine the importance of such activities. On the contrary, it is to heighten the scholar's sense of responsibility; such activity can contribute to or destroy existing forms of cultural life. As the fruits of scholarship come to be tasted by increasing numbers, so the potential for cultural transformation is increased. The feminist concern with the gulf between abstract conceptual work and social praxis is thus averted; for, so long as such theoretical work can be meaningfully communicated it constitutes a form of praxis.

At the same time, this analysis invites the development of critically reflexive dialogue. If scholarly discourse is active in the shaping of the culture, then such discourse should be open to critical scrutiny from all sectors of the society. The kinds of attacks launched by feminists on male practices of knowledge making should be viewed as neither uniquely necessary nor a temporary holding action—awaiting the emergence of new social forms. Rather, as Feyerabend advocated in his *Science in a Free Society,* the reflexive consideration of various forms of discourse should be a continuous undertaking in which all subcultural enclaves should be invested. In this undertaking a premium is to be placed on dialogue. All too often the focus of critique is limited to various outgroups; its logic is shared only by participants in a specialized discourse community—which such critique typically serves to sustain. However, when critique remains insulated from challenge by others—particularly its targets—coordinated interdependence is reduced. The possibilities for hierarchy, subject-object dichotomy, and dehumanizing oppression are all increased. As Keller (1986) advised, we must "negotiate our way between sameness and opposition" and permit "the recognition of kinship in difference and of difference among kin." It is through broadly extended dialogue that we are most likely to accomplish these honorable goals.

CONCLUSION

THIS chapter has attempted to examine the epistemological implications of existing feminist criticism of scientific knowledge. As initially demonstrated, such criticism is not simply an admonishment of the male bias in scientific "truths"; it simultaneously questions the very concept of empirical science itself. The chapter then considers various attempts by feminist scholars to replace the androcentric conception of empirical knowledge with views of science that grant privilege to the feminist perspective. Important shortcomings are also found in this orientation. Finally, the chapter explores the possibilities of a social epistemology that seems deeply congenial with many existing lines of feminist argument. Such an orientation would view knowledge claims as discursive commitments, fundamentally unconstrained by observation, dependent on social process, and constitutive of social pattern. The importance of criticism and conceptual creativity is stressed. Further implications and possible shortcomings of these views are discussed elsewhere (Gergen 1985, 1987). Additional exploration will be required to determine the viability of such an orientation—both as an account of science and as an expression of feminist concerns.

NOTE

1. At times social scientists may appear to test competing theories against each other. However, such "tests" are permitted only when the scholar is willing to suspend belief in a given form of intelligibility and accede to the plausibility of a · competing framework. Such suspension of belief cannot be undertaken on ra-

tional-empirical grounds, as there is nothing in the initial commitment that would grant a potential competitor voice.

REFERENCES

Austin, J. L. (1962). *Sense and sensibilia.* London: Oxford University Press.

Barnes, B. (1974). *Scientific knowledge and sociological theory.* London: Routledge and Kegan Paul.

Barrett, W. (1979). *The illusion of technique.* New York: Doubleday.

Bleier, R. (1984). *Science and gender.* New York: Pergamon.

Chodorow, N. (1978). *The reproduction of mothering: psychoanalysis and the sociology of gender.* Berkeley: University of California Press.

Derrida, J. (1977). *Positions.* Paris: Editions de Minuit.

Evans, J. (1986). *Feminism and political theory.* Beverly Hills: Sage.

Feyerabend, P. K. (1976). *Against method.* Atlantic Highlands, N.J.: Humanities Press.

———. (1982). *Science in a free society.* New York: Schocken.

Flax, J. (1983). "Political philosophy and the patriarchal unconscious: A psycho-analytic perspective on epistemology and metaphysics." In S. Harding and M. Hintikka (Eds.). *Discovering reality: Feminist perspectives on epistemology, metaphysics, methodology and philosophy of science.* Dordrecht: Reidel.

———. (1986). "Gender as a social problem: In and for feminist theory." *American Studies/Amerika Studien,* Journal of the German Association for American Studies 31:193–213.

Frye, M. (1983). *The politics of reality.* Trumansburg, N.Y.: Crossing Press.

Gergen, K. J. (1973). "Social psychology as history." *Journal of Personality and Social Psychology* 26:309–20.

———. (1982) *Toward transformation in social knowledge.* New York: Springer-Verlag.

———. (1985). "Psychological inquiry in an age of social epistemology." Boston Symposium in the Philosophy of Science.

———. (1987). "The checkmate of rhetoric (But can our reasons become causes)." In H. Simons (Ed.). *Case studies in the rhetoric of the human sciences.* Chicago: University of Chicago Press.

Gilligan, C. (1982). *In a different voice: psychological theory and women's development.* Cambridge: Harvard University Press.

Habermas, J. (1971). *Knowledge and human interest.* Boston: Beacon Press.

Hanson, N. R. (1958). *Patterns of discovery.* London: Cambridge University Press.

Harding, S. (1986). *The science question in feminism.* Ithaca: Cornell University Press.

Hartsock, N. (1983a). "Difference and domination in the women's movement: The dialectics of theory and practice." In A. Swerdlaw and H. Lehner (Eds.). *Class, race and sex: Exploring contradictions, affirming connections.* Boston: Hall.

——. (1983b). "The feminist standpoint: Developing the ground for a specifically feminist historical materialism." In S. Harding and M. Hintikka (Eds.). *Discovering reality: Feminist perspectives on epistemology, metaphysics, methodology and philosophy of science.* Dordrecht: Reidel.

Henriques, J., et al. (1984). *Changing the subject: Psychology, social regulation and subjectivity.* London: Methuen.

Hubbard, R. (1983). "Have only men evolved?" In S. Harding and M. Hintikka (Eds.). *Discovering reality: Feminist perspectives on epistemology, metaphysics, methodology and philosophy of science.* Dordrecht: Reidel.

Janssen-Jurreit, M. (1982). *Sexism: The male monopoly on the history of thought.* London: Pluto Press.

Johnson, P. B., and Frieze, I. H. (1978). "Biases in psychology: What are the facts?" in I. Frieze (Ed.). *Women and sex roles: a social psycholgoical perspective.* New York: Norton.

Keller, E. F. (1984). *Reflections on gender & science.* New Haven: Yale University Press.

——. (1986). "The science/gender system, or, is sex to gender as nature is to science?" Women, Health and Technology Conference, University of Connecticut, Storrs.

Kessler, S. J., and McKenna, W. (1978). *Gender: An ethnomethodological approach.* New York: Wiley.

Knorr-Cetina, K. (1981). *The manufacture of knowledge.* Oxford: Pergamon.

——, and Mulkay, M. (1983). *Science observed.* Beverly Hills: Sage.

Koch, S. (1959). Epilogue. In S. Koch (Ed.) *Psychology: A study of a science.* Vol. 3. New York: McGraw Hill.

Kuhn, T. S. (1970). *The structure of scientific revolution.* Chicago: University of Chicago Press.

——. (1977). *The essential tension.* Chicago: University of Chicago Press.

Latour, B., and Woolgar, S. (1979). *Laboratory life, the social construction of scientific facts.* Beverly Hills: Sage.

Long Laws, J. (1971). "A feminist review of marital adjustment literature: The rape of the Locke." *Journal of Marriage and the Family* 33:483–517.

Longino, H. (1981). "Scientific objectivity and feminist theorizing." *Liberal Education* 67.

——. (1983). "Scientific objectivity and the logics of science." *Inquiry* March issue.

Macaulay, J. (1985). "Adding gender to aggression research: Incremental or revolutionary change." In V. O'Leary, R. Unger and B. S. Wallston (Eds.). *Women, gender, and social psychology.* Hillsdale, N.J.: Erlbaum.

MacIntyre, A. (1973). "Ideology, social science & revolution." *Comparative Politics* 5: 321–41.

Mendelsohn, E. (1977). "The social construction of scientific knowledge." In E. Mendelsohn and P. Weingert (Eds.). *The social production of scientific knowledge*. Dordrecht: Reidel.

Mitchell, W. J. (1983). *The politics of interpretation*. Chicago: University of Chicago Press.

Packer, M. J. (in press). "Social interaction as practical activity: Implications for the study of social and moral development." In W. M. Kurtines and J. Gerwirtz (Eds.). *Social interaction and sociomoral development*. Beverly Hills: Sage.

Popper, K. R. (1968). *The logic of scientific discovery*. New York: Harper and Row.

Quine, W. V. (1951). "Two dogmas of empiricism." *Philosophical Review* 60:20–43.

——. (1953). *From a logical point of view*. Cambridge: Harvard University Press.

——. (1960). *Word and object*. Cambridge: MIT Press.

Rorty, R. (1979). *Philosophy and the mirror of nature*. Princeton: Princeton University Press.

Rose, H. (1983). "Hand, brain and heart: A feminist epistemology for the natural sciences." *Signs* 1:73–90.

Ryle, G. (1949). *The concept of mind*. London: Hutchinson.

Scheman, N. (1983). "Individualism and the objects of psychology." In S. Harding and M. Hintikka (Eds.). *Discovering reality: Feminist perspectives on epistemology, metaphysics, methodology and philosophy of science*. Dordrecht: Reidel.

Scully, D., and Bart, P. J. (1973). "A funny thing happened on the way to the orifice: Women in gynecology textbooks." *American Journal of Sociology* 78: 1045–49.

Shotter, J. (1980). "Action, joint action and intentionality." In M. Brenner (Ed.). *The structure of action*. Oxford: Blackwell.

Shweder, R. A., and Miller, J. G. (1985). "The social construction of the person: How is it possible?" In K. J. Gergen and K. E. Davis (Eds.). *The social construction of the person*. New York: Springer-Verlag.

Smith, D. (1979). "A sociology for women." In J. Sherman and E. J. Beck (Eds.). *The prism of sex: Essays in the sociology of knowledge*. Madison: University of Wisconsin Press.

Spender, D. (1981). *Men's studies modified: The impact of feminism on the academic disciplines*. Elmsford, N.Y.: Pergamon Press.

——. (1985). *For the record: The making and meaning of feminist knowledge*. London: The Women's Press.

Stanley, J. L, and Wise, S. (1983). *Breaking out: Feminist consciousness and feminist research*. London: Routledge and Kegan Paul.

Toulmin, S. (1961). *Foresight & understanding*. New York: Harper and Row.

Unger, R. K. (1983). "Through the looking glass: No wonderland yet! (The reciprocal relationship between methodology and models of reality.)" *Psychology of Women Quarterly* 8:9–32.

Weisstein, N. (1971). "Psychology constructs the female." In V. Gornick and B. Moran (Eds.). *Women in sexist society.* New York: Basic Books.

White, H. (1978). *Tropics of discourse.* Baltimore: Johns Hopkins University Press.

Wittgenstein, L. (1963). *Philosophical investigations.* (G.E.M. Anscombe, Trans.). New York: Macmillan.

FOUR

The Reproduction of Patriarchy in Feminist Anthropology

Peggy Reeves Sanday

Our questions are inevitably bound up with our politics. The character, constraint, and promise of our scholarship are informed as much by moral ends and choices as they are by the "objective" postures necessary to research. For feminists, especially, intellectual insight thrives in a complex relation with contemporary moral and political demands.

(Rosaldo 1983, p. 76)

The attempt to view other systems from ground level is the basis, perhaps the only basis, of anthropology's distinctive contribution to the human sciences. It is our capacity, largely developed in fieldwork, to take the perspective of the folks on the shore, that allows us to learn anything at all—even in our own culture—beyond what we already know. . . . Further, it is our location "on the ground" that puts us in a position to see people not simply as passive reactors to and enactors of some "system," but as active agents and subjects in their own history.

(Ortner 1984, p. 143)

INTRODUCTION

TO VIEW other systems from "ground level," to see people as "active agents and subjects in their own history," as Ortner suggested in the above passage, is extremely difficult given the political (and, I would add, theoretical) agendas to which Rosaldo alluded. Questions concerning the position of the sexes—an issue of long-standing interest to feminist anthropologists—are inevitably politicized in any society. If politics can be seen in part as myth making for purposes of social control or social change, it is easy to see how our informants who spin out tales about their position as male or female are engaged in politics. For example, an old man in an African village who complains about his marital status both rationalizes his status and provides a rhetorical basis for marshaling sympathy for his inferior position when he says, "Women make all the choices. It's all up to the women. If a woman doesn't want me, I must be alone. A woman does whatever she wants. A woman is free. She is free to do what she herself feels like doing." In the same village a female elder reinforces the position of women by appealing to the unchangeable and the universal, "Women came to the earth first and bore the children. If men had come first, they would bear the children. Men can do nothing without women. Every woman has her way of saying no. Women decide everything that is big and important. We women are greater than the men. This is true all over the world. Why? Because women bear the man. Women are greatest everywhere. Women everywhere are superior to men" (From the film *Our God Is a Woman* by Leyla Assaf-Tengroth and Ragnar Hedlund).

In another part of the world (West Sumatra), a well-known specialist in the rules of traditional custom proudly lectures me on the superior position of West Sumatran women vis-à-vis Western women by appealing to biblical imagery: "Why was Adam sent into the world by God? To accompany Eve. So Eve is just as important as Adam. Women play a very important role. Without women life would be impossible. So for these reasons women are given more privileges."

Some sort of gender polemic, verbal game playing in which one sex is compared with the other to score a point in some imagined or actual social debate, is probably present in most societies. The maneuvering in sexual politics means that observations of actors acting are relative to a particular context. Because they are derived from a "ground" that is constantly shifting, such observations provide a weak basis for drawing generalized conclusions about the relative status of the sexes. Compounding the problem of research are the political and theoretical agendas the anthropologist brings to the data. My purpose in this chapter is to examine the agendas in feminist anthropologists' theoretical polemic regarding the position of the sexes in human society. This examination provides a forum for discussing the complex interrelationship between ground level observation, intellectual insight, and contemporary moral and political demands.

In selecting the above examples of gender polemic, I purposely allude to one side of a long-standing debate among feminist anthropologists concerning the ethnographic reality of significant female power and authority. On one hand there are those, like myself, who evoke ethnographic examples of sexual symmetry, sexual equality, or matrifocality, and on the other there are those who claim the universality of "male dominance" or "gender hierarchy." Such different views of the position of women in society held by feminist anthropologists must be puzzling to those who look to anthropology for an objective analysis of a long-standing debate in the social sciences.

I will describe the two sides of this debate and discuss the underlying rationale for each. I suggest that the two sides are joined by similar goals. Although differing in strategy—one reproducing a Western vision of a male-dominated social reality and the other introducing a more female-dominated view—adherents of both work to change Western patriarchy; the disagreement is mainly in the method and theory employed for distilling intellectual insight from the discipline of anthropology in order to effect such a change.

THE PATRIARCHAL MODEL OF HUMAN SOCIETY

THE PATRIARCHAL model articulated by feminist anthropologists is of two forms: one emphasizes the structurally peripheral position of women to the system of rights and duties in persons or things; the other concentrates on the symbolic devaluation of women. The first form of the model is articulated by anthropologists Michelle Rosaldo and Louise Lamphere in their introduction to *Woman, Culture, and Society* (1974), one of the first book-length treatments of anthropological issues from the perspective of women anthropologists.

Like others before them, Rosaldo and Lamphere began by rejecting the work of Bachofen and Morgan. In answer to the claim made by these men that "in an earlier stage of human development the social world was organized by a principle called matriarchy, in which women had power over men," they wrote, "most academic anthroplogists have dismissed [such a claim] out of hand" (Rosaldo and Lamphere 1974, p. 2). "[T]he current anthropological view," they continued,

draws on the observation that most and probably all contemporary societies, whatever their kinship organization or mode of subsistence, are characterized by some degree of male dominance.

Whereas some anthropologists argue that there are, or have been, truly egalitar-
iant societies (Leacock 1972), and all agree that there are societies in which
women have achieved considerable social recognition and power, none has observed a society in which women have publicly recognized power and authority
surpassing that of men. . . . Everywhere we find that women are excluded from
certain crucial economic or political activities, that their roles as wives and mothers
are associated with fewer powers and prerogatives than are the roles of men. It
seems fair to say then, that all contemporary societies are to some extent male-
dominated, and although the degree and expression of female subordination vary
greatly, sexual asymmetry is presently a universal fact of human social life. (Rosaldo and Lamphere 1974, pp. 2–3)

Despite the reference to Eleanor Leacock's very convincing work on
sexually egalitarian band societies in this quote, and despite her own short
description (Rosaldo 1974) of the relatively egalitarian relations between
the Ilongot sexes, among whom she worked, Rosaldo remained firm
regarding the issue of universal sexual asymmetry. In a 1980 article
published in *Signs,* she reiterated the empirical reality of the patriarchal
model, saying:

. . . could I cite a single instance of a truly matriarchal—or, for that matter,
sexually egalitarian—social form, I could go on to claim that all appeals to
universal "nature" in explaining women's place are, simply, wrong. But instead, I
must begin by making clear that, unlike many anthropologists who argue for the
privileged place of women here or there, my reading of the anthropological record
leads me to conclude that human cultural and social forms *have always been male
dominated.* (emphasis mine, Rosaldo 1980, p. 393)

Rosaldo's reference to universal "nature" in this quote brings to mind
Sherry Ortner's article in *Woman, Culture, and Society,* which, although
provocative and innovative in its application of symbolic analysis to gender themes, has been widely criticized (see articles in MacCormack and
Strathern 1980). Ortner's primary purpose in her paper was "to explain
the universal secondary status of women" (1984, p. 83). Since a universal
can be explained only by some other universal, she specifically discounted
explanatory variables such as "economy, ecology, history, political and
social structure, values, and world view." She also discounted the ideology
of biological determinism and turned for explanation to the symbolic
refractions and valuations of women's reproduction. She concluded that

"the universal devaluation of women could be explained by postulating that women are seen as closer to nature than men, men being seen as more unequivocally occupying the high ground of culture. The culture/nature distinction is itself a product of culture, culture being minimally defined as the transcendence, by means of systems of thought and technology, of the natural givens of existence" (Ortner 1974, p. 84).

The core of Ortner's paper is devoted to showing why women are universally assumed to be closer to nature than men. The reasons she enumerated are: "Women's physiology, more involved more of the time with 'species of life' "; "woman's association with the structurally subordinate domestic context, charged with the crucial function of transforming animal-like infants into cultured beings"; "woman's psyche," which is oriented to mothering and "tending toward greater personalism and less mediated modes of relating." Such factors appear to place women "more directly and deeply in nature." Since women are also recognized as participating in culture, Ortner concluded that women are "seen to occupy an intermediate position between nature and culture." Such an intermediacy of status "means 'middle status' on a hierarchy of being from culture to nature" (1974).

Although widely criticized for universalizing a Western gender model, Ortner did not substantially change her views in her 1981 introduction to *Sexual Meanings,* coauthored with Harriet Whitehead. Rather than claiming universality for a genderized culture/nature dichotomy, Ortner and Whitehead qualified themselves with such phrases as "in the majority of cultural cases," or "nearly universally." They are also more receptive to other structures in the symbolic refraction of gender meanings, saying that "not all cultures elaborate notions of maleness and femaleness in terms of symmetrical dualisms" (Ortner and Whitehead 1981, p. 6). Despite such qualifications, they claimed that "in the majority of cultural cases . . . the differences between men and women are in fact conceptualized in terms of sets of metaphorically associated binary oppositions" and that certain oppositions recur with some frequency in gender ideologies cross-culturally (p. 7). These oppositions are: some version of the nature/culture opposition; an opposition between self-interest and the social good, which aligns men with the social good and women with self-interest; and the opposition of public and private domains, with men in control of the public and women confined to the private, domestic domain. Reflecting on these oppositions led Ortner and Whitehead back where Ortner concluded her 1974 article: "It seems clear to us that all of the suggested oppositions—nature/culture, domestic/public, self-interest/social good—are derived from the same central sociological insight: that the sphere of social activity predominantly associated with males encompasses the sphere predominantly associated with females and is, for that reason, culturally *accorded higher value*" (emphasis mine, Ortner and Whitehead 1981, pp. 7–8).

The opposition of nature and culture is not universally associated with male and female in the manner Ortner, or Ortner and Whitehead suggested, as anthropologists writing in *Nature, Culture and Gender* showed (see MacCormack and Strathern 1980). Although dialectical thinking associated with pairs of opposites is present in other cultural systems, the matrix of thought in which such oppositions are embedded differs cross-culturally. There are, for example, a diverse array of patterns that align nature with culture or against culture independently of gender. In my own work in West Sumatra, for example (see Sanday and Kartiwa 1984), I show that Minangkabau concepts of nature constitute a model *of* and *for* culture. Each system must be examined separately for the social meaning of gender polemics based on oppositional thinking. Even when applied to Western culture, the dichotomous oppositions nature/culture, female/male, inferior/superior are not simply correlated. As Jordanova pointed out (1980, p. 65) for Western thought, women may be evaluated as both good and bad, inferior and superior, and both evaluations may be represented as stemming from their association with nature.

THE MATRIFOCAL MODEL

THERE ARE other models of gender relations described by feminist anthropologists that do not emphasize either patriarchy or matrifocality. For example, there is the work of Eleanor Leacock (1978) and Karen Sacks (1982), which is derived from the thought of Marx and Engels. There is also the work of Alice Schlegel (1977), Carol MacCormack (1974), Judith K. Brown (1970), and Kay Martin and Barbara Voorhies (1975), whose ethnographic analyses have demonstrated the efficacy and importance of female power. Annette Weiner (1976) followed a very different line of analysis in forging a conceptual framework for examining women's contribution to the reproduction of society and culture. Like the other anthropologists mentioned, she rejected claims for universal sexual asymmetry; however, she went beyond Western-bound notions of power and authority and showed how women's participation in Trobriand mortuary ceremonies constitutes a significant and dominating female area of social and cultural life.

In addition to the above, there is a long-standing tradition in anthropology of writing on matricentered or matrifocal societies (see Tanner 1974; Tanner and Thomas 1985). In my cross-cultural study of female power (Sanday 1981), I documented instances in the ethnographic record in which women in their roles as mothers play a central role in social affairs. I suggested that where matricentered social activities "override the importance of male activities and correspond to the largest sociopolitical unit, the use of the term *matriarchy* is appropriate in order to signify the greater importance of females" (1981, p. 118). I also described instances of male dominance and argued that we must study the social scripts that direct the behavior of the sexes rather than assume universal relations of domination. Contrary to Ortner and Whitehead, I do not begin by assuming male dominance but rather seek the conditions under which it develops. In doing so, however, I slip into the same tendency to oppose the categories male and female and examine relations between them in terms of a hierarchical ordering.

Fieldwork among the matrilineal Minangkabau of West Sumatra, which I began in 1981, convinces me that Weiner's approach is the most suitable for characterizing the contribution of men and women to Minangkabau society and culture. First, it is important to note that Minangkabau women are neither peripheral to the structure of rights and duties nor symbolically devalued. On the contrary, women are central to the prestige hierarchy of the matrilineage and village. The activities that take place in the matrilineal longhouse, owned by women, encompass men's lives rather than women being encompassed by men's activities, as Ortner and Whitehead suggested is generally the case. Women, not men, form the structurally central core that upholds and reproduces the lineage. Men and women play key roles in ceremonies that both affirm political and economic ties in the village and reproduce cultural tradition. Senior women referred to as *Bundo Kanduang* are equated with the eternal aspects of traditional custom, particularly with customs associated with matrilineality. Senior women are likened to the supporting pole of the matrilineal household, a major symbol of matrilineal custom. Women are responsible for the visual idioms of Minangkabau ethnic identity. They weave the distinctive textiles that must be worn on all ceremonial occasions and wear the distinctive headdress that identifies them as member of a certain village. In some areas this headdress takes the shape of buffalo horns, a shape that is repeated in the distinctive roof of the Minangkabau longhouse and is a major symbol of social identity.

Men are defined in terms of their relationship to women as well as in status terms. The roles of father, uncle, and husband define the adult male and encapsulate expectations vis-à-vis wives, children, nephews, sisters and mother. Thus, the kinship activities of men are encompassed by their duties vis-à-vis wives and matrilineal female kin. A male informant, a distinguished traditional leader, described the duties of men as follows:

A man has two responsibilities, he must play two roles: father and brother. There is a saying: the father carries the children (i.e. loves them) and the uncle leads his nephews by the hand (i.e. educates them.) The uncle acts like a teacher. He is treated as a teacher by his nephews. A mother will say to a naughty child: "Look your uncle is coming. Please be good." Father and uncle work together. Uncles are supposed to work together and help with financial problems. An uncle is supposed to be a strong man financially.

Final authority is vested in senior women and in the titled position of clan leader, which is a male position. The *penghulu* (clan leader) is chosen by senior matrilineage members of both sexes to represent the kin group to the outside and to participate in important lineage discussions. Political activities in the village are mainly the responsibility of the clan leaders and men chosen by the Indonesian national government. These men confer in village council houses on matters affecting the village as a whole or other villages. In some villages women participate in council decision making. However, the major role of women is expressed in their economic and ceremonial activities.

Ortner and Whitehead (1981) claimed that the cultural construction of sex and gender "tends everywhere to be stamped by the prestige considerations of socially dominant male actors" (p. 12). They defined prestige in terms of social honor or social value. Sources of prestige are command of material resources, political might, personal skill, connectedness to the wealthy, and concern for the social good. By all considerations they raised, Minangkabau women are equal, if not superior, to men. The importance of women in connection with the social good through their perpetuation of traditional custom was mentioned above, an importance that makes women socially dominant in some ceremonial contexts. In terms of social value and honor there is evidence both in historical folk-tales of the past and in contemporary life that women receive more social honor than men in many contexts. As for command of material resources, men and women alike frequently told me that women are superior to men in their command of a family's material resources and property.

Despite these considerations, the fact that there is no comparable titled position of clan leader for women will be taken by some to indicate sexual asymmetry and male dominance. Such a conclusion, however, would not fit the Minangkabau conceptual model of relative sex status. At the level of ideology the Minangkabau derive ethnic pride from being referred to as a "matriarchate." In everyday conversation, I have heard Minangkabau men complain that they are dominated by women because of the male's peripheral structural position to the matrilineal longhouse. In other contexts the same men will claim that in matters related to traditional custom men are dominant but that in matters of property women are dominant. Both sexes argue for the domination of men in some respects and of women in others. Often discussions with informants end with a laugh as everyone agrees that it is impossible to separate the rights of women and men and the sexes are equal. Given to solving riddles by reference to proverbs, informants often placed gender relations in some metaphorical relationship (such as skin and nail of the finger) to make the more general point that men and women form a single unity of parts that cannot be separated. Compounding the picture are the complexities introduced by Minangkabau history. Undoubtedly, the early semicentralization of the Minangkabau kingdom, the later Dutch colonial domination, and the more recent effects of Indonesian independence produced a series of changes that covaried with the cultural and structural position of the sexes. In view of the density of the information and the equally dense contours of gender relations, I suspect that any definitive statements regarding relations of domination, whether made by informants or anthropologists, are motivated more by a deeper political or theoretical agenda than by ethnographic reality.

THE BASIS FOR THE PATRIARCHAL AND
MATRIFOCAL MODELS

IN THIS section I consider the systems of thought out of which the patriarchal and matrifocal models are constructed. I suggest these models are motivated by political considerations in being tied to concerns emanating from relations of Western male dominance. Additionally, these models are embedded in a Euro-American folk theory of social reality that is most immediately obvious in the work of Simone de Beauvoir but has long-standing roots in Western thought.

In her book *The Second Sex* (1952), de Beauvoir presented three basic propositions. The first proposition is that the symbolic structures defining masculine and feminine conform to a dialectical pattern of binary oppositions in all societies. The dialectic is essentially static, meaning there is no progress in the system of polarities, as suggested by the work of Hegel and Marx, beyond the dialectic of the transformation between nature and culture, as suggested by the work of Lévi-Strauss. The second proposition is that this static dialectic follows a universal pattern: the masculine is associated with culture and the feminine is associated with nature. The final proposition is that the nature of the dialectic places males in a position of dominating and exploiting women as culture exploits nature in the transition between nature and culture.

De Beauvoir introduced the dialectic that patterns her thinking by reference to the work of Aristotle and St. Thomas. These philosophers viewed women in terms of a negation of what the male affirms. Aristotle said: "The female is a female by virtue of a certain *lack* of qualities; we should regard the female nature as afflicted with a natural defectiveness." St. Thomas called woman an "imperfect man," and "incidental." To this de Beauvoir added that this point of view is "symbolized in Genesis where Eve is depicted as made from what Bossuet called 'a supernumerary bone' of Adam" (de Beauvoir 1952, p. xviii).

The necessity of the negation of the feminine, de Beauvoir suggested, derives from the primordial nature of the category of the *Other*. "The category of the *Other* is as primordial as consciousness itself. . . . No group ever sets itself up as the One without at once setting up the Other over against itself" (1952, p. xix–xx). De Beauvoir accepted Lévi-Strauss' proposition that duality is essential in the passage from the state of nature to the state of culture. This proposition was presented by Lévi-Strauss as a given: "duality, alternation, opposition, and symmetry, whether under definite or vague forms, constitute not so much phenomena to be explained as fundamental and immediately given data of social reality" (ibid.). Human society is not simply a fellowship based on solidarity and friendliness, de Beauvoir added. Following Hegel, she said there is in consciousness a fundamental hostility toward every other consciousness; this hostility is necessary in the subject's definition of self. "The subject can be posed only in being opposed—he sets himself up as the essential, as opposed to the other, the inessential, the object" (ibid). Men set themselves up as the subject, the essential, by making women the object. As Lévinas said, "otherness reaches its full flowering in the feminine" (de Beauvoir 1952, p. xix).

In making women the negated Self, men define themselves in superior terms. They do so by claiming the realm of the social and relegating women to the status of the unmarked and the residual Other. De Beauvoir said, "Society has always been male; political power has always been in the hands of men." She asked, "Why is it that women do not dispute male sovereignty?" (1952, p. xxi). Her answer is that women live dispersed among men, "attached through residence, housework, economic condition, and social standing to certain men—fathers or husbands—more firmly than they are to other women" (1952, p. xxii). This statement, perhaps more than any other, demonstrates de Beauvoir's patriarchal bias, for she has overlooked the many societies in the world in which men are attached to their wives' households and the female principle is the focus of descent. This statement also betrays de Beauvoir's strategy for female emancipation; even though women are dispersed in residence they can be united in a common theory of their oppression (see discussion below).

Having established an inherent and essential duality borne by the categories male and female, subject and other, de Beauvoir established the universality of this duality and its association with the duality of culture and nature. Accepting Lévi-Strauss' contention that all duality is aligned along the axis of the movement from nature to culture, it is an easy intellectual step to line up the duality posed by male and female with that of nature and culture: "Man seeks in woman the Other as Nature and as his fellow being. But we know what ambivalent feelings Nature inspires in man. He exploits her, but she crushes him, he is born of her and dies in her; she is the source of his being and the realm that he subjugates to his will" (1952, p. 162).

The dualistic model articulated by de Beauvoir, Lévi-Strauss, and later feminists can also be seen in the social ideology of eighteenth-century French polemic. M. and J. H. Bloch's (1980) suggested that the association of nature-culture with male-female during this period formed the language of challenge in the midst of ideological turmoil. The correlation of nature and female in opposition to that of culture and male provided the terms for clarifying by way of analogy a larger debate during a key period of social transformation. These authors suggested that, when looking at other cultures that oppose nature against something else, we examine the ideological polemic that employs this opposition and relate it to contemporary social or intrapsychic tensions rather than see it as a fundamental matrix of human thought.

Along the same lines, Jordanova (1980) added that oppositional polemic helps clarify blurred categories, especially during a time of social change. Examining the historical importance and social relevance of the nature/culture, male/female dichotomies, Jordanova pointed out that these dichotomies are currently employed by feminists to illustrate a simplistic model of oppression "which is useful because it seems to imply a clear power relationship" (1980, p. 43). This approach in itself constitutes a polemic against such a relationship because, as Jordanova showed, feminists abstract from the dichotomies only one of several historically important dimensions. Historically these dichotomies contained positive as well as negative evaluations of women and negative as well as positive evaluations of men.

The notion of women as natural contained not just women as superstitious but also women as the carriers of a new morality through which the artificiality of civilization could be transcended. In the same way, men as culture implied not just the progressive light of reason but also the corruption and exploitation of civil society. Next to what is presented as the desirable domination of superstition by reason, and women by men, in Mozart's opera *The Magic Flute,* one must put repugnance for the exploitation and inequality generated by masculine domination expressed in the eighteenth-century French novel *Paul et Virginie.* And in the end, it is not the possibility of finding texts with these extreme views clearly expressed which is most interesting, but rather the extent to which they were inseparably intertwined. (1980, p. 43)

Thus, Jordanova argued that thinking in terms of dichotomies, where the two opposed terms mutually define each other, provides a grammar and a lexicon for debating social issues. "Our entire philosophical set describes natural and social phenomena in terms of oppositional characteristics" (ibid.). While each polarity may have its own history, it also develops related meanings to other dichotomies. Transformations between sets of dichotomies can be performed because one provides a structural analogue of the other: "the pairs church and state, town and country also contain allusions to gender difference, and to nature and culture. . . . Thus, man/woman is only one couple in a common matrix" (ibid.). The dialectical relationship between the members of a pair provided a means for thinking about social relationships during times of change.

Regarding gender polemic in nineteenth-century debate, Jordanova pointed out that the goal was to clarify gender categories and to legislate concomitant relations of power and dominance. Enlightenment debates were also fraught with sexual metaphor as Enlightenment writers critically examined forms of social organization. This period was marked by the association in science and medicine of women with nature and men with culture and with a conscious attempt to subordinate women's medicine and women's bodies to male control. Thus, in addition to clarifying blurred categories, the use of sexual metaphors was also associated with changing the power relationship between the categories as social entities.

The polemic of the patriarchal model articulated by twentieth-century feminists both clarifies and reiterates blurred gender categories. Separation and autonomy of the woman from male expectations are the themes of de Beauvoir's concluding section on liberation. De Beauvoir called for women to unite in their oppression in the struggle for their freedom. Participation of the male in female domestic activities, along the lines of the more sexually egalitarian Ilongot domestic situation, is Rosaldo's

(1974: 41) call for change. While de Beauvoir clarified the separateness of the female social category and called for the liberation of female behavior from male expectations, Rosaldo called for a reblurring of gender categories as a device for domesticating men. Both arguments make men the *Other* as women take on the status of *Subject*. In her later work, Rosaldo (1983) noted also that attention by women to their commonalities is fundamental to feminist political demands. One commonality in de Beauvoir's and Rosaldo's model is women's universal oppression argued through the guise of assuming universal male dominance, a point that led them to the call for sisterhood. Both stated that women's universal oppression can be changed by culture and is not to be taken as a fact of nature (see Rosaldo 1983 and de Beauvoir 1952, p. xxii).

Although the content and structure of gender polemic may vary cross-culturally, its social function does not. In Papua New Guinea and tropical forest South American societies, for example, one frequently reads stories told by men in their men's houses about the time when women ruled and men were subordinate to women's wishes. These stories end with the necessity of men overthrowing women and taking command, usually because women could not do something, such as hunt, which became necessary for social survival. These stories operate as polemics that clarify gender identity in situations where the male identity is ontologically tied to female biology. Born of women, the adolescent male takes on a masculine gender only when he has divested himself of his feminine identity. In other words, these stories separate blurred gender categories resulting from males feeling that they carry female biological substances. Such stories also provide men with a rationale for celebrating their solidarity separated from women in societies where men grow up in a woman's world until they reach puberty, when they become more focused on male activities in men's houses.

In the gender polemic of feminists espousing universal male dominance it is men, not women, who are assumed to be naturally dominant. According to the patriarchal model the feminine is ontologically and socially subordinate to the masculine. The polemic this assumption produces may have similar psychological and social consequences as the notion of former female dominance has for tribal men. The assumption of universal male dominance provides a forum for ideologically separating the feminine from the encompassing masculine at the same time it provides a metaphorical house in which women can find solidarity with other women.

The notion of former female dominance characterized nineteenth-century models of the evolution of human culture. These models stressed the importance of female power and authority as mothers. The matrifocal model is part of this tradition. However, those who employ this model in contemporary anthropology do not make evolutionary or universalistic claims. The claim for matrifocality is derived from the perspective of particularistic field research. The goal is to describe meanings and structure in *one* social system that may then be taken as a case study providing an exception to universalistic claims or as demonstrating patterns that differ from androcentric conceptions of power and authority. However, in highlighting the cultural and structural importance of women, the very real importance of men may be underrated. Thus, the thinking displays dichotomous tendencies in which the female part of the dichotomy is clarified while the male part may be understated.

One significant difference separating the matrifocal from the patriarchal model remains to be discussed. The patriarchal model poses the terms of the opposition as a static rather than a progressive dialectic. This means that there can be no progress in the terms of the opposition but only "leaps" or transformations. Thus, although nature may be transformed by culture, in some sense nature always remains opposed to culture. A progressive dialectic, on the other hand, ends with the synthesis of formerly opposed terms in a new term, which then becomes opposed to another new term.

Such a concern for synthesis characterizes the world view of matrilineal peoples such as the Minangkabau, the Hopi, and the Navaho. For example, Witherspoon said (1977) that the Navaho intellectual style is not content with the static nature of simple dualism but "reaches for the unity of creative synthesis" in such figures as Changing Woman, the Navaho Supreme Mother. As the embodiment of the Navaho highest goal, the search for participation in the mystical forces of life and death—she is creative synthesis. As such she goes beyond politics, beyond gender, and beyond the oppositional polemic contained in the notions of matriarchy or patriarchy.

If synthesis occurs at the level of cultural symbolism, we may ask how this may affect, or be affected by, social relations. Martin and Voorhies argued that social structures highlighting the female principle (such as in matrilineal structures) are "accommodating and integrative," while those based on the male principle (i.e., patrilineal structures) are "acquisitive and internally divisive" (quoted in Sanday 1981, p. 177). The accommodating nature of matrilineal forms results from the dispersion of related men due to the practice of matrilocality, a practice promoting cooperation and coordination of groups. The integrative structures of matrilineality, I suggest, promote the "synthesis" of the sexes, not their opposition. This means that we must look at how male and female are synthesized in one area of social life, which then becomes opposed to another area, producing accommodative relations between the sexes in most areas of social life.

For example, while working in West Sumatra I was consistently struck by the accommodating nature of Minangkabau interpersonal relations and by the emphasis on synthesizing the contradictions that to the outsider appear to be inherent in the fact that such a solidly matrilineal society is also, as Abdullah says (1985, p. 141), "one of the most thoroughly Islamized ethnic groups in the Malay world." The accommodative nature of interpersonal relations is evident in everyday village affairs and in Minangkabau traditional literature (see Junus 1985). The contradictions between matrilineal customs and patrilineal Islam are apparent only to the outsider or to those who have rejected one for the other. To most Minangkabau, questions regarding this apparent contradiction, as Abdullah noted (1985, p. 141), incite "ethnic pride on 'the genius of Minangkabau' to synthesize contradictions harmoniously." The accommodative nature of Minangkabau interpersonal relations and contradictory spheres of social life provides an important key for unraveling the ideological and social role of the categories male and female in Minangkabau thought and behavior.

Finally, the political use of the findings of matrifocal research employs different strategies for ending Western patriarchy. The deconstruction of male social dominance—if we are to learn from matrifocal societies— means raising the feminine pole to cultural visibility as well as admitting women to the opportunity structure. Admitting women to the opportunity structure, however, is carried out not so much in opposition to men as in collaboration with men with like-minded goals. The strategy is not separation for solidarity, but accommodation for change. Which strategy ultimately succeeds is a moot point because both strategies are deeply ingrained in Western political thought and activity.

CONCLUSION

THE CULTURAL order is used for political or theoretical purposes by feminist anthropologists who begin with the question of sexual asymmetry. Whether the goal is to unify feminists and their supporters in a shared world view regarding women's oppression or to explore the implications of a matrifocal world view, we must ask whether in the process our subjects are buried by our own political concerns.

It is difficult to disentangle intellectual insight in feminist anthropology from contemporary political and moral concerns. As Rosaldo (1983, p. 93) said, "as critics, we feminists have remained, not surprisingly, the partial victims of the categories provided by our society." It may very well be that all anthropology is a form of comprehending self and society through a detour of the comprehension of other selves in other societies. If this is the case, then it is important to recognize the dialectic in which we are engaged when we study others. If knowledge of others is entangled with comprehension of self, we must understand that the projection of this knowledge onto all of humankind reproduces this age's form of imperialism.

In ending I would like to make a distinction between feminist anthropology and the anthropology of women and argue that both play an important role. Feminist anthropology, I suggest, is myth making for change, while the anthropology of women records the details of women's lives without regard to contemporary political concerns and avoids explaining those lives in universalistic terms. Intellectual insight will come from both endeavors to the extent that practitioners separate projections of self and society from others' realities. I believe that Rosaldo presents a model for feminist anthropology in her honesty regarding her own intellectual development. By sharing the evolution of her thought she has taught us a great deal about ourselves. This kind of intellectual honesty escapes the posturing so prevalent in anthropological writing in which authors struggle to be remembered for having founded some new paradigm rather than for having captured someone else's reality. It is the kind of honesty that allows all of us—colleagues in and out of the field—to be ourselves rather than purveyors or products of a paradigm.

To date feminist anthropologists have been virtually silent on the matter of sisterhood with their informants or how they felt as women in societies with differing gender paradigms. In both respects I experienced a profound exhilaration and an equally profound filling out of my personal understanding of womanhood. For better or worse, I was a feminist in the field, as well as in my home country, as I found myself arguing for women's traditional rights in the provincial capital and complaining about the relative absence of women in the modern urban environment. The gains to understanding by carrying my feminist program with me were great; relations with certain key male informants whom I confronted were, however, somewhat strained. In the villages of West Sumatra, I found that in talking with women a new kind of sisterhood emerged in which self and other were merged rather than distinguished and both parties in the discourse were changed. This kind of sisterhood, I suggest, places the anthropologist where she belongs. Neither looking over the shoulder of informants and friends or constituting herself as the absent voice in the ethnographic product, she occupies center stage where her biases, posturing, and the effect of her presence are clearly evident.

NOTE

This paper has been inspired by the later work of Michelle Rosaldo in which she boldly questions some of her earlier assumptions. Her flexibility and willingness to question past dogma serve as a model for feminist scholarship, which I have tried to emulate (perhaps not as successfully as she). I am also very grateful to Joanne Lind, who brought to my attention the possible existence of an African matriarchy and rekindled in me long-standing questions regarding the reasons I have always been sure that female power and even female rule is more than a theoretical possibility. Joanne's discussion of some of her own problems due to her work on historical matriarchies also stimulated the thinking of this chapter.

REFERENCES

Abdullah, T. (1985). "Islam, history, and social change in Minangkabau." In L. L. Thomas and F. von Benda-Beckman (Eds.). *Change and continuity in Minangkabau*. Athens: Ohio University, Monographs in International Studies, Southeast Asia Series, No. 71, pp. 141–55.

de Beauvoir, S. (1952). *The second sex*. New York: Vintage.

Bloch, M., and Bloch, J. H. (1980). "Women and the dialectics of nature in eighteenth-century French thought." In C. P. MacCormack and M. Strathern (Eds.). *Nature, culture and gender*. Cambridge: Cambridge University Press, pp. 25–41.

Brown, J. (1970). "A note on the division of labor by sex." *American Anthropologist* 72: 1073–78.

Jordanova, L. J. (1980). "Natural facts: A historical perspective on science and sexuality." In C. P. MacCormack and M. Strathern (Eds.). *Nature, culture and gender*. Cambridge: Cambridge University Press, pp. 42–69.

Junus, U. (1985). "Political history and social change in Minangkabau." In L. L. Thomas and F. von Benda-Beckmann (Eds.). *Change and continuity in Minangkabau*. Athens: Ohio University, Monographs in International Studies, Southeast Asia Series, No. 71, pp. 181–206.

Leacock, E. (1972). "Introduction." in F. Engels. *Origin of the family, private property, and the state*. New York: Pathfinder.

——. (1978). "Women's status in egalitarian society: Implications for social evolution." *Current Anthology* 19: 247–55.

MacCormack (Hoffer), C. P. (1974). "Madam Yoko: Ruler of the Kpa Mende Confederacy." In M. Z. Rosaldo and L. Lamphere (Eds.). *Woman, culture, and society*. Stanford: Stanford University Press.

MacCormack, C. P., and Strathern, M. (Eds.). (1980). *Nature, culture and gender*. Cambridge: Cambridge University Press.

Martin, M. K., and Voorhies, B. (1975). *Female of the species*. New York: Columbia University Press.

Ortner, S. (1974). "Is female to male as nature is to culture?" In M. Z. Rosaldo and L. Lamphere (Eds.). *Woman, culture, and society*. Stanford: Stanford University Press.

——. (1984). "Theory in anthropology since the sixties." *Comparative Studies in Society and History* 26: 126–66.

——, and Whitehead, H. (Eds.). (1981). "Introduction." In *Sexual meanings*. New York: Cambridge University Press, pp. 1–28.

Rosaldo, M. Z. (1974)."Woman, culture, and society: A theoretical overview." In M. Z. Rosaldo and L. Lamphere (Eds.). *Woman, culture, and society*. Stanford: Stanford University Press.

——. (1980). "The use and abuse of anthropology: Reflections on feminism and cross-cultural understanding." *Signs* 5: 389–417.

——. (1983). "Moral/analytic dilemmas posed by the intersection of feminism and social science." In H. Haan et al. (Eds.). *Social science as moral inquiry*. New York: Columbia University Press.

——, and Lamphere, L. (1974). "Introduction." In M. Z. Rosaldo and L. Lamphere (Eds.). *Woman, culture, and society*. Stanford: Stanford University Press.

Sacks, K. (1982). *Sisters and wives: The past and future of sexual equality*. Urbana: University of Illinois Press.

Sanday, P. R. (1981). *Female power and male dominance.* New York: Cambridge University Press.

——, and Kartiwa, S. (1984). "Cloth and custom in West Sumatra." *Expedition* 26: 13–29.

Schlegel, A. (Ed.). (1977). *Sexual stratification.* New York: Columbia University Press.

Tanner, N. (1974). "Matrifocality in Indonesia and Africa and among black Americans." In M. Rosaldo and L. Lamphere (Eds.). *Woman, culture, and society.* Stanford: Stanford University Press, pp. 129–56.

——, and Thomas, L. L. (1985). "Rethinking matriliny." In L. L. Thomas and F. von Benda-Beckman (Eds.). *Change and continuity in Minangkabau.* Athens: Ohio University, Monographs in International Studies, Southeast Asia Series, No. 71, pp. 45–72.

Weiner, A. (1976). *Women of value, men of renown.* Austin: University of Texas Press.

Witherspoon, G. (1977). *Language and art in the Navajo universe.* Ann Arbor: University of Michigan Press.

FIVE

The Pervasiveness of Patriarchy: On Finding a Different Voice

John Shotter and Josephine Logan

FEMINIST thought? Does it exist? Our claim is that "feminist thought" is not as yet a distinctive and comprehensive mode of thought *sui generis*. There is not as yet a distinctly feminist *practice* in the conduct of scholarship. Some feminists are simply seeking success, equality, or recognition, that is, to be taken seriously, within existing academic practices, with little or no desire to dismantle them; while many others reject and wish to rearrange or abolish patriarchal (and capitalist) structures. Indeed, major points of conflict for the women's movement can be found in the polarity of the ideas and ambitions within the movement itself (for example, see Rowland 1984). This, we want to argue, is because the women's movement must of necessity develop itself within a patriarchal culture of such a depth and pervasiveness that, even in reacting to or resisting its oppressive nature, the women's movement continually "reinfects" or "contaminates" itself with it. All of us, women and men alike, are "soaked" in it.

More than simply a set of aims, goals, desires or demands, which one can choose to pursue or not, it is, we want to argue, embodied in the very ways we all *do* things together—including, how we reproduce those ways in what we do. Thus, to attempt to understand patriarchy as a simple system of oppression that always serves the interests of men at the expense of women may be far too narrow and misleading a view. Patriarchy is enshrined in our social practices, in our ways of positioning and relating ourselves to one another, and in the resources we use in making sense of one another. And we cannot easily reject these practices. Hence, we need to understand how we can develop new practices while still making use of the resources embodied in the old. We must find a different voice, a new place currently unrecognized, from which to speak about the nature of our lives together. This then is our double project in what follows: to show how pervasive patriarchy is, but also to show that its pervasiveness is illusory, and that it hides from us activities that have to do with mothering and nurturing rather than with originating and fathering.

THE PRACTICAL REPRODUCTION OF PRACTICES

GIDDENS (1979), in discussing the "deeply sedimented" nature of social practices, introduced the important notion of "the duality of structure," by which he meant "the essential recursiveness of social life" (p. 5), its continually self-reproducing nature. For Giddens, social structure is "both medium and outcome of the reproduction of practices" (p. 5); it contains processes for both its development and stabilization. "The duality of structure relates the smallest item of day-to-day behaviour to attributes of far more inclusive social systems: when I utter a grammatical English sentence in a casual conversation, I contribute to the reproduction of the English language as a whole" (p. 78). And, he could have added, in reproducing the English language as a whole one also contributes to the reproduction of its associated forms of life, the patterns of practical social relations constituted in and by the ways of speaking it contains. This means that feminism, while attempting in all good faith to voice an intelligible reaction to patriarchy, *in its concern to be intelligible* can tend to reproduce the very categories and procedures of patriarchy it wishes to displace—a point Mary Daly (1978) appreciated only too well. It is such categories she hoped to subvert in her insistence on speaking 'antistructur- ally', that is, metaphorically, spontaneously, personally, poetically, nonin- strumentally, and (or, but) ambiguously.

Is she right? While we all might agree that our ways of speaking about

ourselves are crucial in determining the kind of sense we make of ourselves, are her de facto declarations of alternative forms sufficient? Can
one, just by the individual determination to do it, *reground* oneself in an
alternative discourse of one's own making? Are subversive attempts of
this kind our only recourse? We have no in-principle answer to this
question; its answer depends upon the exigencies of the present historical
context. In other words, it is a practical question. In some academic
contexts she is laughed at, in others listened to seriously—but to what
practical effect? We question the efficacy of her approach here only in
order to raise the whole question of how one might account, academi-
cally, for the factors influential in people's development of their sense of
themselves. For it seems to us that at the present time there are crucial
and pervasive limitations, not only in the current structures of academic
knowledge, but in our academic ways of gaining knowledge: they lack in
their very nature the resources required if we are to account for the
reproduction of even our patriarchal selves. Indeed, it is just that kind of
process that they hide. While we can account for our biological reproduction of ourselves, we remain somewhat mystified as to the nature of our
participation in the reproduction of our psychological, societal, cultural,
political, and moral selves, the practices in terms of which we position
and relate ourselves to each other. Our current academic practices make
the experiences involved *rationally invisible* to us (Shotter 1986); that is,
they are rendered unaccountable as commonplace events and can exist
only as puzzling, indescribable or inexplicable "feelings," or as feelings of
an illegitimate kind, said to be extraordinary, magical, crazy, stupid, or
just plain wrong.

How is such a state of affairs maintained? Why is it so difficult to
discuss the nature of such reproductive and developmental processes rationally? It is, we feel, the current insistence by men and women alike,
upon warranting our claims to knowledge in patriarchal terms that is
responsible. As Kristeva (1974) has argued, it leads to the repression of
the resources and activities associated with motherhood,[1] that is, with
those activities to do with creativity and nurturance. The patriarchal
attempt to prove already well-formed claims true (the search for certainty,
for the true nature of things), has displaced attention away from cooperative forms of creative communication within which something initially
vague is shaped into intelligible and legitimate forms.

So what we want to do below is: 1) to bring out the nature of the limitations in our current modes of institutional and disciplinary thought; 2) to illustrate their origins and pervasiveness; 3) to discuss the self-defeating nature of resistance to them; 4) to say what is required if we are not to eradicate such modes of thought (for that is, we think, impossible), but to find already present in them another voice that is currently repressed; 5) to show the tragic, continually self-defeating nature of attempts (at least, in academic institutions and settings) to give legitimate expression to such a voice; and very briefly, 6) to point toward an academic practice of a less patriarchal kind that might take that voice more seriously—a practice in which accounts are warranted not in terms of their correspondence to 'reality,' but in terms of their implications for our practical ways of going on together. Academic practices are thus central to our concerns here. For, to repeat, it is the demand feminist thinkers place upon themselves to adhere to disciplinary practices—to speak in certain orderly, intelligible, and legitimate ways, to be in fact *individually* authoritative at all times, able oneself to justify independently all of one's claims on one's own—that necessitates their reinscribing in their speech the very patterns of patriarchal relations they wish to undermine.

It is ironic, isn't it? But perhaps that must be both our recourse and resource here: an appreciation of the irony involved. For if we also cannot legitimately express ourselves in such a setting as the present one in anything but the current academic fashion and the patriarchal ways it embodies, we can perhaps overcome some of the more powerful limitations they exert upon us by an ironic distancing of ourselves from them. Then, instead of remaining subject to them, we can perhaps 1) gain a degree of self-conscious control over them, and 2) take some account of the ways in which they influence the lived experience of those who labor under them—that at least is the aim of the material we want to introduce to you below.

MASTERY AND POSSESSION: DESCARTES' PROJECT

LET US begin then, by exploring what might be taken as the origin of our current, disciplined mode of thought: a statement from Descartes' 1651

Discourse on Method—the full title of which, it is worth adding, is *Discourse on the method of properly conducting one's reason and of seeking the truth in the sciences.* But straightaway, in characterizing its origin in this way, we are clearly making a mistake: Could one man alone have fathered a whole mode of thought, world-wide? The very idea! It is outrageous! Surely, some such tendencies must have been in motion in society at large already. Thus those of us concerned with the historical development of academic practices might feel pulled instead toward, say, Ong's 1958 book on Peter Ramus (1515–72); *Ramus: Method and the decay of dialogue: From the art of discourse to the art of reason;* we may want to argue that Descartes' concern with method, with orderliness and clarity, with systems, and with everything being in its proper place from a single point of view, grew out of the previous schoolroom and the educational practices introduced into it by Ramus almost a century earlier. But there's the mistake again. Was Ramus their sole author? Their father? Ramus actually was known as the world's greatest master of the shortcut. And clearly, what Ramus did was to codify many of the already existing, but somewhat unruly, oral practices in printed, spatial diagrams.

But having said what the mistake is—the authorial fallacy—let us now go on to commit it! If we had to choose just one statement by which to characterize the ethos of our modern age, it would be this one from Descartes' sixth discourse: "Instead of the speculative philosophy taught in the schools, a practical philosophy can be found by which, knowing the power and the effect of fire, water, air, the stars, the heavens and all the other bodies which surround us, as distinctly as we know the various trades of our craftsmen, we might put them in the same way to all the uses for which they are appropriate, and thereby make ourselves, as it were, masters and possessors of nature" (Descartes [1651] 1968, p. 78). Although social realities are more influenced by practices than by theories, and by everyday rather than academic practices at that,[2] we would choose this passage as it seems to us more than any other to state in a clear, simple, and frank manner the interests and intentions implicit in our current, dominant, "scientific" ways of knowing and valuing: *mastery* and *possession.* For quite apart from Descartes' easy equation of *personal powers* (Harré 1970; Shotter 1973) with natural powers, it hardly needs to be said that Descartes was referring in his statement not to men generally but only to *some* elite group of men—to those with sufficient social status to put craftsmen's knowledge (their powers) to what they deem to be their "appropriate" uses, that is, the elite group's own uses. As a part of "nature," women are also available to men of such status for mastery and possession in the same way. It is the mastery and possession of what is deemed to be "nature"—where nature is seen as whatever is an "other-ness," as something mysterious, wild, full of unforeseen possibilities for exploitation—that is, we feel, the not so hidden agenda in much academic discourse calling itself "scientific." So we would like to spend just a few moments now to elucidate the consequences for us as academics in com-miting ourselves to Descartes' project—to the mastery and possession of nature.[3]

First let us explore the consequences of turning that project round upon ourselves. What might be involved in our attempt to make ourselves masters and possessors of our own nature? What could such a project mean? As stated, it contains a number of unfortunate ambiguities:

1) Who is the "ourselves" Descartes was addressing? Not all of us, clearly. But just those who are concerned with mastery and possession, and who are prepared to do to themselves and to others what its pursuit by use of his method requires—those with other concerns, with allowing others their own expression of their own powers,[4] lack a voice in his rhetoric. Strongly antirhetorical in explicit content, Descartes' *Discourse* embodies a masterful (!) use of narrative for persuasive ends (Nelson and Megill 1986); seeming to be addressed to all, generally, his rhetoric hides the hierarchical nature of the society his stance toward knowledge implies.

2) Whose nature is it that is to be mastered and possessed? Here the ambiguity is even more serious. Is it that of others or one's own? Is his method concerned with people's *ontology,* with their developing by in-creasing their recognition of the resources available to them from within their own ecological settings? Clearly, not at all. His talk is only about already ontologically well-formed individuals. His concern is with their increasing, their knowledge of a world external to them, set over against them, of which they are not a part, not their knowledge of their selves. Their ignorance of their own being is left untouched.

3) The ambiguities do not end here, however—with whether his method is concerned with achieving mastery and possession of one's own "self," or of others—for what is one's own *nature* such that one could be said to be master and possessor of it? Is mastery and possession of our self our only relation to ourselves, our only way of being ourselves, of being

someone?[5] Indeed, what must the nature of one's self be if, in order to be oneself, one must continually *resist* the infliction of mastery and possession from without, by another or others? It is in such a situation as this, we suggest, that one becomes acutely aware of one's "nature" or "self"—one's femaleness, blackness, Irishness, or Jewishness, for example. One constructs a self for oneself of an assaulted, embattled, or oppressed kind; one sees oneself as *in opposition* to others. But is this kind of "patriarchy" intrinsic to resisting groups, or is it a secondary, derived patriarchy? In other words, does resistance give rise to an attempt to impose upon others the very violations of selfhood one wants to resist oneself? We think this rarely to be the case. Under the circumstances of resistance, "violation" of others frequently becomes an inevitable (and often undesirable) consequence of opposing violation. It hardly needs pointing out, for example, that most freedom fighters would not be doing what they do but for the perpetration of injustice and violation of one country, class, or race against another.

These ambiguities, and the dilemmas to which they give rise, infect every area of research in the humanities and human sciences today. And the pathologies to which they give rise appear elsewhere in social life. Surely there must be more point to our investigations than the mere "discovery" of yet more techniques of control, use, appropriation, exploitation, domination, subordination, subjection, and so on? Surely there must be another kind of knowing beyond that to do only with power and its economies, a mode of knowing to do with men and women changing their conditions of existence in relation to one another? Well, we think there is. It involves knowing from within a situation, a practical kind of knowing of a particular and contingent kind, to do with relating to and participating with others in maintaining and changing patterns of human relation. This type of knowing contrasts sharply with traditional, patriarchal patterns. Patriarchy leads to a general, decontexted kind of theoretical knowledge that can be possessed by individuals of their *external* world. This knowledge is expressed in a hierarchically arranged, closed system of binary oppositions; it is concerned with achieving a unity of vision and thought, with everything in its proper place and all conflict eradicated, once and for all. Feminist thought can be seen as different in every respect: as a practical, particular, contexted, open, and nonsystematic knowledge of the social circumstances in which one has one's being, concerned with achieving a heterarchy of times and places for a plurality of otherwise conflicting voices.

But while we are bombarded by class, cultural, racial, and gender oppression and injustice, we are forced to reckon with patriarchal and capitalist techniques of use, power, and control. Other kinds of knowing are thus blocked, first and foremost by original patriarchy, which is to some degree perpetuated by a responding secondary patriarchy of resistance.

THE PERVASIVENESS OF PATRIARCHY

JUST TO emphasize the difficulties we all face in recognizing the continued and ever-present nature of the repressed aspects of the relational processes within which we all have our being, let us spell out the deep and detailed degree to which we are all infected.

Possessive Individualism and Genderless Sexism

To be controversial—very controversial—let us examine what is entailed in current accusations of "sexism." From our point of view, it would seem to be a *genderless sexism*, a sexism based only upon claimed "natural" differences among people. For modern "persons" apparently have no intrinsic gender; they are free to develop and define themselves by making their own choices. They possess their "selves" as they possess other property. Macpherson described the "possessive" quality of modern individualism thus: "Its possessive quality is found in its conception of the individual as essentially the proprietor of his [sic] own person or capacities, owing nothing to society for them. The individual, it was thought [and many still do think], is free inasmuch as he is proprietor of his person and capacities. The human essence is freedom from dependence upon the wills of others, and freedom is a function of possession" (1969, p. 3). In other words, one is free in all but one's *economic* relations to others; one is a wholly self-contained entity, owing nothing to one's embedding and participation in a network of interdependencies with others for the nature of one's being. This, at least, is how we all treat one another. And the fact is, within this economic scheme of things, women as a sex seem to possess less of the basic human "essence"—freedom from dependence upon the wills of others—than men.

Why do we call this a genderless sexism? Because, while allowing us a sense of freedom to be the makers of ourselves, this conception of our individuality *decontextualizes* us. We end by being classed in relation to one another only by our possessions. Hence at base (in the basest possible terms) men are differentiated from women solely by their sexual and secondary sexual characteristics. "A characteristic but quite secondary bulge[6] in the blue jeans is now all that differentiates and bestows privilege on one kind of human being over another," said Illich (1983, p. 13), from whom we have drawn some of the analysis presented here. In such a scheme, differences in *gender,* a whole network of differences between men and women—differences in behavior, distinctions in terms of times, places, tasks, tools, forms of speech and dress, gestures, perceptions, forms of life with their associated voices—a whole scheme of *contexted* differences is ignored, repressed, and rendered rationally invisible. The way of life in which men and women have their respective statuses and roles disappears. A world of *gendered* individuals, living interdependently within a web of complementary, mutually supportive relations with one another, is treated (at least for the purpose of all supposedly *rational* transactions) as if consisting of a world of *sexed* but otherwise indistinguishable individuals, now all in competition with one another for scarce resources.

And the point Illich (1983) made about such a situation is that (whatever other kinds of injustices men have perpetrated against women) the *economic* exploitation of women by men cannot exist without the (apparent) abolition of contexted, vernacular forms of life, and the social construction of a genderless sexuality—indeed, the very notion of exploitation, of "putting other people's powers to use," is, as we have seen, a part of Cartesian patriarchy.

Secondary Patriarchy: Resistence Does Not Lead to Exorcism

Women are born into societies that often isolate them.[7] Women's achievements and political stuggles are, by and large, omitted from recorded history and have little place in men's *and women's* consciousnesses.

Thus women do not easily become aware of a solidarity with other women, or with women and men: "The suppression of women's movements in history isolates every women; there is nothing by which she can orient herself to bring her personal experience into continuity with the past" (Janssen-Jurreit 1982, p. 33). In other words, women have to an extent been alienated from experiences appropriate to their experience as women. Likewise, a woman's definition of herself is not her own or that of her foremothers; it is a man's, a subjective vision of what "he wishes her to be and what he fears her to be" (Figes 1966, p. 17).

Ironically, what this means is that to struggle to get her head above the mire of patriarchy, women must apply patriarchal methods: In the face of overwhelming physical and economic exploitation and manipulation, women are bound to concern themselves with patriarchal preoccupations of mastery, possession, and power (as is the case with any oppressed group). Women's bodies and capacities are taken out of their own control for exploitative purposes, and regaining control—or at least attempting to redress the balance—becomes an issue. Where it does not become an issue, one submits to the continuation of injustice, inequality, and domination. Thus either way, the rules of patriarchy are applied.

From *within* patriarchy it is difficult for women to avoid an initial patriarchal attitude—if this is how resisting inequality and injustice must be interpreted. Having said that, however, movements which appear to be individualistic, narcissistic, and (secondarily) patriarchal in approach must be considered from the lived experience of those who make up these movements. Ideas and theories may be transcended, but it is more difficult to transcend experience; indeed, it can be positively dangerous, even suicidal. For example, for women, black Africans, republican Irish, revolutionary Chileans, Nicaraguans, or Argentinians (this list could be extended indefinitely) to surrender their self, nationalist, or identity concerns would be a white flag invitation to continued plunder, exploitation, and injustice.

Where there exist class, racial, cultural, and gender inequality and political struggles, in terms of a concern with self/nationalism/identity, there must surely be considered positive and necessary forms of resistance. Of course, similar approaches are used in the interest of exploitation, and more insidiously in *concealing* exploitation. Thus, patriarchy at present reproduces itself in both its supportive *and* its resistive elements, and perhaps it will not be until the latter slowly begins to change places with the former (herein lies our hope) as the prevailing world order, that nonpatriarchal approaches to structuring and restructuring our social and political worlds can begin to emerge.

The Invisibility of the Community: Joint Action

Let us turn now to another related manifestation of our difficulties. Those of us who want to explore social constructionist themes (e.g., Gergen 1982, 1985; Kessler and McKenna 1978; Shotter 1984) as we do here, want to modify the whole notion of authorship, of individuals as originators; we want to suggest that in fact social outcomes are *jointly* produced. That is, they cannot be traced back to any plans, desires, or purposes of any particular individuals. In being independent of the wishes or intentions of individuals, they appear to have an objective quality, to be a third term in people's relations to one another, something with a life of its own, belonging neither, say, to authors nor their readers, but to be *between* them. Norbert Elias put the matter thus: "plans and actions, the emotional and the rational impulses of people, constantly interweave in a friendly or hostile way. This basic tissue resulting from many single plans and actions of men [sic] can give rise to changes and patterns that no single individual person has planned or created. From this interdependence of people arises an order *sui generis,* an order more compelling and stronger than the will or reason of the individual people composing it" (1982, p. 230). And along with many other such writers (e.g., Mead 1934; and Vygotsky 1962 [see Kozulin 1986]), Elias sees features of our psychological make-up historically, that is, as being produced or constructed in the following social process: 1) they are first expressed unconsciously and spontaneously[8] as an outcome of practical activities *between* people; 2) in the course of such *joint action,* individuals notice its results and discover how themselves to arrange the conditions for their occurrence, in other words, they discover how to act *deliberately;* 3) the original social function of the joint activity is now transformed to serve an individual's purpose; and 4) the social origins of the ability to act deliberately and self-consciously in such a way, although still present, need no longer be acknowledged, for the individual is now able to act, so it seems, autonomously. Indeed, it is in the very nature of the experience of self-conscious individuals to find their abilities as if *belonging* to them, with their social, communal origins repressed or forgotten.

It is precisely this process that we can see at work in the formation of "possessive individualism". A particular pattern of social relations[9] constructs a form of inner experience in individuals that is then attributed solely to them *as individuals,* with the still present pattern of social relations constructing it rendered rationally invisible. That is, these relations become unaccountable by the very mode of individualistic and scientistic talk maintained by those relations. The tragedy of the repressed or forgotten social nature of such a process is this: that vernacular resources available to all may be socially reconstructed as individually owned and then subjected to an economics of scarcity.

The Scientific Management of Ourselves: The Social Construction of a Scarcity of Human Resources

About the vernacular knowledge and skills possessed by workers, F. W. Taylor said: "The ingenuity and experience of each generation—of each decade, even, have without doubt handed over better methods to the next. This mass of rule-of-thumb knowledge or traditional knowledge may be said to be the principle asset or possession of every tradesman . . . which is not in the possession of the management" (1947, p. 32). But this state of affairs can be remedied by applying "the principles of scientific management" in which, as he said, "The managers assume . . . the burden [!] of gathering all the traditional knowledge which in the past has been possessed by the workman and then by classifying, tabulating and reducing this knowledge to rules, laws and formulae . . " (p. 36). In his *History of Sexuality,* Foucault discussed the point of the drive to classify and tabulate in the same vein: "One had to speak of [sex] as of a thing to be not simply condemned or tolerated but managed, inserted into systems of utility, regulated for the greater good of all [here he speaks ironically], made to function according to an optimum" (1980, p. 24). The optimum was to be set, of course, by the tabulators.

In fact what is at work here is a process at work everywhere in the human sciences:[10] the conversion of an unruly, disordered, spontaneous, contexted form of life into an ordered, self-controlled, decontexted form. It is a process that produces not only an order but a political economy, a set of rules for behaving that, to the extent one "masters" them, determines one's access to the goods of life. And, of course, in mastering the rules, one learns how to subject oneself to the system: one becomes dominated by one's own techniques of domination, and, as we have said, by one's techniques of *resisting* domination. No wonder that Taylor said in praise of his "principles": "In the past the man has been first; in the future the system must be first" (p. 7).

To live and work within a system, to feel that one *must* conform oneself to *rules* in one's actions, to experience oneself as if split into a master and a slave, is the outcome of being continually subjected, or subjecting oneself, to such a process. It is as if one's every move were being watched over by a hostile critic. And as Foucault said: "He who is subjected to a field of visibility, and knows it, assumes responsibility for the constraints of power; he makes them play spontaneously upon himself; he inscribes in himself the power relation in which he simultaneously plays both roles [master and slave]; he becomes the principles of his own subjection" (1979, pp. 202–3). This, we feel, *is* our fate under patriarchal forms of life—if, that is, such forms of life could ever become total. As it is, the repressed, that is rationally invisible vernacular, continues to function, ensuring the continual recreation and nurturance of our moral, social, political and psychological selves.

CONCLUDING REMARKS

RATHER than exploring the implications of what might be a more interdependent, creative, processual, contexted, and historical image of persons, one that allows for the possibility of *gendered* as well as *sexual* existences, we have been exploring here the barriers in the way of such explorations, the limitations we encounter in our current attempts to understand how we, as a culture, can reproduce and develop ourselves. In doing so, we have invoked Descartes' image of us as engaged in a process of mastery and possession. For it is that image that today still continues to inform, not just our psychological theorizing, but how we actually *feel* about ourselves—indeed, that is why it is so difficult to cure ourselves of it: it reflects how we actually experience ourselves. But to cure ourselves we must. For it is an image of ourselves that is so antisocial that: 1) it has left us totally mystified and quite ignorant of the interrelated social activities required for the production and reproduction of both a social cohesion *and* of genuine individualities—to the extent that we have relegated many activities such as drama, play, poetry, ceremony, and ritual to the realm of leisure activities or pastimes, for individual recreation, but not to be taken seriously as important for the re-creation of our sense of ourselves and of our social orders. 2) It has misled us into assigning human beings a basically nonsocial, mechanistic nature, thus rendering the *moral* and *political* nature of their personhood, the social point of their capacity for self-control, self-determination, and self-transformation, opaque to psychological investigation. It has directed our attention towards knowledge of the so-called 'external' world—something that individuals can do on their own—but not to investigations of how they gain their knowledge of their personhood—something they clearly cannot learn on their own. And 3) it misleads us about the nature of 'reality': as academics we worry about ways of talking that correspond to reality, because we feel that before we can pass our knowledge on, before it can be "put into practice," it has to meet certain criteria. We cannot fully explicate here the social and political nature of these criteria (see Hubbard this volume). Suffice it here to say that they must be of a form such that no new scientific knowledge can question the intelligibility of our belief in the efficacy of science as a prominent social institution. In other words, they work to ensure the reproduction of the prevailing social order, in which we authorize a small group of scientific experts (by their meeting of such criteria) to make authoritative pronouncements as to what all of us should take to be factual; it is an order in which a nondialogical, context-free way of talking is basic, an order in which just the social processes required to change it are denied.

Our concern is with an alternative, more communitarian practice (a practice engaged in at the opening session of this conference, in which people spoke not with the voice of professional academics, but with a voice more rooted in their personal circumstances). A feminist practice would allow a conversation within which the creative, formative power of talk could be put to use in reformulating, redistributing, and redeveloping both people's knowledge of themselves and their immediate circumstances, and the nature of their practical-historical relations to one another. Rather than acting irrespective of our circumstances, it would be concerned precisely with how we can act in ways that are rooted in our social, moral, and political circumstances; with how a community of understanding functions in its joint action to produce and maintain the ways of being and understanding that make it the community it is. A first step in empowering ourselves and releasing ourselves from the disabling consequences of Descartes' image of ourselves as concerned only with mastery and possession is to recognize that it is not simply *that* that disables us. The sins of omission and commission are to be found not in our thoughts, but in our immediate practical relationships to one another, here and now; in what voices we allow to speak and which ones we take seriously; our sins are in our actual ways of going on together—whatever they are. Who is to say? How might they best be described? Ah, what stories there are still to tell—about who we might be and what it is we might be doing to one another, ourselves, and our world.

NOTES

1. Many men (and not a few women) mistakenly believe "feminists" to be antagonistic toward home, motherhood, and the family, whereas in fact, what many people in the women's movement are objecting to is the *degradation* of women's role (thus far) as mother and homemaker, and her economic dependence and exploitation within that role.

2. See also Carolyn Merchant (1980) who also argued, but with a rather different focus from Ong, that practices precede theories, and everyday practices academic ones.

3. Few modern writers express this theme in a more undisguised form than Freud, where the whole theme in, for example, *The introductory lectures* (Freud [1922] 1973), is that of mastery. Freud's attitudes are typically expressed in the following quotation from *Civilization and its discontents* in which he said:

> We are threatened with suffering from three directions: from our body, which is doomed to decay and dissolution . . .; from the external world, which may rage against us with overwhelming and merciless forces of destruction; and finally from our relations to other men. Against the dreaded external world one can only defend oneself by some kind of turning away from it, if one intends to solve the task by oneself. There is, indeed, another and better path: that of becoming a member of the human community, and, with the help of a technique guided by science, going over to the attack against nature and subjecting *her* to the human will ([1929] 1961, pp. 25–26).

4. And there were other voices even then:

> No man is an *Island,* entire of it self.
>
> Any man's *death* diminishes *me,*
> because I am involved in *Mankind;*
> And therefore never send to know
> for
> whom the bells tolls; It tolls for *thee.*
> Donne, 1571–1631, *Devotions*

Such "poetic" views seemed to cut little ice, however.

5. See Erich Fromm (1979), who in his book, *To have and to be,* explored the implications of a nonpossessive relation to others and oneself.

6. And by a bulge in the blue jeans he could mean, but he doesn't, the bulge of the wallet in the person's back pocket.

7. As Giddens noted: "Anthropological research indicates that all societies which have been reliably studied are patriarchal, although the degree and nature of male domination has varied considerably," (1982, p. 128). However, see Sanday this volume. Gidden's own blindness to patriarchal values is, perhaps, revealed in his concern only with societies that have been studied *reliably.*

8. By spontaneous, we do not mean occurring with no *social* antecedents at all; we simply mean spontaneous on the part of individuals, i.e., unplanned by them.

9. Presumably, the formative social relations in question are those induced by capitalism and relations of trade.

10. See Marx and Engels ([1929] 1977, p. 67), *The German ideology.* They traced the process whereby, in the human sciences, "ruling ideas," or more accurately "ruling illusions" are substituted for the actual ruling individuals, and people are mystified into misidentifying the reasons for rulers ruling, and think of themselves as accidental victims of 'natural' occurrences. Marx and Engels explained the process as a three-part trick. Below, we reproduce Smith's (1974, p. 41) more succinct version:

Part 1. Separate what people say they think from the actual circumstances in which it is said, from the actual empirical conditions of their lives, and from the actual individuals who said it.

Part 2. Having detached the ideas, they must now be arranged. Prove then an order among them which accounts for what is observed.

Part 3. The ideas are then changed 'into a person,' that is they are constituted as distinct enties to which agency (or possibly causal efficacy) may be attributed. And they may be reattributed to 'reality' by attributing them to actors who now *represent* the ideas.

Modern recommendations on theory construction in the human sciences look uncomfortably like this recipe for making ideologies, according to Smith.

REFERENCES

Daly, M. (1978). *Gyn/Ecology: The metaethics of radical feminism*. Boston: Beacon Press.

Descartes, R. [1651] (1968). *Discourse on method*. Harmondsworth: Penguin.

Elias, N. (1982). *Power and civility: The civilizing process:* Volume 2. Oxford: Blackwell.

Figes, E. (1966). *Partriarchal attitudes*. London: Macmillan.

Foucault, M. (1979). *Discipline and punish: The birth of the prison*. Harmondsworth: Penguin.

——. (1980). *The history of sexuality:* Volume 1: *An introduction*. New York: Vintage.

Freud, S. [1929] (1961). *Civilization and its discontents*. (Trans. and Ed. J. Strachey). New York: Norton.

——. [1932] (1973). *Introductory lectures on psychoanalysis*. (Trans. J. Strachey, Eds. J. Strachey and Angela Richards). Harmondsworth: Penguin.

Fromm, E. (1979). *To have and to be*. London: Cape.

Gergen, K. J. (1982). *Toward transformation in social knowledge*. New York: Springer-Verlag.

——. (1985). "The social constructionist movement in modern psychology." *American Psychologist* 40:266–75.

Giddens, A. (1979). *Central problems in social theory: Action, structure and contradiction in social analysis*. London: Macmillan.

——. (1982). *Sociology: A brief but critical introduction*. London: Macmillan.

Harré, R. (1970). Powers. *British Journal for the Philosophy of Science* 21:11–19.

Illich, I. (1983). *Gender*. London: Marion Boyars.

Janssen-Jurreit, M. (1982). *Sexism: The male monopoly on history and thought*. London: Pluto Press.

Kessler, S. J. and McKenna, W. (1978). *Gender: An ethnomethodological approach*. New York: Wiley.

Kozulin, A. (1986). "The concept of activity in soviet psychology." *American Psychologist* 41:264–74.

Kristeva, J. (1974). *La revolution du langage poétique*. Paris: Seuil.

Macpherson, C. E. (1969). *Possessive individualism: Political theory from Hobbes to Locke*. Oxford: Oxford University Press.

Marx, K. and Engels, F. [1929] (1977). *The German ideology*. (Ed. C. J. Arthur). London: Lawrence and Wishart.

Mead, G. (1934). *Mind, self and society*. Chicago: University of Chicago Press.

Merchant, C. (1980). *The death of nature: Women, ecology and the scientific revolution*. San Francisco: Harper.

Nelson, J. and Megill, A. (1986). "Rhetoric of Inquiry." *Quarterly Journal of Speech* 72:20–37.

Ong, W. J. (1958). *Peter Ramus: Method and the decay of dialogue*. Cambridge: Harvard University Press, reissued 1983.

Rowland, R. (Ed.). (1984). *Women who do and women who don't join the women's movement*. London: Routledge and Kegan Paul.

Shotter, J. (1973). Acquired powers: The transformation of natural into personal powers. *Journal for the Theory of Social Behaviour* 3:141–56.

——. (1984). *Social accountability and selfhood*. Oxford: Blackwell.

——. (1986). *"The rhetoric of theory in psychology."* In J. F. H. van Rappard, A. W. staats, and M. E. Hyland (Eds.). *Proceedings of the founding conference of the International Society for Theoretical Psychology*. Amsterdam: North Holland.

Smith, D. (1974). "Theorizing as ideology." In R. Turner (Ed.). *Ethnomethodology: Selected readings*. Harmondsworth: Penguin.

Taylor, F. W. [1918] (1947). *Scientific management*. New York: Harper.

Vygotsky, L. S. (1962). *Thought and language*. Cambridge: MIT Press.

SIX

Toward a Feminist Metatheory and Methodology in the Social Sciences

Mary M. Gergen

IN THE past decade, feminist intellectual endeavors have blossomed. A radically expanded spectrum of ideas has become available for feminist scholars through the development of theoretical works (cf. Chodorow 1978; Daly 1978; DuBois et al. 1985; Evans et al. 1986; Flax 1983; Gilligan 1982; Jaggar 1983; Kelly 1984; Miller 1976), metatheoretical and philosophical contributions (cf. Crimshaw 1986; Gould 1984; Harding, 1986; Keller 1982) and practices (cf. Henriques et al. 1984; Reason and Rowan 1981; Roberts 1981; Spender 1981; Wilkinson 1986). The academic world may not have welcomed these and other contributions with open arms, but as is becoming increasingly apparent, wide-ranging intellectual endeavors have been influenced by their introduction. The creation of women's studies courses and programs in the university and the introduction of feminist perspectives into "mainstream" disciplines of inquiry have become commonplace (Spender 1978, 1981).

While growth and development have occurred in theory and teaching, less has been accomplished in the practice of scholarly research within the university setting. The implications of feminist theory and metatheory for methodology has not been spelled out. For example, within the social sciences, a fountainhead of feminist theory, many scholars who align themselves with feminist causes continue to practice within a traditional methodological framework (cf. Bem 1974; Deaux 1985; Eagly and Carli 1981; Spence and Helmreich 1978). That no well-articulated alternatives have been formulated within conventional academic circles is a matter of grave concern because methods are often considered the true hallmark of the practitioner. New theories may be allowed into a discipline, but methods that deviate markedly from the old ones or that challenge or ignore traditional assumptions are strongly suspect. Thus many so-called feminist social scientists continue to practice their sciences in forms that violate the precepts of an enlightened feminist perspective.

But if the challenges of feminism are to be taken seriously, feminist social scientists need to develop new methods, ones that support the feminist metatheories. We must reject many of the traditional methods of economics, psychology, political science, and sociology, for example, as violations of our feminist beliefs. This leads to the problem of trying to ascertain what a feminist methodology might be. How might a feminist science be created? What means fulfill the evaluative and intellectual demands of feminism? There may be several modes for reaching this goal; my effort in this chapter is to spell out some of the central goals of a feminist methodology, and to illustrate these with one pilot study designed for this purpose.

The feminist critique of existing methodology in the social sciences (and also in the natural sciences) is drawn from many sources beyond those traditionally associated with feminist pursuits. The feminist critique is not a unique intellectual creation, but is a collective one, dependent on many diverse strands of intellectual thought. It shares perspectives with the interpretive (Taylor 1971), social constructionist (Gergen 1985); and critical (Jay 1973) schools of thought, among others. These perspectives have illuminated various critiques of the sciences. Within the social sciences critical work by scholars such as Apfelbaum and Lubek 1976; Berg and Smith 1985; Harré and Secord 1972; Israel and Tajfel 1972; Sampson 1978; Shotter 1975; and Strickland, Aboud, and Gergen 1976) has delineated profound difficulties with the current empiricist paradigms. I will briefly review some central criticisms of the traditional methodology in the social sciences that are relevant to feminists, focusing on psychology as a prime example of the social sciences. As counterpoint to these criticisms, I will suggest how a feminist methodology might be developed.

EMPIRICIST SHORTCOMINGS AND THE FEMINIST ALTERNATIVE

THERE ARE several major criticisms of the empiricist paradigm in psychology that are relevant to a feminist appraisal of the social sciences. Within each of these criticisms the elements for an alternative metatheory and attendant methodology are suggested. Of critical interest is the relationship of the scientist to the subject matter. At issue is nothing less than the nature of scientific objectivity. Six aspects of this issue will be treated below.

Independence of Scientist and Subject Matter

Psychologists have traditionally supported the necessity of maintaining objectivity in their research (Alexander 1982; Coser 1975; Giddens 1974; Polkinghorne 1983). To achieve this goal the scientist ideally is an independent observer who minimizes any relationship between him/herself and the subject of study (Alexander 1982). It is thought that as long as the scientist is distant, uninvolved, and neutral, subjects will not be influenced by the scientist, and reliable data will be collected. If there is any form of personal relationship between the scientist and the subject this interaction will, as it is said, "contaminate the findings."

Many feminist writers have criticized this perspective (Chodorow 1978; Gilligan 1982; Harding 1986; Keller 1982). They have suggested that for various reasons this view is limited and androcentric. For example, Nancy Chodorow (1978) has argued that men develop a personal identity by separation and differentiation from their mothering agents. This pattern of separation encourages the development of a more general preference for separateness over interdependence. Many feminists believe that what many scientists consider the proper method for organizing social reality is merely an outgrowth of male developmental history. Of course, the irony in the traditional argument is that any form of relationship, distant or close, between the scientist and the subject, constitutes a message of relatedness, regardless of the content, to the subject. It is not possible for humans to simply have "objective" contact within the scientific process, or anywhere else.

The alternative possibility, one that is perhaps more in harmony with female development, is one that admits the interconnectedness of persons. In this view the most feasible approach to scientific investigation is to recognize this bond between people in social contexts, and to construct scientific methods on these grounds (Becker 1986; Oakley 1981; Stanley and Wise 1983). A feminist metatheory and methodology would thus incorporate the tenet that the investigator and the subject are interdependent.

Decontextualization of Phenomenon

Traditional empiricist psychology attempts to establish general laws of human functioning. This means that any given phenomenon is viewed as an expression of universal law. The major problem for the scientist is to determine these laws by testing the relationship among isolated entities. In order to clarify the relationships of the entities under study the scientist typically removes the analytical units of interest from their cultural and historical context. Such context stripping often involves moving the entities into the laboratory—so that they may be studied in isolation from all of their "contaminants" (Reason and Rowan 1981; Weinreich 1977). For example, the complex problem of when to help in an emergency becomes codified into a simple choice of informing an experimenter of a possible emergency in a tidy laboratory setting.

A second form of decontextualization involves the removal of the study from the life circumstances of the scientist (Heron 1981). For example, scientists do not normally report the extent to which the research was inspired because of a certain personal problem or by pressure from department chairpersons to publish. The research is made to seem free-standing, without regard to institutional interests of sponsors or the personal gain that might accrue to the investigator.

The objections of feminists to the decontextualization process have often centered on the consequences that have accrued to women-as-subjects. Decontextualized women subjects are often studied in isolation from their personal circumstances. Frequently scientists attribute women's personal traits, which may stem from their position as an oppressed group, to their "natural dispositions." A tendency to be depressed, for example, might be attributed to a biological cause rather than to difficult social conditions. Often these theories support androcentric biases (Marshall 1986). This decontextualized type of science overlooks important social and cultural factors that influence the lives of women (Bernard 1973; Mednick and Tangri 1972; Minton 1986; Parlee 1979; Sampson 1978; Sherif 1979; Snyder 1979; Vaughter 1976). In accord with the argument for interdependence of researcher and subject, feminist thinking suggests that subjects of research often depend on their context to provide their identity. It is not possible to decontextualize a phenomenon without changing its significance. Thus research should be conducted insofar as possible without violating the social embeddedness of the subject. In addition scientists should consider the historical contingency of the phenomena and the extent to which research aims and outcomes are dependent on the personal circumstances of the scientist (Meyer, this volume).

The Possibility of Value-Free Theory and Practice

A third questionable assumption in the traditional paradigm is that the scientist can and should produce research in a value-free mode. Personal prejudices, ethical principles, and other evaluative concerns should not influence the research endeavor, its outcomes or conclusions. The bad scientist is one who allows scientific conclusions, to become tainted by personal values. In contrast, feminist scholars refute the assumption that knowledge and its creation can be value-free. Instead it is assumed that all work must be value-laden. The claim that science is value-free is a self-deception or an attempt to deceive others.

In *Feminist Philosophers,* Jean Crimshaw illustrated how values are embedded in a supposedly value-free theoretical exposition. She wrote, "A theory like behaviorism, for example, implies that human beings and human behavior can be thought of as material to be 'modified,' and the term 'behavior modification' is often given to programmes which offer to apply behaviorist theory in order to effect changes in human behavior. Such programmes . . . imply a sharp distinction between 'controllers' and 'controlled' and are intrinsically and profoundly anti-democratic" (1986, p. 91). Sociologist Shulamit Reinharz has summarized the feminist position on value-free science: "The feminist critique of social science supports the view that since interest-free knowledge is logically impossible, we should feel free to substitute explicit interest for implicit ones. Feminism challenges us to articulate our values and, on the basis of these, to develop new theories and formulate new research practices" (1985, p. 163).

Many feminists have suggested how women might benefit from the explicit, self-conscious application of values within scientific practice. For example, Vaughter (1976) has advocated that scientists create research that advances the status of women and adds to the quality of their lives; Gilligan (1982) has supported the need for new theoretical formulations about women that enlarge their potentials. Young-Eisendrath (this volume) has discussed how women might redefine personal qualities that have been made negative through male-dominated theorizing. Others have argued for an emancipatory psychology that will liberate men as well as women from the ideological constraints of gender stereotyping (Minton 1986; Pleck 1981).

The Possibility of Brute Facts

A fourth assumption of the traditional paradigm is that facts are independent of the scientist who establishes them. That is, the world is assumed to be as it is, independent of the observer. It is the task of the scientist to reflect that world in his/her theories. In addition, all persons using proper scientific methods should come to the same conclusion regarding the nature of the world.

Feminist critics of the social sciences disagree with this view of objectivity. Rather a feminist perspective holds that all aspects of the scientific method require acts of interpretation. Interpretations are required to select or create a relevant vocabulary and a theoretical framework, to make distinctions among objects, to formulate explanatory systems and to summarize findings. Thus, what becomes established fact is not reflective of the world as it is, but the world as subjected to an a priori linguistic framework.

In this light, feminist thinkers are particularly critical of the ways in which scientific language has been shaped to produce an androcentric world of "facts" that often give men advantage over women. The ongoing conflict between feminist psychologists and defenders of the *Diagnostic and Statistical Manual for Mental Disorders III,* is illustrative. The thrust of the feminist arguments is that male-dominated groups have fashioned categories of mental illness that apply only to women and are discriminatory against them. The contention that languages are tools of male domination has been made by many feminist writers (cf. Daly 1978; Spender 1980). Efforts to recreate language in forms more suitable to women are in progress.

The problem of how language shapes scientific work is particularly central to feminist methodological concerns. Often important concepts are based on preexisting assumptions concerning gender relations. For example, to study "sex-typed behavior" is to accept the notion that males and females have very different patterns of social behavior and to perpetuate this idea by writing about it (See Morawski's chapter in this volume for further reflections on feminist linguistic issues). Even the metaphors in scientific work reflect androcentric assumptions. Pauline Bart (1971) has illustrated the use of the adjectives "hard" and "soft" in the sciences. She wrote: "We speak of hard data as being better than soft data, hard science better than soft science, hard money better than soft money. . . . This is of course a male metaphor, so since discovering this, I have substituted a metaphor based on female sexual experience and refer to wet and dry data" (p. 1).

The Superiority of Science and the Scientist

An empiricist theory of science holds that the only way to establish valid knowledge is through scientific procedure. Thus, all other claims to knowledge are by definition inferior. This assumption of the superiority of science manifests itself among scientists in a variety of common methodological practices.

For one, the researcher is assumed to be more knowledgeable and competent than the subject. As a result the researcher tends not to be interested in finding out what subjects know or are capable of doing, except in the predetermined area mapped out in the design of the study. Second, the researcher expects to have complete control over the way in which the study proceeds. The context, methods, procedures, analyses, outcomes, and recommendations for application are all regulated by the psychologist, and the subject is indeed subjugated. Third, the scientist never shares his/her views with subjects prior to the research because such sharing would supposedly "contaminate" the results.

As feminist thinkers maintain, presumptions of experimenter superiority and the subjugation of the research subject recapitulates the traditional patterns of gender relationships in the culture (See Hubbard's chapter in this volume on this topic). In effect, scientific dominance is simply another manifestation of sexual dominance. As an alternative, feminists argue for the enhanced voice of research participants. Rather than considering subjects' views as inherently inferior, the scientist should respect the potential value of the subjects' ideas and be maximally sensitive to the perspectives of the subjects and their experiences. Subjects should also become participants with status equal to the scientist in the research effort (Freire 1976; Mearns and McLeod 1984). Feminists' views would favor research that placed the investigator's orienting presumptions and modes of practice at risk (Elden 1981).

In summary, feminist thinkers reject the following traditional empiricist methodological principles:

1. The independence of scientist and subject;
2. the decontextualization of the subject matter from the field in which it is embedded, physically and historically;
3. value-neutral theory and practice;
4. the independence of "facts" from the scientist;
5. the superiority of the scientist over other people.

Feminist-inspired research would endeavor to recognize that scientists, subjects, and "facts" are all interconnected, involved in reciprocal influences, and subject to interpretation and linguistic constraints. In addition, scientific endeavors would be treated as value-laden and would be formed with specific value orientations in mind. This research approach would treat scientists as participants in the research project along with the subjects of the research and not as superior beings who maintain a knowledge monopoly among themselves.

A STUDY OF MENOPAUSE: AN APPLICATION

MOST psychological research published today, including sex role and gender research, has been formed within the dominant empiricist paradigm. (Cf. Wetherell's 1986 critique of the Bem Sex Role Inventory research domain.) However, there are growing numbers of investigators who have written and experimented with various research ideas suggested by a feminist perspective. Some innovative materials are reported in volumes such as *Exploring clinical methods for social research,* edited by David Berg and Kenwyn Smith (1985); *Doing feminist research,* edited by Helen Roberts (1981); *Feminist social psychology,* edited by Sue Wilkinson (1986); *Human inquiry, a sourcebook of new paradigm research,* edited by Peter Reason and John Rowen (1981); *Changing the subject,* edited by Julian Henriques et al. (1984); and *Beyond method,* edited by Gareth Morgan (1983). Psychological studies reported in this volume by Verena Aebischer and Joan Meyer also highlight the emergence of feminist methods in the social sciences.

Background of the Study. What follows is a brief description of a study I designed specifically with feminist criteria in mind. The topic centered on women's construction of menopause and their related image of themselves as women in their forties. I chose this topic because I had been distressed in reading psychological and popular literature concerned with middle-aged women. The general theme of such material is that during this period women suffer a steady decline in a variety of valued human traits such as beauty, strength, worth as a human being, function, and intelligence. As a result, it seemed, women over forty might be vulnerable to many negative side effects, for example, depression, anomie, and overcompensation. The major impact of such theorizing seemed to me the creation of a cultural expectation that women after forty experience a sharp decline in important human capacities and life satisfaction. A belief in the expectation might further serve to produce some of the very effects that are predicted. (Interestingly we do not find such dire predictions in the literature for men from forty to sixty, and we do not have cultural expectations that such degenerative events must occur to them.)

My goal for this study was to present to a group of my peers through a dialogical procedure the notion that middle age marked a new era in a woman's life during which she could become freer, more self-actualized, and more satisfied with life than in her preceding years. I chose to focus on menopause as the topic under discussion because this process encompasses the major negative stages associated with the passage of women through middle age. Because I wanted to emphasize my role as equal participant, I did not attempt to lead the discussion group in a forceful way. I also invited the other group members to share in the development of the research project and its outcomes.

Method of Exploration. The research event took place in my home in June 1985. Seven women, all familiar with each other, primarily through playing tennis together, were invited to participate with me in "a discussion group about the lives of women between forty and sixty." At the time of the study these women were all married, living with their husbands, and mothers. They ranged in age from forty-one to forty-eight. Most had worked at least part-time in the previous year, although only two were then involved in full-time careers. They were all upper-middle-class suburban homeowners. One woman was Australian, living temporarily in the United States while her husband was on a job rotation with an American corporation.

Upon arrival, each woman privately filled out several questionnaires, including an attitudinal measure about menopause and a self-image scale. The *Opinions about menopause questionnaire* was designed to tap agreement with traditional medical and psychiatric views about menopause, for example, "Menopause is basically a medical problem" and "Women usually get emotionally more unstable after menopause." The participants could indicate agreement or disagreement with these items on a 7-point scale. A self-image scale, *Images of a woman,* was designed to give a measure of respondents' self-images at twenty, thirty-five, and as projected to fifty. Using a semantic differential scale participants rated themselves on twenty paired adjectives at each of the three ages. These two questionnaires were viewed as the instruments that would potentially be sensitive to change following the discussion. My goal for the discussion was to influence these women to feel more positively about themselves and their futures as a result of their participation in the experience. Additional questionnaires were thus given to the participants to take home so that they could fill them out the morning following the session, and then mail them back to me. In addition, the postsession questionnaires included a comment sheet on which participants could describe reactions to the session, any new ideas they had been exposed to about menopause, and any suggestions for future research. In being given the opportunity to make suggestions for further research endeavors they were given the opportunity to be coplanners in this project.

A one-and-one-half-hour tape-recorded discussion was the major event of the research session. As the discussion facilitator, I introduced topics at various times. The first hour was devoted to the exploration of beliefs and feelings about the process of menopause and the lives of women in middle age. In the last half hour, I spoke briefly about my views about menopause and women in middle age. I tried to emphasize the socially constructed nature of developmental events such as menopause, and how no one formulation was necessarily true. I argued that it would be possible to see menopause as coordinated with a transition to a new, very positive period of life. I encouraged comments about this perspective and tried to pursue the exposition of this view with the group. The participants included this issue in their discussion during the last portion of the session.

An Analysis of the Discussion. The major underlying supposition of the study was that through the interaction of the group and exposure to a social constructionist view of menopause and middle age the participants would alter their attitudes about these issues in what I would consider a more positive direction. The presuppositions of the study included the assumptions that most women are aware of the negative images of middle-aged women in the culture, feel personally concerned about the process of menopause, feel negative about its impact on their lives, and dislike being middle-aged themselves.

The discussion proved enlightening and broadened my understanding of the dimensions of the topic greatly. As the conversation revealed, in general the participants resisted thinking about menopause and their identity as "middle-aged women." Their sense of what it means to be in their forties seems to be in a transition from an older vision of decline to a newer one of freedom, health, and prosperity. I think the discussion brought out some of their shared concerns, especially centered on the process and signification of menopause, and helped to redefine these concerns again as peripheral to their plans and goals in life. The discussion seemed therapeutic in that certain fear-provoking and dismal ideas were shared and perhaps reduced in power by their exposure.

The emancipatory framework of this study was designed so that the participants would be exposed to a model of menopause that emphasized menopause as part of a role transition to a positive new form of womanhood. The social construction of menopause as a medical problem, with negative physical and psychological consequences, was to be abandoned. I wanted to encourage these women to consider the possibility that all concepts of social life are social constructs, which are open to negotiation of meaning, particularly by the members of the affected groups. The discussion group did seem to negotiate new meanings for the menopausal time of life, achieving a synthesis of my intended outcomes and the participants' original opinions. In terms of reorganizing the thoughts of the participants to accept that events such as menopause are not "real," but socially constructed, I was generally unsuccessful. While discussants seemed willing to accept a variety of interpretations of what menopause might include, they did not focus on the social negotiation aspects of the construct itself. In philosophical terms, my coparticipants tended to be naive realists. The major social strategy I saw emerging from the discussion was that of "beating the old system." By this I mean that participants plan to rely on exceptional personal resources to cope with menopause, rather than to change the social construction itself. Let me expand briefly.

The tendency I noted in our group was implicitly to support the medical model as long as one did not suffer personally from it. So, for example, the need to look young and fertile is not questioned. However, keeping eternally young is a goal that many upper middle-class women can pursue quite successfully. As long as it works, the need to bring new value and new attributes to the image of the aging woman is not essential. In fact, to renegotiate the standards of what it means to be attractive so as to give aging women a more positive position would serve to negate the efforts of certain women to evade the role. If having bodily fat, wrinkles, and grey hair is acceptable for a fifty-year-old woman, then why struggle with diet and exercise regimes?

Yet, it was also clear as the discussion developed that the participants saw many very positive aspects to life in the period from forty to sixty. These women became very supportive of the idea that life might even be better then than it had been when they were in their twenties and thirties.

Many mentioned ways in which they felt freer, more competent, more powerful, and less frustrated by obligations to family. In this respect they were able to see the potential to construe for themselves a life different from what is currently part of the medical/psychiatric model, in which women grieve over their empty nests and lost youth. While it is impossible to judge how much the group as a whole changed to become more positive toward middle age during the discussion, it seemed clear that the tendency for making these more positive comments did occur after I brought up the possibility of middle age being a time for growth and change. Thus, I believe that my goal of improving perceptions of women in mid-life was met in the study, if only to a small extent.

Analysis of Questionnaires

Analyses indicated that the discussion had an influence on participants' attitudes as judged by the difference scores between questionnaires filled out before and after the group discussion. In general the participants became less committed to the medical/psychiatric model of the ill-effects of menopause following the discussion. Participants disagreed more strongly with the view that "Most women would rather continue to menstruate than not," ($X = 2.63$ prediscussion and 1.88 postdiscussion, with $1 =$ strongly disagree and $5 =$ strongly agree) and "feel negative about their loss of fertility" ($X = 3.13$ prediscussion and $X = 2.13$ postdiscussion). In fact most women in this study indicated that the freedom from worry about pregnancy is one of the chief gains of menopause. Discussants were also more likely to disagree that women "keep menopause a secret, as something shameful" ($X = 2.63$ prediscussion and $X = 2.25$ postdiscussion) and that women "become less attractive after menopause" ($X = 2.38$ prediscussion and $X = 2.0$ postdiscussion). Participants also disagreed more with the statement that "Women usually get emotionally more unstable after menopause" ($X = 2.38$ prediscussion and $X = 2.25$ postdiscussion) and "less interested in sex" ($X = 2.88$ prediscussion and $X = 2.25$ postdiscussion). The means are presented here to indicate the general tendency for the participants to reject these ideas, not to illustrate statistically significant changes.

Comparing the self-image scales, I noted the changes in discrepancies the group found between being a younger women and being a fifty-year-old (the average age of menopause) both before and after the discussion group. As the results showed, the group tended to project a positive self-image into the fifties even at the beginning of the study. Thus there was little room for positive change. The only area in which substantial enhancement did occur was in the trait *strength* ($X = 3.75$ prediscussion and $X = 2.57$ postdiscussion). As a result of the discussion, the participants rated strength as increasing in the fiftieth year. Overall the group characterized themselves at fifty as being active, attractive, dominant, sexual, intelligent, logical, outgoing, practical, relaxed, stable, and successful, as well as strong. In these respects the panel chose to describe themselves in ways that fit my vision of what the new middle-aged woman could be.

CONCLUSION

AS MENTIONED this research was merely a preliminary attempt to put feminist metatheory into action in a research design. In its inception the design of the study tried to respect the interdependency of myself, as the manager of the study, and the other participants. In many respects I endeavored to take an equal place with the others in the discussion. I chose for my panel social peers who knew very little about my professional career. The topic of research was one that interested me personally and was relevant to my future. I attempted to conduct the research in a setting that would be similar to other situations in which women exchange confidences (on my back porch, for lunch). The research was organized in such a way that the values I espouse were to be advanced. In addition, it was intended to support a social constructionist metatheory of science. While these abstract goals directed and informed my efforts, the realizations were not without flaw.

While it seemed that there were some effects that resulted from the dialogical approach to attitude change, the method was not by any means perfect in its form. There are many ways in which this research could have been improved. In future research one might want a greater range of participants, of scientist-facilitators, and of analytical tools. The participants frequently suggested that it would have been worthwhile to have had the comments of women who had already been through menopause.

One could imagine other groups of participants who could contribute unique perspectives to the topic. The study might have been more in keeping with feminist goals if the participants had been involved in planning the study from its inception (cf. Elden 1981). However, as a result of all participants having equal access within the discussion group, the control of the outcomes was decentralized and the processes of social negotiation enhanced. It is sobering to recognize that giving the power away means that certain of one's perceived goals for organizing a study are less directly achievable. At the same time, I acquired new ideas about social change as a result of being a member of this group. I recognized that the women I talked with had developed a strategy for evading the traps of becoming middle-aged. This would not have been possible if I had controlled and manipulated most of the process and proceedings. Lastly, I might have tried to incorporate into the study more outcomes that would have been immediately and directly useful to the participants.

For the future, I am enthusiastic about the opportunities for exploring new methodologies, for socially negotiating new realities, and for finding new ways of creating challenging situations that have an impact on the social realities of people. I believe that the feminist perspectives on knowledge will help promulgate fruitful new modes of social science. What is necessary is that communities of scholars and other interested people take up the challenge to create together concrete instantiations of abstract ideals.

REFERENCES

Alexander, J. (1982). *Theoretical logic in sociology: Positivism, presuppositions, and current controversies.* Berkeley: University of California Press.

Apfelbaum, E., and Lubek, I. (1976). "Resolution vs. revolution? The theory of conflicts in question." In L. Strickland, F. E. Aboud, and K. J. Gergen (Eds.). *Social psychology in transition.* New York: Plenum.

Bart, P. (1971). "Sexism in social science: From the iron cage to the gilded cage, or the perils of Pauline." *Journal of Marriage and the Family* 33:742.

Becker, C. S. (1986). "Interviewing in human science research." *Methods* 1:101–24.

Bem, S. (1974). "The measurement of psychological androgyny." *Journal of Consulting and Clinical Psychology* 42:155–62.

Berg, D. N., and Smith, K. K. (Eds.). (1985). *Exploring clinical methods for social research*. Beverly Hills:Sage.

Bernard, J. (1973). "My four revolutions: An autobiographical history of the American Sociological Association." *American Journal of Sociology* 78:773–91.

Chodorow, N. (1978). *The reproduction of mothering: Psychoanalysis and the sociology of gender*. Berkeley: University of California Press.

Coser, L. (1975). "Presidential address: Two methods in search of a substance." *American Sociological Review* 40:691–700.

Crimshaw, J. (1986). *Feminist philosophers: Women's perspectives on philosophical traditions*. Brighton, England: Wheatsheaf Books.

Daly, M. (1978). *Gyn/ecology: The Metaethics of radical feminism*. Boston: Beacon Press.

Deaux, K. (1985). "Sex and gender." *Annual Review of Psychology* 36:49–81.

DuBois, E. C., et al. (1985). *Feminist scholarship, Kindling in the groves of the academe*. Urbana: University of Illinois Press.

Eagly, A., and Carli, I. I. (1981). "Sex of researchers and sex-typed communications as determinants of sex differences in influenceability: A meta-analysis of social influence studies." *Psychological Bulletin* 90:1–20.

Elden, M. (1981). "Sharing the research work: Participative research and its role demands." In P. Reason and J. Rowan (Eds.). *Human inquiry: A sourcebook of new paradigm research*. London: Wiley.

Evans, J., et al. (1986). *Feminism and political theory*. Beverly Hills: Sage.

Flax, J. (1983). "Political philosophy and the patriarchal unconscious: A psychoanalytic perspective on epistemology and metaphysics." In S. Harding and M. B. Hintikka (Eds.). *Discovering reality*. Dordrecht: Reidel.

Freire, P. (1976). *Education: The practice of freedom*. London: Writers and Readers Publishing.

Gergen, K. J. (1985). "The social constructionist movement in modern psychology." *American Psychologist* 40:266–75.

Giddens, A. (1974). *Positivism and sociology*. Portsmouth, N.H.: Heinemann.

Gilligan, C. (1982). *In a different voice*. Cambridge: Harvard University Press.

Gould, C. (Ed.). (1984). *Beyond domination: New perspectives on women and philosophy*. Totowa, N.J.: Rowman and Allenheld.

Habermas, J. (1971). *Knowledge and human interests*. Boston: Beacon Press.

Harding, S. (1986). *The science question in feminism*. Ithaca: Cornell University Press.

Harré, R., and Secord, P. F. (1972). *The explanation of social behaviour*. Oxford: Blackwell and Mott.

Henriques, J., et al. (1984). *Changing the subject*. London: Methuen.

Heron, J. (1981). "Philosophical basis for a new paradigm." In P. Reason and J. Rowan (Eds.). *Human inquiry*. New York: Wiley.

Israel, J., and Tajfel, H. (Eds.). (1972) *The context of social psychology: A critical assessment*. New York: Academic Press.

Jaggar, A. (1983). *Feminist politics and human nature.* Totowa, N.J.: Rowman and Allenheld.

Jay, M. (1973). *The dialectic imagination.* London: Heinmann.

Keller, E. F. (1982). "Science and gender." *Signs: Journal of Women in Culture and Society* 7:589–602.

Kelly, J. (1984). *Women, history and theory: The essays of Joan Kelly.* Chicago: University of Chicago Press.

Marshall, J. (1986). "Exploring the experiences of women managers: Toward rigour in qualitative methods." In S. Wilkinson (Ed.). *Feminist social psychology.* Milton Keynes, England: Open University Press.

Mearns, D. J., and McLeod, J. A. (1984). "A person-centered approach to research." In R. F. Levant and J. Shilen (Eds.). *Client-centered therapy and the person-centered approach: New directions in theory, research and practice.* New York: Praeger.

Mednick, M. S., and Tangri, S. S. (1972). "New social psychological perspectives on women." *Journal of Social Issues* 28:1–16.

Miller, J. B. (1976). *Toward a new psychology of women.* Harmondsworth, England: Penguin.

Minton, H. L. (1986). "Emancipatory social psychology as a paradigm for the study of minority groups." In K. S. Larsen (Ed.). *Dialectics and ideology in psychology.* Norwood, N.J.: ABLEX.

Morgan, G. (Ed.). (1983). *Beyond method: Strategies for social research.* Beverly Hills: Sage.

Oakley, A. (1981). "Interviewing women: A contradiction in terms." In H. Roberts (Ed.), *Doing feminist research.* London: Routledge and Kegan Paul.

Parlee, M. B. (1979). "Psychology and women." *Signs: Journal of Women in Culture and Society* 5:121–33.

Pleck, J. H. (1981). *The myth of masculinity.* Cambridge: MIT Press.

Polkinghorne, D. (1983). *Methodology for the human sciences.* Albany: SUNY Press.

Reason, P., and Rowan, J. (Eds.). (1981). *Human inquiry, A sourcebook of new paradigm research.* New York: Wiley.

Reinharz, S. (1985). "Feminist distrust. Problems of context and content in sociological work." In D. Berg and K. Smith (Eds.). *Exploring clinical methods for social research.* Beverley Hills: Sage.

Roberts, H. (1981). *Doing feminist research.* London: Routledge and Kegan Paul.

Sampson, E. E. (1978). "Scientific paradigms and social values: Wanted-A scientific revolution." *Journal of Personality and Social Psychology* 36:1332–43.

Sherif, C. W. (1979). "Bias in psychology." In J. A. Sherman and E. T. Beck (Eds.). *The prism of sex: Essays in the sociology of knowledge.* Madison: University of Wisconsin Press.

Shotter, J. (1975). *Images of man in psychological research.* London: Methuen.

Snyder, E. C. (1979). "That half of 'mankind' called women: An introduction to women's studies." In E. G. Snyder (Ed.). *The study of women: Enlarging perspectives of social reality*. New York: Harper and Row.

Spence, J., and Helmreich, R. (1978). *Masculinity and femininity: Their psychological dimensions, correlates and antecedents*. Austin: University of Texas Press.

Spender, D. (1978). "Notes on the organization of women's studies." *Women's Studies International Quarterly* 1:255–75.

——. (1980). *Man made language*. London: Routledge and Kegan Paul.

——. (Ed.). (1981). *Men's studies modified*. New York: Pergamon.

Stanley, L., and Wise, S. (1983). *Breaking out: Feminist consciousness and feminist research*. London: Routledge and Kegan Paul.

Strickland, L. H., Aboud, F. E., and Gergen, K. J. (Eds.). (1976). *Social psychology in transition*. New York: Plenum.

Taylor, C. (1971). "Interpretation and the sciences of man." *Review of metaphysics* 25 (1).

Vaughter, R. (1976). "Psychology: Review essay." *Signs: Journal of Women in Culture and Society* 2:120–46.

Weinreich, H. (1977). "What future for the female subject? Some implications of the women's movement for psychological research." *Human Relations* 30:535–43.

Wetherell, M. (1986). "Linguistic repertoires and literary criticism: New directions for a social psychology of gender." In S. Wilkinson (Ed.). *Feminist social psychology*. Milton Keynes, England: Open University Press.

Wilkinson, S. (Ed.). (1986). *Feminist social psychology*. Milton Keynes, England: Open University Press.

SEVEN

Feminist Thought and Social Psychology

Joan Meyer

SIMONE de Beauvoir began her classic work *The Second Sex* by remarking that the subject of women is especially irritating to women themselves. And indeed, research in recent years (Pheterson 1982) has borne out the fact that individuals do not enjoy belonging to a psychological minority group and tend to minimize differences between themselves and the dominant group (e.g., "I may be a woman, but I feel most at ease with the men . . ."). Interestingly, the dominant group tries to evade the issue in similar ways. Apparently, the situation is painful to both parties. However, thanks to the women who had the courage to tackle this difficult issue, we are able to discuss feminist scholarship today. In this chapter I would like to evaluate the impact of feminist thought on psychology, and more specifically, on social psychology. As a feminist and a social psychologist, I shall give you a very personal view of the relation between these two areas of knowledge.

I will start with a very rough impression of the communication process between mainstream social scientists and feminists. I believe this process has in itself been instrumental to some of the insights gained. I will devote a few words to the position of social psychology in the social sciences and then move on to what I consider to be some of the most significant contributions of feminist thinking. From there, I will consider the impact

of feminist thought on social psychology and then conclude on an opti-
mistic note by pointing out promising ways of thinking and investigating
made possible by feminist scholars and as yet not sufficiently explored.
Along the way, I hope to acquaint you with some of the research done in
my own country, the Netherlands.

THE RELATIONS BETWEEN FEMINIST SCHOLARS
AND MAINSTREAM SOCIAL SCIENTISTS

FEMINIST scholarship had its origins not in the academic world, but in a
social movement and social consciousness. How did this movement begin? At a certain moment, a reasonable number of women were participating in traditionally male territory—the domain of paid employment,
specifically in the academic professions.

Comparing themselves to their male colleagues, they began to realize
that their situation was the same in name, but very different in practice.
The discrepancy between the democratic ideals of society and the differential treatment of women in so-called "male" territory gave rise to the first
step: the demand for equality. Reactions from the male counterparts
proved to be disappointing, so women started to substantiate their claims
with meticulous studies, analyzing and pinpointing differential treatment
or even differential effects of similar treatment, due to various factors
influencing men and women in our society. (Stacey, Béreaud, and Daniels
1974; Abramson 1975; Epstein 1970; Fidell and DeLamater 1971; Graham and Birns 1979; Briscoe and Pfafflin 1979) Support and acclaim for
these efforts were conspicuously lacking from the male world, thus forc-
ing women to admit that their own interpretations of reality differed in
important respects from the interpretations of their mainstream colleagues.

Accepting the existence of different interpretations led to further developments. Women began to scrutinize the so-called "male" world and its
products—among those the fruits of social science—and to discover
flaws in the everyday interpretations of social life paralleled by flaws in
the "scientific" interpretations of social life, flaws, that is, from a viewpoint
of feminist consciousness. The discovery was frustrating, but exhilarating

at the same time. In any case it enabled feminist scholars to voice critiques of social science products and launch sharp attacks, some bitter, some witty, on the "male bias" of the very content of social science (Bart 1971; Long Laws 1971; Millman 1971; Schwendinger and Schwendinger 1971; Scully and Bart 1973; Weisstein 1971).

Reactions, once again, were illuminating. Instead of being "shamed into silence and consequently mending their ways" as could naively have been expected, a number of different reactions could be distinguished. The most conservative social scientists reacted by closing the ranks of the brotherhood and bolstering their position with increased stress on hard-core approaches emulating the natural sciences. The content of feminist critiques was either ignored (by far the most common and most effective reaction) or met with vicious counterattacks labeling feminist scholars as unscientific, emotional, and wooly-minded.

A second reaction was slightly more positive. These social scientists did not spend time trying to understand feminist critics, but they did at least become more scrupulous about noting and reporting sex differences in research. They also prefaced their presentations with remarks intended to show their personal nonsexist attitudes, such as, "While I was cooking the Sunday dinner for my family as I usually do, it suddenly dawned on me . . ."

Finally, and happily, there were others who became genuinely interested in the feminist discourse. Individually or in collaboration with feminist colleagues, they became absorbed by its diverse influences on men and women and started taking a critical look at the male role, and its impact on themselves as people and as scientists.

Although it is quite possible that some of these people were just following a trend, by and large I think they have not received due credit. On the contrary, many found themselves regarded with distrust by feminists and at the same time excluded from the ranks of their more conservative male colleagues.

In the Netherlands for example, a well-known and generally respected educational psychologist, inspired by feminist writings, conducted some important research that resulted in a book on the subtle influences in the classroom that discouraged girls from becoming too proficient in mathematics (Jungbluth 1982). The book received much publicity. Later, at a conference, the researcher stated that since the publication of the book all of his contacts with mainstream social scientists had disappeared into thin air. He received no more invitations to lecture or write articles. He stated that from a content point of view the research was probably the best he had done, but from a career point of view it was definitely the worst.

What becomes increasingly clear from the later developments in the relations between feminist and mainstream social scientists is that there are different interpretations of events. However, it is no coincidence that some interpretations are to be found in the curriculums of compulsory courses for social sciences, whereas others have been relegated to the fringe of an occasional workshop or seminar. In other words, the relevance of the power dimension between the sexes comes to the force. At this point I shall conclude my general impressions of relations between feminist and mainstream social scientists, and take a look at the impact feminist thinking has had in social psychology.

FEMINIST SCHOLARSHIP AND
SOCIAL PSYCHOLOGY

SOCIAL psychology purports to study the influence of society on the individual as well as its complement, the influence of the individual on society. Since feminist scholarship has its roots in social developments, one would be justified in expecting social psychologists to be among the most advanced in making use of feminist insights. But this unfortunately would be incorrect. The impact of feminist scholarship has been far greater in the clinical and therapeutic approaches in psychology and in developmental psychology than it has in social psychology.

Yet the development of feminist thinking has not bypassed social psychology altogether. Thanks to a large number of highly qualified and competent female social psychologists, there are quite a few achievements, including nonsexist experimental work and research that explores the specific ways in which men and women behave differently in various contexts. In addition, there has been an ordering of research to illustrate the differential ways various social contexts influence men and women (Deaux 1976). And there is an analysis of ways in which sexism has operated in theories and research in the past, and consequently of how to avoid sexism in the future (Johnson and Frieze 1978). Finally, quite a few of the aforementioned female social psychologists have taken up issues evidently inspired by the feminist movement for theorizing and research.

Much as these gains are to be appreciated in their own right, if we take a look at mainstream journals and textbooks, it is impossible to say that there has been a significant impact of feminist thinking on the discipline as a whole. A fundamental discussion and reevaluation of content and method has not come about as yet, and feminist social psychologists are in danger of falling into the age-old female trap of clearing up after the men. Why is social psychology so particularly inaccessible to modification, compared to clinical and developmental psychology? A number of reasons seem plausible.

First, in developmental psychology it is impossible not to deal with the question of how psychological sex differences come into being; in tackling this problem, inevitably fairly broad theories about the relation between the individual and society are developed. Theories within a psychoanalytic framework, cognitive development theory, and social learning theory have all been criticized from a feminist viewpoint, but the important common denominator is that they offer connecting parts to build from. In contrast, social psychology has limited theorizing to very small, restricted areas. Instead of broad visions or perspectives, we find a patchwork quilt of minitheories and subsequent inconclusive research. Clinical and therapeutic approaches in psychology cannot ignore subjective experience. Moreover, there is a direct interface with the general public, since clinicians have clients. In the long run, clinicians have to take account of significant social developments and of modifications in the ways individuals define their situations if they are to continue their work (Moulton 1977; Wittkower and Robertson 1977). Feminist self-help groups and radical feminist therapy groups developed in the period when discrepancies between mainstream clinical interpretations and feminist interpretations were at a maximum. These clinical groups may also have influenced more traditional therapists in their practices and views.

Again in contrast, two important factors lacking in social psychology are a genuine 'reality testing point' and a legitimate place for the subjective experience. There is some reality testing in applied social psychology, but theorizing is usually narrow and restricted to the specific problem at hand.

In addition, there is no two-way communication process between applied and academic "theoretical" social psychology, since applied social psychology is generally regarded as a branch of lower order by academics. As for the subjective experience of subjects, the most frequent conception in social psychology is that these are contamination of data, or delusions to be unmasked by the experiment. Though subjects are labeled as such, they are often subjects in name only to laboratory experimenters. Their subjective experiences are out-of-bounds (Meyer 1983).

GENERAL CRITIQUE FROM FEMINIST SOCIAL SCIENTISTS

TWO IMPORTANT main issues raised by feminist scholars are especially relevant to social psychology as a whole. The first issue used to be called "the invisibility of women," but could now be more accurately termed the "pars pro toto" phenomenon. By this I do not simply mean the traditional practice of using only male subjects for experiments, or a majority of male subjects, and later removing the female minority from the data because they supposedly confounded the results. The problem is much broader since choosing an area for theorizing, formulating research questions, developing and operationalizing hypotheses are all vulnerable to a social scientist's personal outlook, commonsense knowledge, and cultural or subcultural molding.

All other things being equal, a male in a predominantly male academic setting is more likely to choose achievement as an area for research than nurturance, and choosing achievement, is more likely to operationalize it in terms of solving abstract or rational problems than, say, household management problems. If an experiment is built on everyday experiences common to most men but uncommon to most women, and in the final stages of the research the female subjects don't seem to fit in properly, this is hardly surprising.

Let me give you a concrete example of the "pars pro toto" phenomenon in a series of well-known experiments in social psychology. The subject matter is interpersonal attraction between women and men. Is interpersonal attraction between women and men intensified by fear? This question was tested by Dutton and Aron (1974) under two conditions: in one, men walked over a narrow, high, unstable bridge; in the other, they walked over a low, broad, stable bridge. The men were approached with a questionnaire by an attractive woman who gave them her telephone number to call "if they wanted any further information about the survey." The criterion for attraction was whether the men later made use of the phone number. Did the men in the high-fear condition call the woman more often than the men in the low-fear condition? (They did, but that is another story).

The same question was tested in another setting (Berscheid and Walster 1969). Men were invited to take part in an experiment purported to deal with the learning process. They were introduced to an attractive woman who was to be their partner in the experiment. In the high-fear condition they were led to expect a series of extremely painful electric shocks in the experiment; in the low-fear condition they were told the shocks would barely cause any sensation. Thereupon the experimenter approached the men confidentially to ask them how attracted they were to their partner in the experiment. The experimenter legitimated the questions by saying that such things could influence the results of the experiment and therefore had to be taken into consideration.

The subject of these experiments is the effect of fear on interpersonal attraction between men and women, and the experimental situation includes both men and women, so maybe the "pars pro toto" phenomenon is not too obvious at first glance. However, at the end of these experiments we may or may not know something about conditions under which men feel attracted towards women; however, we know nothing about conditions under which women feel attracted to men. In these experiments women do not figure as subjects but as a stimulus to which the men react.

In yet another example, a whole series of experiments was devoted to "playing hard to get" (Walster et al. 1973), to find out whether this strategy heightened attraction between men and women. All possible variations were tried out, even to the point of using a prostitute in the experiment. Only one aspect was constant throughout the experiments: who used the strategy (the woman) and whose feelings of attraction were researched (the man's).

These examples all reveal a one-sidedness in gathering data. The longer this bias exists, the more difficult it is for subsequent researchers to break the cycle, especially if it has all been classed under a general heading ("interpersonal attraction") supposedly covering both men and women. The argument thus is *not* that one cannot ask partial questions—certainly if one wants to do laboratory experiments this is inevitable—but that in doing so, one must be aware of what is omitted. And being aware, to make this explicit, one invites others to look into the questions one has left aside.

A second area of general concern for feminist scholars has been that of method. I believe there is no competition between research methods, or at least there need not be. But each method has its own limitations. Regarding the so-called hard-boiled approach, I quote Lillian Rubin: "What difference does it make to society if we have methodologically perfectly constructed studies about something that any twelve-year-old child know?" (Rubin 1982a). But I feel the position taken by feminist scholars is more accurately described by the following quotation from *The Little Prince* by Antoine de Saint-Exupéry:

Grownups love numbers. When you tell them about a new friend, they never ask you questions about the essential things. They never say to you: "What does his voice sound like? Which games does he prefer? Does he collect butterflies?" Instead they ask you: "How old is he? How many brothers has he got? How much does he weigh? How much does his father make?" Only in that way do they get the feeling that they know him. If you tell grownups: "I saw a beautiful house made of pink bricks with geraniums in the windows and doves on the roof. . . ." they cannot imagine such a house. You have to tell them: "I saw a house of a hundred million dollars." And then they will exclaim: "Oh, how beautiful." (1946, p. 14)

Feminist scholars who advocate and are instrumental in the development of alternative methods for research in the social sciences have good grounds for doing so. A thesis by Komter (1985) titled "The power of what is taken for granted: Relationships between men and women" is an example of an alternate methodology.

This study was developed from a critique of mainstream family sociology, where power is usually operationalized by counting the number of decisions each partner makes. Joint or segregated decision making as well as the number of decisions taken by each partner individually are taken to reflect the relative power of husband and wife. Although this method has received a good deal of critical attention (cf. Gillespie 1971), after twenty years of research into marriage and family life, decision making is still viewed as one of the most important indicators of power. Points of criticism raised concerning this method are: 1) often only the wife is subjected to interviews or questionnaires (family life is the woman's domain); 2) social resources such as formal education, status, and income are structurally unequally divided between men and women; and, 3) different decisions do not carry the same weight.

Still it is easy to see why this indicator was and is so attractive to mainstream social scientists: it leads to a seemingly orderly and simple treatment of a complex phenomenon. Once you have reduced the concept of power to the number of decisions taken, you can go ahead and do your arithmetic and ignore the spoilsport who points out the meaninglessness of equating the choice of where to live with choosing the family toothpaste three times.

In her theoretical analysis, mainly based on Lukes (1971) and Gramsci (1971), Komter outlined as the main question for her study on power in marital relationships the following: through which mechanisms and processes is power inequality between husbands and wives maintained and ideologically legitimated? Behind the mainstream sociological question "who has more power, the husband or the wife?" the conceptualization of power is again quantitative: one party "owns" more of it than the other. However, power is not a personal attribute or possession, but an aspect of the relation between people or groups of people. As such, Komter defined it as the ability, purposefully or not, to affect the feelings, attitudes, cognitions, or behavior of the other. It is important to note here that power is conceived as a two-way process, and that the central focus has moved from "who has more?" to ways and means by which power differentials come into being and are maintained, reinforced, or shifted.

Consequently, Komter's operationalizations of power concentrate on *change:* what would one like to change in the relationship, what has one tried to change, strategies used to effect or impede change, reactions of one's partner to change, obstacles to the process of change, and conflicts. Five areas were chosen, which were considered nontrivial and therefore suitable for studying these processes: household work, children, sexuality, social contacts, leisure, and finances. It will be clear that this theoretical model is a good deal more sophisticated than counting decisions.

The major gains from this type of study lie not in quantification, since that is elementary, but in the qualitative aspects, such as ambivalences and contradictions. Systematic differences in the ways husbands and wives answer certain questions throw light on the psychodynamics of the marital relationship in a specific social and cultural context. More qualitative research and studies approaching the subject from different angles, more profound analyses both before and after research, will make possible theoretical models more apt to the main subject matter: relations between people and groups of people against their cultural and historical backgrounds, in a structured social setting.

Social life is richer and more complex by far than the means we have devised to describe it. We use unilinear models, whereas interpersonal relations are full of ambiguities and inconsistencies. Relations are dynamic, whereas we can take only one picture at a time. People will say different things on different levels; this does not mean that one of the things they said was untrue, but that it must be placed in a different context.

There are many examples that reveal greater complexities of social life. For example, a husband and wife both agree that they have equal power in their relationship. Yet when a researcher comes to interview the wife, the husband refuses to leave the room, and no matter what the wife and the interviewer say, they cannot make him leave the room. A week later the researcher returns to interview the husband. He refuses to allow his wife to stay in the room, and she leaves. What can be said about their power relationship?

One is interviewing a woman who stresses that she has chosen to be a housewife and that she finds complete fulfillment in home making and pities women who feel they need to do a man's job. Yet when asked what she would do with five extra hours in a day, she replies she would take a computer course. How can one interpret this data? The traditional solution to these problems would have been to devise some exact-looking means to determine which of the contradictory data was "true." For instance, it would not be difficult to devise an experiment that would demonstrate either of these alternatives to be the "true" one. But a truth dependent on the combined intuition and ingenuity of the experimenter is hardly a serious solution. Moreover, if one is dealing with different levels of communication, one experiment simply is not enough.

Perhaps I can illustrate this point by reviewing a study I did in 1979–

1981 (Meyer 1983). As is well-known, the kind of answers one gets in social research depends in part on the kind of questions one asks. Social scientists are familiar with the phenomenon of social desirability. Social desirability has often been regarded as an obstacle in research, biasing the "true data" by making people answer or act in ways they perceive as socially desirable rather than answering "truthfully" or acting "naturally." However, in everyday life we accept that there are often discrepancies between the way we would like things to be and the way things go, or between the way *we* would like things to be and what is generally considered fitting in our culture or subculture.

Many of the forces that drive us to take action or help us to develop originate in these very discrepancies. So it is not very logical to look for one simple straightforward answer the moment we closet ourselves in the research laboratory.

The study I want to describe dealt with the changing position of women and men in the Netherlands and with the reactions of young men and women to these changes. Subjects were asked about the relationship in terms of "what ought to be," for instance: "If husband and wife both have jobs outside the home, housework should be divided equally between them" (agree-disagree, 5-point scale). Then, they were asked how they would like things to be in specified situations, for instance: "For me, it would be (pleasant-unpleasant, 5-point scale) to have a partner who usually does the cooking." People were then given a questionnaire that gave them an opportunity to put equality principles into practice; different settings were described in a written test where subjects could either accept a more or less egalitarian approach or reject a very dominant or very submissive approach.

Note that the method was orthodox in the sense that the usual laboratory written tests were used. The general trend of the results is as following: The first test mentioned showed the most egalitarian results; both men and women perceived social norms to be egalitarian. The second test described (what one would find pleasant or unpleasant in specific instances) showed more variable responses, with the more conservative groups coming out less in favor of equality. Finally, the third test described left still fewer equality-minded subjects, as was to be expected. Especially when the context given was a romantic one, men tended to prefer the submissive approach and women the dominant approach.

Now what do these results tell us? That the third test described is the best one, so we can leave out the other two since they don't give us the "true" picture?

If we take our subjects seriously—and surely there is no a priori reason to do otherwise—the interpretation will be something along these lines: There is a process of change taking place in our society regarding the relation between women and men. Our subjects see as socially desirable a situation where there is equality between men and women in a number of important areas of life. At the same time they are not sure they would enjoy all concrete manifestations of such equality; and it appears harder to put equality principles into practice if the context is romantic rather than businesslike. Conclusion: the changes seen as socially desirable will take some time coming about, especially in people's private lives. It seems to me that this kind of multifaceted approach does more justice to people, situations, and the issues at stake than a simple two-by-two design. It is important to stress two ways in which such an approach differs from mainstream methods: first of all, a difference in methodology—to know what responses mean, it is essential to take account of the cultural setting for individual behavior and of the different emotional coloring of situations. The other difference is one of interpretation: people do not need to be either logical or internally consistent to qualify as sincere. On the contrary, it is taken for granted that people are usually fairly sincere; if their answers seem contradictory in the light of the theoretical model, the theoretical model is probably inadequate and needs reworking.

To summarize the main points of feminist critique described here, we need a methodology to make explicit the limitations of any particular research question, area, group, and generalizability. And we need models of human relationships that allow for ambivalence, ambiguity, and inconsistencies, in order to do justice to the variable responses and behavior of people. This may sound like a small step, but in fact it alters the whole concept of the social sciences. Instead of the former authoritative role: "replacing the amateurish conceptions people have in everyday life with the 'true' story of what 'really' makes them tick," the social scientist is faced first with the task of understanding what different interpretations mean to the people using them in their respective contexts and then of devising some kind of topography to chart these data.

USEFUL PRINCIPLES FOR SOCIAL SCIENCE
THEORIZING AND RESEARCH

PERHAPS the task I have just outlined for social scientists seems impossible. However, feminist scholars have covered a good deal of ground and unearthed quite a few useful tools for tackling these problems. If the impact of their writings has not been great up until now in the social sciences and in social psychology in particular, this can, of course, be partly due to the power differential involved in the communication process between feminist scholars and mainstream social scientists. But it is at least in part also a result of the fact that many feminists have simply put these principles into practice and not bothered to translate them into formal statements. In conclusion I would like to state some of these principles because I believe they could considerably further development in the social sciences, not only concerning relationships between men and women, but in other areas as well.

1. *The investigator should take stock of the material context.*
The first principle involves taking account of the material context in which social behavior takes place. How are scarce resources like time, money, space, discretionary power, and schooling distributed among different groups in society? Which formal hierarchies are involved? What consequences does this distribution have for the groups and relations you want to study? In feminist writings, these factors are taken into account. What should persuade other social scientists to do likewise is the fact that, unlike so many other variables involved in social processes, the distribution of scarce resources lends itself to exact measurement. The material context provides us with a firm basis upon which actions and interpretations of groups and individuals can be imposed. It also provides us with a baseline against which the partiality of research questions or the limited generalizability of results can be checked out.

Let me illustrate this principle with a study based on Kanter's theories about the effect of different ratios between groups in organizational settings (Kanter 1977). Kanter spoke of skewed groups when the ratio of the dominant group versus the minority is from 85:15 percent to 99:1

percent (tokens), tilted groups when the dominants constitute 65 to 85 percent, and balanced groups when the difference is no more than 30 percent.

The ratio of the dominant and minority group has important consequences for minority group members: minorities in skewed and tilted groups have been considerably hampered in performing up to their normal standards due to the psychological effects of their conspicuousness (Spangler et al. 1984). This study (Ott 1985) poses the question whether the described effects are due purely to ratios or whether other factors are involved as well. It is comparative research in two different settings:

a) Nursing, a traditionally female occupation where male nurses form a minority of new members; and

b) Police work, a traditionally male occupation where women are in a similar minority position.

The research shows that the consequences of being a minority are very different for the men in nursing and for the women in the police force. Whereas both groups are more highly visible in the skewed contexts, for the men in nursing this appears to be an advantage, specifically in regard to informal contacts with colleagues and career possibilities. For the women the reverse holds true: fewer career possibilities and fewer informal social contacts, or social contacts of an unfavorable nature.

There is no way to account for such findings without paying attention to the material context. True, nursing is a female-dominated profession, but it is also an enclave in a hierarchical organization where the higher echelons are again male-dominated, against the backdrop of a society where most professions and paid jobs are male-dominated. (In only 6 percent of all paid functions in the Netherlands is the number of women proportionate to the number of women in the labor market, Oudijk 1983.)

2. *The investigator should take account of the normative context for social processes.*

The second principle involves taking account of the cultural and historical setting for social actions. Specifically, it is important to know which cultural norms are shared by which groups in society, relevant, of course, to the area under study. The normative context forms a theme on which groups and individuals construct their own variations, be they conforming or counternormative. Individual and group actions acquire their meaning against a historical and cultural background. For instance, to understand what it means to dye one's hair green, one has to know about the fashion rules in the culture and subculture in which this action takes place.

It is also important to check out the relationship between the normative context and the material context; some cultural norms are firmly rooted in a material substructure, whereas others are not. In the Netherlands for instance, cultural norms in the sixties prescribed getting married and starting a family at the age of twenty. These norms are supported by material consequences: many financial benefits were attached to marriage, and the only way for a large group of people in society to qualify for housing was as a married couple. Also, the more children they had, the larger the house they were granted. At the same time the cultural norms were under discussion—mainly from those groups who did not have the same material benefits attached to marriage (students, for example). Now in the eighties, cultural norms regarding marriage and having a family are less stringent, but the material substructure has undergone a much more radical change. Unemployment figures are high, especially among young people, and for those receiving any kind of social benefit, getting married means less housing space and a reduction of at least 40 percent in joint income. The point I am trying to make is that it is impossible to do meaningful research about relationships between men and women if you do not take account of such factors.

3. *The investigator should give the subjective experience a legitimate place in social science.*

The third principle has to do with the way we treat subjective experience. Feminist scholars have always attached importance to subjective experience, and rightly so. It is impossible to know what one has actually done with a laboratory experiment if one refrains completely from checking the subjective experiences of subjects. The fact that such procedures have often been omitted in many well-known experiments in social psychology (Milgram 1965) has left social scientists guessing about the way to interpret results. The subjective experience of subjects need not be consistent with behavior or with the experimenter's interpretation to provide useful information and even if it confirms what we expected, there is nothing unscientific about a double check.

The subjective experience of the social scientist has been handled by feminist scholars in two ways: first of all as a criterion against which existing theories and research are tried out. This does not mean that if I cannot come up with a subjective experience to support existing interpretations it invalidates them, but rather that if a certain interpretation feels especially strange to me, I might not be the only person in the world to experience this, and so the matter is worth closer scrutiny. Social norms often give the individual the idea that he or she is the one exception violating them. Sharing and exchanging subjective experience has been an important way for feminists to order social life and arrive at an understanding of their position.

The second way in which subjective experience is relevant is as a factor influencing the social scientist's steps in the gathering of knowledge for which we have no proper methodology: choosing an area for theory building and research, formulation of the problem and hypotheses, and interpretation of the results. Feminist scholars have been especially scrupulous in describing how their own subjective experiences have influenced their work. No matter that critics have predictably capitalized on such utterances by invalidating the work as too emotionally involved and so unscientific, since it is hardly scientific to ignore such issues. Making use of one's own subjective experience in a positive sense in social science can be a safeguard against objectifying one's research subjects, as well as being a fruitful source of inspiration.

4. *The investigator should be aware of the impact of the research on society.*
The last principle to be mentioned here has to do with the relation between social science and the society in which it takes place and to which it is addressed. Here again, the fact that feminist scholars have usually been explicit about the social aims or relevance of their work does not imply that there are no social aims hidden under other theoretical models or problem formulations. To pose the question of which groups or problems in society a particular piece of research might address is not only part of the responsibility of the social scientist; but it is also illuminating as a means of structuring an area of study. A good example of this is provided in the Netherlands by trend reports commissioned by the national committee for women's studies and emancipation research; research concerning major themes such as motherhood, sexuality and sexual violence, language, arts, and the media, over a period of roughly fifteen

years, was reviewed with special attention to development in problem formulations over time, the relation between funding, executing, agent and problem formulation, and applicability of results.

REFERENCES

Abramson, J. (1975). *The invisible woman: Discrimination in the academic profession.* San Francisco: Jossey-Bass.

Bart, P. B. (1971). "Sexism and social science: From the gilded cage to the iron cage, or the perils of Pauline." *J. Marriage and the Family* 33:734–46.

Beauvoir, S. de. (1949). *Le deuxième sexe* (The second sex). Paris: Gallimard.

Berscheid, E., and Walster, E. H. (1969). *Interpersonal attraction.* Reading, Mass.: Addison-Wesley.

Briscoe, A. M., and Pfafflin, S. M. (1979). *Expanding the role of women in the sciences.* New York: New York Academy of Sciences.

Deaux, K. (1976). *The behaviour of women and men.* Belmont: Wadsworth.

Draayer, N. (1984). *Seksueel geweld en heteroseksualiteit* (Sexual violence and heterosexuality). Den Haag: Ministerie van Sociale Zaken en Werkgelegenehid.

Dutton, D. G., and Aron, A. P. (1974). "Some evidence for heightened sexual attraction under conditions of high anxiety." *J. Personality and Social Psychol.* 30:510–17.

Epstein, C. F. (1970). *Woman's place.* Berkeley: University of California Press.

Fidell, L. S., and DeLamater, J. (1971). *Women in the professions: What's all the fuss about?* Beverly Hills: Sage.

Gillespie, D. L. (1971). "Who has the power? The marital struggle." *J. of Marriage and the Family* 33:445–58.

Graham, M. F., and Birns, B. (1979). "Where are the women geniuses? Up the down escalator." In C. B. Kopp and M. Kirckpatrick (Eds.). *Becoming female.* New York: Plenum.

Gramsci, A. (1971). *Selections from the prison notebooks.* Q. Hoare and G. Nowell-Smith (Trs.). London: Lawrence and Wishart.

Johnson, P. B., and Frieze, I. H. (1978). "Biases in psychology: What are the facts?" In I. H. Frieze (ed.). *Women and sex roles: A social psychological perspective.* New York: Norton.

Jungbluth, P. L. (1982). *Docenten over onderwijs aan meisjes: Positieve discriminatie met een dubbele bodem* (Teachers on educating girls: Positive discrimination with a false bottom). Ph.D. diss., Nijmegen: Instituut voor Toegepaste Sociologie.

Kanter, R. M. (1977). *Men and women of the corporation.* New York: Basic Books.

Komter, A. (1985). *De macht van de vanzelfsprekendheid: Relaties tussen vrouwen en manne* (The power of what is taken for granted: Relationships between women and men). Den Haag: VUGA.

Long Laws, J. (1971). "A feminist review of the marital adjustment literature: The rape of the locke." *J. Marriage and the Family* 33:483–517.

Lukes, S. (1971). *Power: A radical view.* London: Macmillan.

Meyer, J. L. (1983). *Sekse als organisatieprincipe: Veranderende normen in de asymmetrisch machtsrelatie tussen mannen en vrouwen* (Gender as an organizational principle: Changing norms in the asymmetrical power relationship between men and women). Ph.D. diss., Amsterdam. Universiteit van Amsterdam.

Milgram, S. (1965). "Some conditions of obedience and disobedience to authority." *Human Relations* 18:57–76.

Millman, M. (1971). "Observations on sex role research." *J. Marriage and the Family* 33:772.

Moulton, R. (1977). "Some effects of the new feminism." *Amer. J. Psychiat.* 134:1–6.

Ott, M. (1985). *Assepoesters en kroonprinsen: Een onderzoek naar de minderheidspositie van agentes en verplegers* (Cinderellas and crown princes: A study of the minority position of female police officers and male nurses). Ph.D. diss., Amsterdam: SUA.

Oudijk, C. (1983). *Sociale atlas van de vrouw 1983* (Social atlas of women in 1983). Den Hag: Staatsuitgeverij.

Pheterson, G. (1982). "Alliance between women: A group process report and theoretical analysis of opression and liberation." *Psychologie en Maatschappij* (psychology and society) 20:399–425.

Rubin, L. (1982a). *Social science research, the subjective dimension.* Lecture at the Rijksuniversiteit Groningen, the Netherlands.

Rubin, L. (1982b). On a qualitative method based on interviewing. Lecture at the Rijksuniversiteit Utrecht, the Netherlands.

Saint-Exupéry, A. de. (1946). *Le petit prince* (The little prince). Paris: Gallimard.

Schwendinger, J., and Schwendinger, H. (1971). "Sociology's founding fathers: Sexists to a man." *J. Marriage and the Family* 33:783–92.

Scully, D., and Bart, P. (1973). "A funny thing happened on the way to the orifice: Women in gynecology textbooks." *Amer. J. Sociol.* 78:1045–49.

Spangler, E., Gordon, M. A., and Pipkin, R. M. (1984). Token women: An empirical test of Kanter hypothesis. *Amer. J. Sociol.* 84(1):160–70.

Stacey, J., Béreaud, S., and Daniels, J. (1974). *And Jill came tumbling after: Sexism in American education.* New York: Dell.

Trendreports VBEO. (1983). *Moederschap, huishoudelijke arbeid, politieke macht en taal, kunst en media.* (Motherhood, housework, and political power in language, the arts and media) Den Haag: Ministerie van Sociale Zaken en Werkgelegenheid.

Walster, E., et al. (1973). "Playing hard to get: Understanding an elusive phenomenon." *J. Personality and Social Psychol.* 26:113–21.

Weisstein, N. (1971). "Psychology constructs the female." In V. Gornick and B. Moran (Eds.). *Women in sexist society.* New York: Basic Books.

Wittkower, E. D., and Robertson, B. M. (1977). "Sex differences in psychoanalytic treatment." *Amer. J. Psychother.* 31:66–75.

EIGHT

Psychological, Feminist, and Personal Epistemology: Transcending Contradiction

Rhoda K. Unger

IT IS impossible to discuss the relationship between feminist epistemology and psychological epistemology without critiquing psychology as a scholarly discipline. Psychology, more than other social sciences, has been largely unaware of the way its definition of appropriate methods and content has created the phenomena with which it deals. At the same time, more important phenomena have been either ignored or excluded by means of these same definitions.

In this chapter I will review briefly some of the epistemological assumptions of behaviorism that, until recently, represented the dominant paradigm within psychology. Next, I will discuss how explicit and implicit definitions influenced the study of females and males. I will then discuss one potentially useful model through which feminist psychologists may offer an alternative way to explain sex-related differences. And, last, I will point out some current problems involving the conflicting epistemological assumptions of psychology and feminism that, I believe, pose particular difficulties for those attempting to synthesize psychological and feminist scholarship.

BEHAVIORISM AND THE STUDY OF WOMEN

THE juxtaposition of the words "behaviorism" and "the study of women" seems to some of us to be a contradiction in terms. The essence of behaviorism is to restrict psychology to a few simple easily observable and categorizable behaviors in order to facilitate the examination of the relationship between behavioral output (so-called operants) and its outcomes (e.g., reinforcements). In so doing, however, psychology has limited itself to the study of behaviors that are devoid of much meaning for the human subject—of either sex—and has had to examine these subjects in a context that eliminates any opportunity for the selection of alternative behaviors. Obviously, a "science" that seeks to determine universal "laws of behavior" from an examination of the behavioral similarities among pigeons, rats, and human beings has had little to say about the similarities or differences among various groups of humans.

Although it is obvious that behaviorism precludes the study of sex by virtue of its assumptions, it is less obvious that the basic set of epistemological assumptions from which behaviorism derives—the positivist-empiricist model—also results in a narrow definition of "appropriate" questions about males and females. The positivist-empiricist model assumes that general laws of behavior exist and may be extracted by means of the use of careful scientific methodology. Proper psychological methodology is assumed to be akin to experimental methodology in chemistry or biology.

Briefly, random selection of subjects is mandated, as well as random distribution of subjects into experimental conditions. In order to minimize the effect of "extraneous variables," a laboratory setting is the usual locale for such manipulations. The relationship between experimenter and subject is assumed to be an impersonal one. And, if the mandates of proper experimental technique are carried out, results are expected to be reproducible at another time and place with another investigator in charge. Control of irrelevant variables ensures what is known as the internal validity of the study—it enables the investigator to make cause and effect statements about the relationship between the variables manipulated and the behavior of the subjects.

Sex and the Study of Individual Differences

The variable of sex has always posed problems for this model of research. Sex has long been viewed as a subject or organismic variable. It is manifestly impossible for a researcher to select or assign subjects randomly without reference to their sex. One cannot ask a male to become a "female" because statistical rules dictate that a female is needed in that particular cell of the experiment. Since sex cannot be manipulated experimentally, it has tended to be relegated to the area of individual difference research along with other such nuisance variables as race, ethnicity, size, and physical appearance. Since cause and effect relationships could not be inferred, the area was composed of lists of differences among various groups with a weak theoretical framework that permitted researchers to make any causal statements they wished. Usually, biological explanations were given and social explanations ignored.

Biological factors and social roles and norms are inextricably confounded in the study of individual differences. Nevertheless, explanations for sex- and race-related differences have been heavily influenced by biological determinism from the very beginning of the field. It has been noted that Galton, the founder of individual difference research, viewed women and dark-skinned peoples as inferior to men and the British (Buss 1976; Sherif 1979; Shields 1975a). The theoretical background for the study of sex differences was behavioral Darwinism, that is, a theory that states that group differences in behavior are a result of evolution. The differences between women and men are seen to have an adaptive function for individual humans, and reproduction of sex-related traits is seen to shape society rather than the other way around. Of course, this theory is still popular in contemporary sociobiology.

Some critiques of the behavioral Darwinist model for human behavior emphasize its acultural and ahistorical nature. That is, current social reality with its sex- and race-related differences is seen as the "universal" norm. Since biological sex differences exist, psychological and behavioral sex differences are presumed to exist, are looked for, and are found. Much less attention is paid to sex similarities (Unger 1979). Assumptions about biological causality have led to a confusion of descriptions of differences between the sexes and explanations of such differences. Specification of hormonal or neural mechanisms does not appear to be required. In addition, social perceptions and cognitions relating to biological events are presumed to have little effect upon such events (Unger 1983).

The Feminist Response to Exclusion and Misdirection

Feminist psychologists have long been dissatisfied with the data base on which assumptions about sex differences have been made (c.f. Rosenberg 1984; Shields 1975b). Early researchers worked to demonstrate that many so-called sex differences could not be empirically verified. The list of sex differences, however, is potentially infinite, and thus a more recent focus has been to examine the size and implications of so-called sex differences (c.f. Block 1976). Studies using a sophisticated statistical technique called meta-analysis call into question the meaningfulness of differences that account for such a small amount of variability in the behavior of males and females (Eagly and Carli 1981; Hyde 1981).

Another group of feminist researchers in psychology has concentrated on the situational conditions in which sex-related differences are likely to appear. For example, sex differences are more likely to appear in the natural than in the laboratory environment (Unger 1981). It could be argued by experimentalists that this phenomenon is due to the lack of control of extraneous variables in the natural environment. One can also argue, however, that it is extraneous variables such as status and roles—inextricably confounded with biological sex—that produce most of the differences found in "real life." (Eagly 1983; Henley 1977; Unger 1976, 1978). The artificial laboratory environment, which mandates a lack of relationship between participants and assumes that subjects have no personal or cultural history, restricts the usual range of male-female relationships. In other words, one can argue that sex has little explanatory value outside of normative social relationships.

The failure to take into account situational context, social role, and historical circumstances has led even feminist psychologists to overestimate the importance of personality as an explanation of behavior. A number of trait theories designed to be more favorable to women have been the focus of much study in the psychology of women. These include Matina Horner's work on fear of success (1972); the concept of androgyny developed by Sandra Bem (1974) and Janet Spence and Robert

Helmreich (1978); and, most recently, Carol Gilligan's (1982) work on female moral development. Unfortunately, these concepts contain some unexamined assumptions that may have antifemale consequences even when this is the last thing the researchers intended. A number of methodological criticisms of these theories exist (c.f. Tresemer 1977; Kelly and Worrell 1977; Pedhazur and Tetenbaum 1979; Benton et al. 1983). For the purposes of this essay I will concentrate on epistemological issues with regard to these theories.

One of the major epistemological problems of trait theories is the extent to which they seek to increase predictability between groups by decreasing the variability within groups. Although the groups are no longer labeled "male" or "female," the procedures used to define them are logically akin to those developed for the study of sex differences. Individuals are categorized in terms of their response on some measure and their behaviors are explained in terms of their relative scores. In the measures discussed above, sex is not an absolute category, but is highly related probabilistically to the trait being measured. Thus, many more females than males are found to be high in fear of success, and gender identity (sex-typed, sex-reversed, androgynous, etc.) is distributed differentially in terms of biological sex.

In trait theories little attention is paid to the meaning of the trait for its possessors or to the consequences of its possession in terms of life in a nonegalitarian reality. Moreover, traits are assumed to have a situational universality (otherwise, they would be useless for predicting an individual's behavior) that may give them more of a global significance than they actually possess. And, since relatively little empirical attention is paid to their origin as compared to their measurement, suppositions about irreversibility may lead to pessimism about the possibility of individual change.

Perhaps the most important criticism from a constructionist point of view is that the individualistic focus in trait measurement may induce lack of concern about society's responsibility for the differential distribution of various traits in women and men. This issue is particularly important because traits—even when posited by feminists—are not value-free. It is clearly better to be unafraid than afraid, and possession of the qualities of both genders is seen as better than being bound to only one. Only Carol Gilligan's typology asserts the superiority of women, but it may do so at the risk of substituting gynocentrism for androcentrism.

FEMINIST PSYCHOLOGY AND THE
COGNITIVE PARADIGM

MANY fine papers have investigated the social conditions under which sex-related traits may or may not appear (c.f. Dion 1985; Eagly and Wood 1985; Macaulay 1985). These researchers are aware of the importance of social context in eliciting role-relevant behaviors in individuals of either sex. They are also concerned with the impact that deviation from normative gender and role prescriptions has upon the individual's interpersonal relationships.

This way of looking at sex treats it as a cognitive rather than a biological variable. In the new psychology of sex and gender, maleness and femaleness are seen as social stimuli that provide information for both actor and observer. The observer's beliefs about sex as a social reality are confirmed by gender-characteristic styles of self-presentation and by the differential distribution of females and males into different status roles. Behavioral distinctions between individual males and females are maintained both by intrapsychic needs for self-consistency and pressure from others to behave in a socially desirable manner.

There is a very extensive body of research in the area of sex as a cognitive structure, and I will only briefly sketch the outlines here. First, it may be demonstrated that sex is a salient social category even in the most impersonal of circumstances. Thus, sex is the category chosen first by most people when asked for a description of an individual with whom they have had a brief interaction. People will also choose sex as a category in a problem-solving task even when more relevant and statistically useful cues are available (Grady 1977).

Sex appears to be an unquestioned given in most people's perception of themselves (Spence and Sawin 1985). However, both males and females appear to use different information for the perception of their own and others' gender identity. The importance of sexual category appears to be heightened when one's sex is in a numerical minority. When asked "Who are you?" both children and adults respond with sex-related information when their category is rare within their family or classroom (McGuire, McGuire, and Winton 1979).

Numerous studies also document the fact that men and women are evaluated differently even when their actual performance is identical (for a review of such studies see Wallston and O'Leary 1981). More important, perhaps, explanations for identical performance in males and females differ as well. High achievement in males is explained by more stable internal causes than is the equivalent performance in females (Deaux 1976; Frieze et al. 1978; Hansen and O'Leary 1985). Males are seen as "smarter" whereas females are seen as "luckier" and/or more "hard-working."

Different implicit causal assumptions about identical outcomes obviously have implications in terms of expectations for future performance. Therefore, researchers have sought laboratory models of the so-called "self-fulfilling prophecy." A few creative studies demonstrate that gender-characteristic behaviors may be produced by the beliefs of others with whom the individual interacts. Thus, Snyder, Tanke, and Berscheid (1977) demonstrated that women were more socially adept when they held a brief telephone conversation with men with whom they were unacquainted who believed that these women were physically attractive in comparison to women whose partners believed they were less attractive. Attractiveness labels were randomly assigned and therefore could not account for the differences in social skills obtained.

The cognitive paradigm views sex as a form of information similar to other forms of information we use to organize our world. Stereotypes move from being seen as inherently negative and prejudicial to potentially neutral categories that operate in the same way as other cognitive categories (Deaux 1985). Thus, research has moved away from an examination of stereotyping as a form of individual pathology to the exploration of the social processes by which sex-related stereotypes are maintained. Biased perceptions of all kinds appear to be maintained because people select information that confirms their own beliefs (c.f. Hamilton 1979). Individuals may be given a deviant label or their normal behaviors described as deviant if they are perceived as distinctive within a group (Langer and Imber 1980; Taylor and Fiske 1978).

People may even use their own sex as a cue for gender-appropriate behaviors. It is, of course, difficult to discriminate predictions based on such a cognitive model from predictions based on sex-related trait differences. One useful conceptual tool is to compare differences in the behavior of females and males by themselves with the behavior of comparable individuals in group settings. Several provocative studies have indicated that people behave in more sex-stereotypical patterns when in a group than when alone. For example, males are more likely to deviate from their customary pattern of preferring equity (reward by merit) and females from their pattern of preferring equality (equally shared reward) when allocating rewards anonymously rather than in public (Kidder, Belletirie, and Cohn 1977). Similarly, males are much more nonconforming in public than they are in private, although there is little change in females' behavior depending on whether or not it is being observed by others (Eagly, Wood, and Fishbaugh 1981). These studies suggest we must look at how individual rewards and punishments are mediated by gender-related societal norms.

CONTRADICTORY CONSTRUCTS: AN ALTERNATIVE FEMINIST PARADIGM

WHILE research on the cognitive aspects of sex and gender may have opened many rich areas of study, concentration upon these aspects may also blind us to real societal constraints. Prejudice is not all in our heads. Individuals often have only a limited choice of potential behaviors available to them even though their behavioral options may appear to the observer to be unlimited (c.f. Fine 1983–1984, for an excellent discussion of these processes in terms of minority women). Assuming that effective behavior is a matter of individual effort or choice may lead us to assume that the victims are responsible for their circumstances.

Feminist psychologists may have a potentially crucial role in analyzing the nature of sociostructural constraints on individual behavior. Important questions that may be addressed are: Under what conditions are specific social norms activated, especially when the behavioral consequences of behaving in a gender-specific manner may have negative results for the individual at that time? What social processes are responsible for individuals' acquiescing to societal norms that are harmful to themselves as well as to groups of which they are a member?

I believe these questions and others like them require an analysis that recognizes the existence of contradiction at all levels of human existence. For example, it is clear that many contradictory social norms exist and, as yet, we have no theory that helps to explain when one rather than another will be evoked. We also know that sex stereotypes in our society appear to be virtually universal, but we are unable to explain why some people are more immune to sexist assumptions than others. On a more individual level, it is clear that people use different sources of information to explain their own and other's behaviors. What cognitive mechanisms permit them to consider themselves exceptions to rules that seem unbreakable for others?

One such analysis involves the nature and function of the so-called "double-bind" in the structuring of female as compared to male behavior (Unger 1985). Double-binds represent a form of contradiction for individuals—they are situations in which persons may incur some social penalty regardless of their behavior. We are all familiar with the statement "Damned if you do and damned if you don't" or "Out of the frying pan and into the fire." What I would argue is that such contradictions are not the result of accidental circumstances, but are due to the way social roles for women in our society are constructed and behaviorally maintained.

Although my model bears a relationship to cognitive paradigms discussed earlier, the focus is on consensually defined reality rather than on an interior cognitive world. The model forces one to focus on the nature of the categories used to describe women versus men, how these definitions are sustained, and the implications of these consensual definitions for the control of both self-definition and behavior.

A careful analysis of the nature of stereotypes about women reveals some interesting contradictions. Women are not the object of stereotypes under all circumstances. They are most apt to be the target of negative perceptions when they step outside of their normative roles. According to Ashmore (1985), the most important dimensions by which female prototypes are evaluated are working inside the home versus working outside of it and being respectable versus not respectable. This distinction between domestic and public spheres does not exist for prototypes of men. Feminist anthropologists, however, have noted that it is a basic distinction for women in many societies besides our own (Rosaldo and Lamphere 1974).

When women step outside of their "proper sphere," they become subject to contradictory categorizing, which makes them susceptible to double-binds. These categorizations have several properties:

1) It is the stimulus aspects of femaleness rather than some other role or trait that activate assumptions that make her appear to be out of place. Under some circumstances a woman's mere presence outside the home may evoke a set of socially mediated assumptions that betray the presence of usually invisible social controls. For example, sexual harassment on the job is seen by some as the price women pay for working outside of their homes. Similarly, rape by a stranger outside the home is usually punished less severely than a similar rape that takes place within the home.

(2) A woman may be demarcated as "out-of-place" by differential linguistic usage (as, for example, a *woman* doctor or a *female* executive). Linguistic marking does not appear to occur when the out-of-place characteristic may be attributed to some reproductive property that is unique to women such as menstruation or pregnancy.

(3) Exclusionary strategies, such as harassment and discrimination, are necessary only when women cannot be excluded by "legitimate" means—by law or social fiat. Such strategies are employed when the woman's presence produces discomfort in individuals with power to define that particular reality. They may not be attended to consciously by those involved in the situation and may be triggered as much by assumptions about the relative social status of women and men as by biological assumptions.

(4) A woman may not be aware of her property as a social stimulus because her evaluations of the self and others may have a different informational base. For her, but not for others, biological status may be largely irrelevant because she sees her role-relevant characteristics as most important (Laws 1975; Spence and Sawin 1985).

(5) The woman's presence in the situation is seen as a matter of choice by herself as well as others. Ironically, double-binds appear to occur only in contexts where a wide range of behavioral options seem to be available to women. They do not appear to exist in traditional societies—where they are not needed as a social control mechanism. They may be a product of rapid periods of social change and the changes in norms that accompany these changes.

(6) A double-bind is most likely to occur when any of the behaviors in which the woman engages has both positive and negative consequences

for her. This is possible because so many contradictory stereotypes about women exist that one can be evoked to match a almost any possible behavior. It is difficult to find a behavior that does not "fit" some feature of "mother," "sex object," "pet," or "iron maiden," which have been described by some theorists as the four archetypal roles for women in Western society (Wood and Conrad 1983). Behavior conforming to any of these prototypes may be rewarded, while at the same time, behavior inconsistent with another prototype may be ignored or punished. These roles are particularly problematic for the target individual because she has not constructed them herself, nor can she be sure what definition is being used by other participants in the interaction.

This analysis makes it clear that the dilemmas for women in these contexts are produced by situational constraints rather than by personal flaws. Behavior is in response to demands embedded in the social context. But because these demands are largely a result of implicit theories about women and their place and are shared by most participants in an interaction, they become social reality. Acceptance of personal responsibility for problems posed by double-binds is facilitated by lack of awareness of their existence, lack of a vocabulary to describe them, and lack of comparison with the experiences of similar others. Because of the relative isolation of women in the public sphere, they have little opportunity to validate alternative versions of reality.

It is important to stress that not all versions of reality have equal validity in our society. Members of groups with higher status have the power to control interpersonal transactions with individuals from groups with lower status than their own (Henley 1977). Thus, if there is disagreement about the construction of a particular reality, the males in the situation are likely to have the power to define that reality. Females enmeshed in a double-bind have a double disadvantage. They are likely to possess lower status than the males in the situation and they are likely to be a numerical minority as well.

Some Examples of Double-Binds and Their Implications

It is easy to find examples of double-binds involving women in our society. For example, because of mutually exclusive definitions of professionalism and womanliness, it is impossible for women to fulfill both roles at the same time (Wood and Conrad 1983). A similar contradiction exists for physical attractiveness in women and assumptions about their perceived ability to function in executive or managerial positions (Heilman and Saruwatari 1979). Other double-binds involve the contradiction between active sexuality and respectability (Rubin 1976) and between pregnancy and assertive behavior (Robinson and Unger 1983).

All of these double-binds appear to fit a common pattern. They are most likely to emerge when the woman's behavior is defined as unexpected in terms of role and place. They are more likely to occur in public than in private contexts. In addition, behavioral control appears to be more effective when relatively few people are involved in an interaction and/or when these individuals are linked by habitual bonds. Norms are evoked and enforced more easily under such circumstances.

Although the woman's out-of-place quality may appear to threaten other people in the situation, she herself may not constitute the "real" threat here. The more potent threat may be to consensually defined reality —to the way things "ought" to work. Double-binds are also fundamentally uncomfortable situations for those who have the power to control the situation. They function, however, to focus the responsibility for the discomfort upon the target individual. She is defined as the "intruder" in the situation—either by her mere presence or by her out-of-place behavior. The target individual may accept responsibility for the discomfort for a number of reasons. First, her sense of personal control may be preferable to feeling at the mercy of external forces. Second, the individual is exposed to only one double-bind at a time and may not recognize the pattern connecting apparently disparate events. And last, since double-binds are largely invisible, individuals may lack both the means to identify them as a class of event as well as a vocabulary with which to discuss them.

Double-binds are a subtle and destructive form of social control. They make it difficult to locate the source of conflict, and therefore may make it more likely that the source of problematic behavior is located within the individual. Invalid problem definitions convince the target group of its own blameworthiness (Caplan and Nelson 1973). This invisible use of power may facilitate the development of disorders such as learned helplessness, agoraphobia, and depression—disorders seen to be more characteristic of women than of men.

Other aspects of double-binds that I have discussed elsewhere (Unger 1985) include the adequacy of various individualistic responses to double-binds, the consequences for theories about the feminine personality of ignoring structural determinants of sex-related behaviors, and the relationship between the acceptance of social contradiction and personal change. In terms of the latter issue, it is noteworthy that social activists appear able to maintain a contradictory cognitive schema that acknowledges both social injustice and the efficacy of individual efforts to change society (Forward and Williams 1970; Sanger and Alker 1972). Such contradictory belief patterns may be particularly adaptive to a contradictory reality.

Although a social constructionist personal epistemology appears to be related to the ability to accept multiple interpretations of a single reality, it is not clear how such an ideology is developed. There is some evidence that social constructionist beliefs are associated with a problematic relationship with society and enhanced by identification with reference groups with marginal characteristics such as feminism (Unger, Draper, and Pendergrass 1986). Feminist scholars share a belief that reality is created rather than discovered, in contrast to be a more positivist epistemology characterized by belief in an objective, stable, and determinist reality (Unger 1984–1985). Feminist students also show a tendency to seek out courses whose assumptions appear to be consistent with their personal epistemologies (Unger, Draper, and Pendergrass 1986).

THE PROBLEMATIC RELATIONSHIP BETWEEN FEMINIST PSYCHOLOGY AND FEMINIST EPISTEMOLOGY IN OTHER AREAS

FEMINISTS need to be aware of potential epistemological biases in their own thinking. In a recent examination of the epistemological assumptions of nonfeminists and feminists, I found that feminists were more likely to view power as a socially mediated process than as a personal characteristic of particular individuals; to view individual efforts to change society as efficacious rather than disruptive; to see science as value-laden and relativistic rather than objective and value-free; and, of course, to see explanations of group differences to be more plausibly social than biological in nature (Unger 1984–1985). These assumptions may lead us to undervalue certain disciplinary practices used to analyze people and their world. Thus, when I presented data from a scale used to measure belief in social constructionism to a group of feminists from various scholarly disciplines, I was criticized by them for stripping beliefs of their social context. Yet, simultaneously, data from this same feminist group confirmed their belief in social constructionism.

I mention this anecdote because I believe that feminist psychologists are caught in a double-bind similar to the ones described above. The dominant ideology within psychology is shifting from a form of empiricism driven by logical positivism to a more cognitive perspective. Nevertheless, the attempt to infer cause-and-effect relationships about human behavior using the tools of empiricism is one of the few unique contributions that psychology as a discipline can offer to the rest of scholarship. If such tools may not be used by feminist psychologists there is little likelihood that their insights will be taken seriously by the rest of the discipline. Disciplinary attention will continue to be on those theories of women's experience that "explain" women's deficiencies or treat them as victims.

Feminist psychologists are well aware of the deficiencies in the methods and practices of psychology. However, they are also becoming aware of the dangers of social constructionism taken too far. For example, if reality is all "within one's head," how do we explore a shared reality? It is obvious that socio-structural barriers constrain the personal development of women, and shared symbolic and definitional constraints appear to be as important as external societal barriers. These psychological barriers have meaning for the individual. But, if they are consensually defined and, therefore, may be redefined, whose definitions have more validity? Some people's definitions clearly have more power than others personally, socially, and professionally. What vehicles of analysis are we to use to examine deep belief structures that maintain nonegalitarian dialogues? Paradoxically, we may have to use some of the tools of logical positivism to examine socially constructed reality.

It is ironic that at the beginning of this chapter I attacked psychology as too constrained by laboratory methodology to add to our knowledge about sex and gender. It may seem like a contradiction if at the end of the chapter I suggest that much information can be gained by the use of empirical techniques. Part of the reason for this shift is the change to cognition as psychology's dominant paradigm. This paradigm leaves more room for multiple perspectives about the relationship of the person to herself, about the relationship between persons, and about the relationship between the person and society.

An additional reason for this change is my belief that the tools of psychology are of less significance in themselves than by whom they are used. Psychology must be viewed as a reflexive discipline (Unger 1983). Conceptualization cannot be divorced from the circumstances of the investigator. Thus, as more women become involved in empirical research and as they continue (unfortunately) to find themselves enmeshed in contradictory and/or ambivalent social and professional interactions, their questions will continue to be enriched by their multiple roles and perspectives. As long as we are willing to question ourselves, feminist scholarship may serve as evidence for the positive power of deviance.

REFERENCES

Ashmore, R. D. (1985). "Thinking about the sexes: From sex-role stereotypes to gender belief systems." Paper presented at the Second Interdisciplinary Conference on Sex and Gender, Nag's Head, N.C.

Bem, S. L. (1974). "The measurement of psychological androgyny." *Journal of Consulting and Clinical Psychology* 42:155–62.

Benton, C. J., et al. (1983). "Is hostility linked with affiliation among males and with achievement among females? A critique of Pollak and Gilligan." *Journal of Personality and Social Psychology* 45:1167–71.

Block, J. H. (1976). "Debatable conclusions about sex differences." *Contemporary Psychology* 21:517–22.

Buss, A. R. (1976). "Galton and sex differences: An historical note." *Journal of the History of the Behavioral Sciences* 12:283–85.

Caplan, N., and Nelson, S. D. (1973). "On being useful: The nature and consequences of psychological research on social problems." *American Psychologist* 28:199–211.

Deaux, K. (1976). "Sex: A perspective on the attribution process." In J. H. Harvey, W. J. Ickes, and R. F. Kidd (Eds.). *New directions in attribution research*. Hillsdale, N.J.: Erlbaum.

———. (1985). "Sex and gender." *Annual Review of Psychology* 36:49–81.

Dion, K. L. (1985). "Sex, gender, and groups: Selected issues." In V. E. O'Leary, R. K. Unger, and B. S. Wallston (Eds.). *Women, gender, and social psychology.* Hillsdale, N.J.: Erlbaum.

Eagly, A. H. (1983). "Gender and social influence: A social psychological analysis." *American Psychologist* 38:971–81.

———, and Carli. L. L. (1981). "Sex of researcher and sex-typed communications as determinants of sex differences in influenceability: A meta-analysis of social influence studies." *Psychological Bulletin* 90:1–20.

———, and Wood, W. (1985). "Gender and influenceability: Stereotype versus behavior." In V. E. O'Leary, R. K. Unger, and B. S. Wallston (Eds.). *Women, gender, and social psychology.* Hillsdale, N.J.: Erlbaum.

———, Wood, W., and Fishbaugh, L. (1981). "Sex differences in conformity: Surveillance by the group as a determinant of male nonconformity." *Journal of Personality and Social Psychology* 40:384–94.

Fine, M. (1983–1984). "Coping with rape: Critical perspectives on consciousness." *Imagination, Cognition, and Personality* 3:249–67.

Forward, J. R., and Williams, J. R. (1970). "Internal-external control and black militancy." *Journal of Social Issues* 26:75–92.

Frieze, I. H., et al. (1978). "Attributions of the causes of success and failure as internal and, external barriers to achievement." In J. Sherman and F. Denmark (Eds.). *Psychology of women: Future directions of research.* New York: Psychological Dimensions.

Gilligan, C. (1982). *In a different voice.* Cambridge: Harvard University Press.

Grady, K. E. (1977). "The belief in sex differences." Paper presented at the meeting of the Eastern Psychological Association, Boston.

Hamilton, D. L. (1979). "A cognitive attributional analysis of stereotyping." In L. Berkowitz (Ed.). *Advances in experimental social psychology,* vol. 12, New York: Academic Press.

Hansen, R. D., and O'Leary, V. E. (1985). "Sex-determined attributions." In V. E. O'Leary, R. K. Unger, and B. S. Wallson (Eds.). *Women, gender, and social psychology.* Hillsdale, N.J.: Erlbaum.

Heilman, M. E., and Saruwatari, L. R. (1979). "When beauty is beastly: The effect of appearance and sex on evaluations of job applicants for managerial and nonmanagerial jobs." *Organizational Behavior and Human Performance* 23:360–72.

Henley, N. M. (1977). *Body politics: Power, sex, and nonverbal communication.* Englewood Cliffs, N.J.: Prentice-Hall.

Horner, M. S. (1972). "Toward an understanding of achievement-related conflicts in women." *Journal of Social Issues* 28:157–75.

Hyde, J. S. (1981). "How large are cognitive gender differences? A meta-analysis using ω^2 and α." *American Psychologist* 36:892–901.

Kelly, J. A., and Worrell, J. (1977). "New formulations of sex roles and androgyny: A critical review." *Journal of Consulting and Clinical Psychology* 45:1101–15.

Kidder, L. H., Belletirie, G., and Cohn, E. S. (1977). "Secret ambitions and public performance: The effect of anonymity on reward allocations made by men and women." *Journal of Experimental Social Psychology* 13:70–80.

Langer, E. J., and Imber, L. (1980). "Role of mindlessness in the perception of deviance." *Journal of Personality and Social Psychology* 39:360–67.

Laws, J. L. (1975). "The psychology of tokenism: An analysis." *Sex Roles* 1:51–67.

Macaulay, J. (1985). "Adding gender to aggression research: Incremental or revolutionary change?" In V. E. O'Leary, R. K. Unger, and B. S. Wallston (Eds.). *Women, gender, and social psychology.* Hillsdale, N.J.: Erlbaum.

McGuire, W. J., McGuire, C. V., and Winton, W. (1979). "Effects of household sex composition on the salience of one's gender in the spontaneous self-concept." *Journal of Experimental Social Psychology* 15:77–90.

Pedhazur, E. J., and Tetenbaum, T. J. (1979). "Bem sex role inventory: A theoretical and methodological critique." *Journal of Personality and Social Psychology* 37:996–1016.

Robinson, D., and Unger, R. K. (1983). "Attitudes toward the pregnant professional." Paper presented at the meeting of the Eastern Psychological Association, Philadelphia.

Rosaldo, M. Z., and Lamphere, L. (Eds.). (1974). *Women, culture, and society.* Palo Alto, CA: Stanford University Press.

Rosenberg, R. (1984). "Leta Hollingworth: Toward a sexless intelligence." In M. Lewin (Ed.). *In the shadow of the past: Psychology portrays the sexes.* New York: Columbia University Press.

Rubin, L. B. (1976). *Worlds of pain: Life in the working class family.* New York: Basic Books.

Sanger, B. P., and Alker, H. A. (1972). "Dimensions of internal-external locus of control and the women's liberation movement." *Journal of Social Issues* 28:115–29.

Sherif, C. W. (1979). "What every intelligent person should know about psychology and women." In E. C. Snyder (Ed.). *The study of women: Enlarging perspectives of social reality.* New York: Harper and Row.

Shields, S. A. (1975a). "Functionalism, Darwinism, and the psychology of women: A study in social myth." *American Psychologist* 30:739–54.

———. (1975b). "Ms Pilgrim's progress: The contribution of Leta Stetter Hollingsworth to the psychology of women." *American Psychologist* 30:852–57.

Snyder, M., Tanke, E. D., and Berscheid, E. (1977). "Social perception and interpersonal behavior: On the self-fulfilling nature of social stereotypes." *Journal of Personality and Social Psychology* 35:656–66.

Spence, J. T., and Helmreich, R. (1978). *Masculinity and femininity: Their psychological dimensions, correlates, and antecedents.* Austin: University of Texas Press.

——, and Sawin, L. L. (1985). "Images of masculinity and femininity: A reconceptualization." In V. E. O'Leary, R. K. Unger, and B. S. Wallston (Eds.). *Women, gender, and social psychology*. Hillsdale, N.J.: Erlbaum.

Taylor, S. E., and Fiske, S. T. (1978). "Salience, attention, and attribution: Top of the head phenomena." In L. Berkowitz (Ed.). *Advances in experimental social psychology*, vol. 11, New York: Academic Press.

Tresemer, D. W. (1977). *Fear of success*. New York: Plenum.

Unger, R. K. (1976). "Male is greater than female: The socialization of status inequality." *The Counseling Psychologist* 6:2–9.

——. (1978). "The politics of gender: A review of relevant literature." In J. Sherman and F. Denmark (Eds.). *Psychology of women: Future directions of research*. New York: Psychological Dimensions.

——. (1979). "Toward a redefinition of sex and gender." *American Psychologist* 34:1085–94.

——. (1981). "Sex as a social reality: Field and laboratory research." *Psychology of Women Quarterly* 5:645–53.

——. (1983). "Through the looking glass: No Wonderland yet! (The reciprocal relationship between methodology and models of reality)" *Psychology of Women Quarterly* 8:9–32.

——. (1984–1985). "Explorations in feminist ideology: Surprising consistencies and unexamined conflicts." *Imagination, Cognition, and Personality* 4:395–403.

——. (1985). "Between the "no longer" and the "not yet": Reflections on personal and social change." First Carolyn Wood Sherif Memorial Lecture. Presented at the meeting of the American Psychological Association, Los Angeles.

——, Draper, R. D., and Pendergrass, M. L. (1986). "Personal epistemology and personal experience." *Journal of Social Issues* 42:67–79.

Wallston, B. S., and O'Leary, V. E. (1981). "Sex and gender make a difference: The differential perceptions of women and men." In L. Wheeler (Ed.). *Review of personality and social psychology*, vol 2, Beverly Hills: Sage.

Wood, J. T., and Conrad, C. (1983). "Paradox in the experience of professional women." *Western Journal of Speech Communication* 47:305–22.

NINE

Knowledge as a Result of Conflicting Intergroup Relations

Verena Aebischer

WHEN I recall the moment I first tried to shape ideas about women's language and women's small talk into an academic subject, and when I compare that moment not so very far away with the issues under debate, in and outside universities, today, I cannot help but be amazed by the qualitative changes that the world around me has since undergone. Subjects that twelve or thirteen years ago were still considered frivolous, not important enough for academic exploration, were hushed up, voluntarily ignored or, under seal of confession, confined to the specialist, have become a matter of public knowledge, seriously analyzed, discussed on television, in newspapers, textbooks and among friends and relatives. From abstract, often politically colored subjects, interest has turned to topics connecting with personal aspects of people's lives. Our passions no longer seem to turn around politics, and if they do, only in the way politics affect our lives. We are interested in medical discoveries, in birth, sexuality, death, in communication among people. Society has undergone and continues to undergo a cultural and "climatic" change, modeling a new subject made not only of reasoning and work, but also of emotions and imagination. It has become possible intellectually to study aspects of everyday life and of everyday people and to be taken seriously. In the following text I shall try to adumbrate the part played by feminism in this change of focus. There were no dazzling victories of feminism; it has, however, had an effect on people's general state of mind, on their sensibility to ethical and cultural questions, and their awareness of new models of domination.

My own curriculum has been shaped by feminism and evolved within its context. My involvement with it has moved from topics reflecting above all personal concern into broader issues of a more general nature. One issue that has captured my attention has been the strikingly uneven distribution across job situations of men and women in one of the most interesting and promising fields of the future, that of advanced technologies. One cause of this imbalance is that girls at a very young age are channeled away from science and technology into more "women specific" fields of study or apprenticeships. Women also self-censor their capacities and their ambitions according to stereotypical attitudes about feminity and about what women are or have to be like. In this chapter I would like to describe research directed toward this problem. My study is an action research in which I attempt to intervene in the professional choices of girls and boys, and, especially, to help girls who want to break into male territory, that is into science and technology.

THE TRANSITION FROM A POLITICAL MODEL TO A CULTURAL MODEL

AS ALAIN Touraine (1987), the eminent French sociologist, recently put it in an interview, thinking in Europe, and especially in France, has been dominated over the past three hundred years by a modernistic model in which mankind would strive for a rational and universal understanding of the world, turning his/her back on irrational belief systems. This modernistic, essentially political and ideological model, which aims at the domination of nature through science and technology, has shaped past historical periods such as the Enlightenment, the French Revolution, liberalism, socialism, and so forth. It is loosening its grip today. Political categories have lost their relevance. We are witnessing a general transition from one value system to another, which culturally, politically, and socially heralds a new type of society. Indeed society today is discovering the importance of personal experiences and a new sensitivity and concern with people's concrete personal lives and needs, their bodies, their personal and intimate relationships, and their immediate ecological environment. Knowledge has become available in fields that had been neglected. And private issues have become public ones.

It is my contention that feminism and the changing prescriptions concerning women have had a liberating consequence on the creation of knowledge in general and on the creation of scientific knowledge in particular.[1] Indeed, women for centuries were on the "underside of history" (Boulding 1976). Feminists started to uncover it when they analyzed the minority status of women in their everyday lives: in the couple, in relation with institutions, and at work. This research also helped open up new topics that affected scientific knowledge. With the aim of analyzing, inventing alternative solutions, and consciously acting against the oppression of women in society, feminists not only developed new items of knowledge,[2] but also contributed to the shaping of new research procedures that would integrate personal concerns into the process of research. Thus they seriously questioned the prevalent relationship between theory and practice in science and society (see also Ley 1982).

This first step in the creation of women-specific knowledge would be followed by new fields of interest. As if the first step had activated a hidden energy and determination and had allowed them to break away from traditional issues of concern, feminists would seek out new ones closely connected with personal knowledge and experience not only of women but of men and children as well. Feminists have joined or formed groups that pool information, analyze it and suggest new approaches in various domains such as medicine, psychiatry, architecture, education, science, and so on. Pinpointing, for example, the prevailing asymmetrical relationship between doctors and patients, they have encouraged and helped to set up alternative ways of treating patients in medicine and psychiatry. By highlighting the collusion of economical and political interests, they have fought the politicians' and architects' decisions to construct highways in cities or to demolish houses instead of renovating them. They have put into question the altruistic intentions of politicians and scientists accused of underinforming the public and of minimizing the potential threat of nuclear power or of genetic manipulations. Dem-

onstrating against the implementation of nuclear power stations and genetic research, many feminists also have suggested alternative ways of
producing energy or asked geneticists to account publicly for what is
going on in their laboratories. Feminists have thus contributed to the
awareness of new models of cultural domination in medicine, mass media,
information, education, science, and so on.

I have followed with great interest a large number of these social
movements, especially feminist groups, which from the start were preoc-
cupied with the idea of a woman-specific culture. I became personally
involved when I realized that I was not listened to when talking in groups
with male friends. This first triggered my interest in language and in the
way language for me as a woman was special. My gradual awareness of
my powerlessness and frustration in the way language was used by most
people around me incited my involvement. It was a growing tiredness of
ideologically imprinted discussions about such abstract theories as struc-
turalism, Marxism, psychoanalysis, and so on, which all were then in their
heydays. It was the exclusion of everything personal: worries, ambitions,
and needs (banished from discussions because they were considered to be
remnants of bourgeois preoccupations), that made me want to explore a
new direction.

French society in the beginning of the 1970s was in turmoil, still under
the cultural and political shock of May '68 with its liberating consequences not only on people's libido but also on the way people continuously committed themselves to causes.

On the one hand there was almost exclusive focus on political issues
such as the revolution in Portugal, the domination of the Third World by
the Western countries, the victories of communism in Angola, Vietnam,
Laos, and so on. The ensuing discussions were instrumental in the development of categorizing processes that separated those who considered
themselves as the liberating agents of change from those supposed to be
under the spell of vile bourgeois ideology. Within that context feminism
was considered to be a reactionary movement that would only divert
attention from the real issues concerning oppression in this world. But
feminist consciousness and determination were often a product of and a
reaction to precisely that context. On the other hand, there were the social
movements of the '70s: ecologically oriented movements, regionalism,
feminism, which, while questioning bureaucratic and technocratic opti-

mism, would also herald the breakdown of traditional ideologies and bring about new forms of action and a new appreciation of the world. Within that context of political and cultural change it became conceptually possible for me to deviate from the Saussurian model of language. And although at that time this was still considered an awkward thing to do, my interest in the study of language and the way it was related to an individual's speech would nevertheless (to my great surprise) find a sponsor and an advisor. From a feminist point of view my attention was caught by the variable *sex* in speech.

In France, at that time, there were a handful of marginal women writers such as Hélène Cixous, Claudine Herrmann, Nathalie Sarraute, and of philosophers such as Annie Leclerc (1974) and Luce Irigaray (1974), who had elaborated the concept of gender-modeled language. Empirical feedback could be found in the writings of Anglo-Saxon authors such as Robin Lakoff (1975), Dale Spender (1980), Mary Ritchie Key (1975), and Barry Thorne and Nancy Henley (1975).

My interest, though was not so much in the creation of what could be a language specific to women only, but in the way women would react and relate to what has universally (as many proverbs from all over the world claim) been considered to be a woman's way of talking: small talk or gossip. Men gossip, too. But when women's gossip is described something in the expression insidiously conveys negative connotations such as: futility, frivolity, indiscretion, wordiness. These negative connotations are not present in descriptions of men's gossip. These negative evaluations are the result of conflicting intergroup relations between men and women, and are present in men's minds as well as in women's minds (Aebischer 1979).

What interested me (Aebischer 1985) was how women coped with these negative connotations, how they could communicate and make themselves understood, although they knew that they were not listened to. What self-images could they have when they thought that what they said was not interesting or not worth saying? My hypothesis was that there were qualities in small talk other than simple wordiness and trivial topics, which women would intuitively recognize, and which would make them want to talk to other women and be silent when with men. The results of this research were not quite as schematic as my personal experiences, which were glittering through the hypothesis. Women reacted in differentiated ways depending on their idea of femininity and the way they perceived "women's talk." Grossly, four types of reactions were elicited: 1) The traditional type of woman saw herself as different from man as a cat from a dog. She thought that there was something like a barrier between them, which would prevent them from really understanding each other when trying to communicate. Accepting and even accentuating the differences between men and women, she shamefully accepted her tendency to gossip. Enjoying it with her equals, she would in addition stress some of what she considered to be inherent positive qualities of this type of communication with other women, which men could not understand. 2) The modern, more career-oriented woman viewed herself as different not from men but—from other women! She thought of them, and especially of the traditional woman, as an inferior species who was as futile, unworthy, and empty-headed as her gossip. 3) The feminist suffragette, like the career woman, held gossip in abhorrence. But unlike her she thought that it was only a reminder of women's past submissiveness to men. Aiming at the transformation of the status quo she claimed that gossip would disappear when women had reached equal status with men. 4) Yet another type of feminist, aiming to transform a world made by men for men into a world made by women for both, held a different view of small talk. Unlike the suffragette, this other type of feminist appreciated its cultural significance. Similar to the traditional woman, she valued gossip, but, instead of feeling shameful about it, she saw it as a cultural means to transform and to humanize the world.

Toward the end of the '70s most of these social movements, such as the ecological movement, had disappeared as organic entities or were reduced to insignificance. Interestingly enough, despite having been vilified by many when they were at their peaks, the ideas carried along by these movements seem to have become autonomous, detached from the initial sources, and have gradually entered people's minds. Even the man in the street cares now about what people eat, what their environment is made of, and so on. In addition, changes can be seen in the academic disciplines. Recently, one of the most eminent geneticists in France publicly renounced his research on genetic manipulations for ethical reasons. Also recently I reviewed a study (Rimé 1987) that demonstrates the essential role of sharing emotions in everyday life. Rimé found that evoking emotional experiences during conversations not only helps to structure com-

munications cognitively, but also helps speakers to achieve better psychological and physiological health. Rimé even claims that people should be
encouraged to develop these capacities without, however, mentioning
that this is the stuff of gossip, and that women are said to be experts in it.
Politicians cannot totally sweep these new values under the table. They
find themselves compelled to accept, or at least pay lip service to the right
of women to their bodies and to decide if they want abortions or not
without having first to refer to a political or moral authority, or the right
of girls to have the same opportunities as boys at school, at work, and
within relationships.

There remain, however, important strongholds that seem unaffected by
this new mentality. The world of science and technology, especially of
computer science and business, has produced a subculture that can hardly
be said to include women. Women are channeled away from it by teachers, husbands, and managers, but they also seem to discourage themselves
even after having passed the first thresholds with flying colors. In France
more girls succeed in high schools than boys do, but out of one hundred
bachelors' degrees in science and technology, only thirty are girls. Compared to the boys these thirty girls do better, however, they do not benefit
from their good results at school in the same way as boys do, and as they
could expect to do. Computer business and new technologies are astound-
ingly open to adolescents. Young people create inventions, set up companies, and acquire capital. But in the specialized technology magazines we
read success stories only of boys. Whereas the doors are open to boys,
they seem to be closed to girls. Disproportionately few women reach
upper professional echelons in science and technology, obtain prominent
high-level management positions, or occupy the various leadership positions available in private enterprise or academia (see also Apfelbaum
1986). Women remain at the lower levels, teaching the computer alpha-
bet to students in universities, working as journalists or as press agents,
or in capacities in which they assist male executives. They hardly climb up
the ladder of success themselves. Sex-role standards are so well internalized by most women that they shape their own—low—levels of aspirations. Women lack positive models of identification with women who
have "made it" in science and technology and who have successfully
reconciled the traditional idea of femininity with the requirements of a
leading role in the field. Women would censor themselves less in regards
to their own aspirations for achievement, if they didn't have the insidious

feeling that acknowledging such aspirations, especially in the field of science and technology, comes close to a deviant behavior that leads inevitably to loneliness and to exclusion.

It is upon considerations of this kind that, together with a French association against sexist education, I have started an action research project in several high schools in France. The idea is to destabilize acquired patterns of socialization among girls and boys aged fourteen to fifteen by making alternative standards available and attractive to their minds. Indeed, at the age of fourteen to fifteen boys and girls orient their professional perspectives according to the options (science, technology, languages, etc.) available to them at school. With the help of four professional role-playing actors, scenes of everyday life involving girls, boys, parents, teachers, and so on, are staged. In these role plays various stereotypical situations are presented to the boys and the girls. These situations introduce the girl who behaves in the traditional way as the unattractive loser. After each scene, a girl (or a boy) is invited to take over the part of the girl. The actors role-play their parts again, when it is left to the imagination of the participating adolescent to invent, within the same setting, new patterns of behavior for his or her part. The same setting is staged several times, inviting other girls and boys to play the part of the girl and, ultimately, to take over all the parts initially held by the professional actors. Different role plays will be presented to the pupils over a period of two to three months. It is hoped that they will lead to a change of attitude as well as to less traditional choices of options decisive for the professional perspectives of both boys and girls. The change of attitude will be measured by the administration of a questionnaire before the role-playing "treatment" and afterward, and in comparison with a control group.

Interestingly enough, this action research, which is financially backed by the European community, is actively encouraged by the French Ministry of Education of the French government, which seems to be concerned about the inequality in schools between girls and boys and eager to bring more girls into science and technology. I am encouraged to believe this support is part of the growing feminist influence on current social affairs in France. I hope that this action research project will serve as a prototype for others interested in claiming a place for women in the expanding world of opportunity in computer science and technology.

NOTES

1. I do not mean that there were not other influences as well. However, I find it interesting that ethnomethodology, for instance, and the subjective approach it advocates, seem to have had less importance as a separate discipline, and more influence as a softening impact on the "hard" ways social sciences have approached social phenomena (and in the process killed the essence of the topic under study).

2. Since industrialization, for instance, labor has been the word for paid bodily and mental work, with theoreticians and politicians being exclusively interested in aspects of work that had to do with forms of work, job positions, social mobility, working conditions, and so on. Labor was man's job. What women did was not even given a thought. The work of housewives, mothers, servants, and so on, became an issue only to and with feminism.

REFERENCES

Aebischer, V. (1979). "Wenn frauen nicht sprechen" (Women who do do not talk). *Osnabrücker beiträge zur sprachtheorie* (Osnabrück contributions to the theory of language) 3:85–95.

——. (1985). *Les femmes et le langage: Représentations sociales d'une différence* (Women and language: Social representations of a difference). Paris: Presses Universitaires de France.

Apfelbaum, E. (1986). *The Henri Tajfel Memorial Lecture 1986: From governess to prime minister: Women in leadership positions.* Paper presented at the Annual Conference of British Psychological Association in Sussex.

Boulding, E. (1976). *The underside of history: A view of women through time.* Boulder, Colo.: Westview Press.

Irigaray, L. (1974). *Spéculum de l'autre femme* (Mirror of the other woman). Paris: Editions Minuit.

Key, M. R. (1975). *Male/female language.* Metuchen, N.J.: Scarecrow Press.

Lakoff, R. (1975). *Language and woman's place.* New York: Harper and Row.

Leclerc, A. (1974). *Parole de femme* (Woman's speech). Paris: Grasset.

Ley, K. (1982). Frau und Wissenschaft (Woman and science). *Schweizer Zeitschrift für Soziologie* (Swiss Journal of Sociology) 8:315–22.

Rimé, R. (1987). *Social sharing of emotions.* Paper presented at the Symposium on Social Psychology and the Emotions. Paris: Maison des Sciences de l'Homme.

Spender, D. (1980). *Man made language.* London: Routledge and Kegan Paul.

Thorne, B., and Henley, N. (Eds.) (1975). *Language and sex. Difference and dominance*. Rowly, Mass.: Newbury House.

Touraine, A. (1987). "Die umrisse einer neuen modernität." Interview mit Alain Touraine (To adumbrate a new modernity. Interview with Alain Touraine). *Basler Magazin der Basler Zeitung* 3:6–7.

TEN

The Female Person and How We Talk about Her

Polly Young-Eisendrath

For Descartes . . . an epistemological chasm separates a highly self-conscious self from a universe that now lies decisively outside the self.

(Bordo 1986, p. 144)

WE ALL come into being within a social context of beliefs about selfhood, intentionality, power, emotion, intelligence, and other personal qualities. We are entirely dependent on each other for our experiences of ourselves as persons, as members of a social group we can call "the human body." As John Shotter and Josephine Logan (this volume) point out, we feel the influence of this body of people most frequently and commonly as communication about how to "go on being." All characteristics of our personal psychologies are individually appropriated from the communicative practices of our particular tribe. At different points along the life-cycle continuum, the tribe is differently constituted—as parents and siblings, as peers and friends, as spouse and children, as community and mentors, whatever is focal to personal meaning.

In the following account, I will trace a feminist epistemology for how to go on being as a feminist in patriarchy. Although even the activity of epistemology making is patriarchal in its social origins, I can exploit the activity to assist myself and others in uncovering the assumptions and limitations of ordinary concepts that refer to the female person in North American society.

My desire to study the ordinary assumptions about being a female person arises directly out of my practice as a psychotherapist and educator. In my daily efforts to persuade and influence women to claim the authority of their own experience, I constantly come up against the concepts we use in our knowledge systems about personal being. My desire to increase vitality and life satisfaction in women is assisted by the task of elucidating ordinary gender concepts that I encounter in conversations with friends, students, and clients. Increased personal authority, as the experience of making one's own decisions and having the wherewithal to live enthusiastically, appears to contribute to life satisfaction in North American culture.

Although it is clear that personal freedom is an illusion, the concept of personal freedom has much meaning in our culture. Its meaning must be clarified if we are to support an increasing participation of women in the philosophical, political, and interpersonal systems of the society in which we live. A feminist epistemology must attend both to aspects of personal authority, as they are enacted by women and men, and to the fact that we are bound and limited, both by our existence as persons and by our complete dependence on a world of living beings who are not persons. Still, the illusion of personal freedom is central to the experience of being a person in North American society. Our principles and ideals for social participation as valid individuals include most prominently "equality," "liberty," and the "pursuit of happiness."

Because epistemology is specifically the study of knowledge systems, in reference especially to limits and assumptions that bind the systems, I believe that epistemology is a worthy topic for feminist remaking. As Emily Grosholz (this volume) says, ". . . practical deliberation, not scientific theory, is the right model for understanding what we are about when we engage in feminist . . ." activities and methods. By grounding ourselves in practical deliberations, we move away from vulnerability to believing that theories and concepts show us the truth, and towards the fact that theories and concepts are used by particular groups to keep themselves and their projects going.

My approach to unraveling the androcentric concepts associated with female persons has the practical concern of displaying the effects of patriarchy on women's self-concepts. I want to help women become increasingly their own authorities so that we can freely validate our experiences, and in this way make claims to our truths.

Because I am limited by my purposes of enabling ordinary women, I am not immediately and directly envisioning broad social and political reforms. In my practical interactions with women and men, I work on methods by which we may eventually arrive at such reforms, but my current conceptualizations are not directly focused in that way.

To be as clear as possible on this issue, I do not consider myself to be a "cultural feminist," nor do I believe it useful to think along the lines of such distinctions among feminists. I believe that we have not yet extricated a feminist methodology from the languages and theories of patriarchy. Although I am convinced that we can build such conceptual frameworks for the practice of feminism, I do not believe we have achieved them yet. An example may help me to illustrate my concern.

The psychology of separation-individuation is often used by feminists implicitly or explicitly in defense of individual rights. This psychology, founded on an illusion of independence, results in a problematic fallacy of conceiving human life as a specifically individual matter. Concepts such as uniqueness, genius, spontaneity, independence, and individualism are privileged. They are offered as ideals against a background of belief that people are by nature "unique individuals." Concomitantly, concepts of ordinariness, shared intelligence, limitation, dependence, and collectivity are devalued or denigrated. Much of our philosophical and cultural heritage in North America is rooted in the fallacy of individualism, the shared belief that separate physical bodies endow us with separately unique and creative minds. The corollary of most ideologies of mental separatism is that some minds are better than others—whether they are better adapted for survival (Social Darwinism) or for esthetic expression (Kantian idealism). Consequently people imagine themselves to be in competition for the privilege or the right to have the best (or at least one of the best) minds. Naturally, the authority of masculinist forms of culture seems to carry us into belief that individual men—such as Charles Darwin, Karl Marx, Sigmund Freud, Albert Einstein, Jean Piaget, and so on—have been our true visionaries. Although we are entirely ignorant of the contributions made by their lovers, wives, children, servants, neighbors, and others, to their knowledge systems, we believe that we trace the accounts of individual genius in recording the thoughts of the "originators." How might a historical account of knowledge read if we included the roles of these people, animals, and objects that formed a shared intelligence with the so-called originators of exemplary knowledge?

I have presented this rather elaborate single illustration of the interplay between individualism and dominance-submission in support of my position that we do not yet have the feminist methods and cultural forms by which to avoid the masculinization of our thought as androcentrism.

FEMINIST EPISTEMOLOGY

WHAT IS the purpose of a feminist epistemology? From my perspective, feminism assists me along a dimension of deconstruction and reconstruction. In terms of deconstruction, feminism offers a critique of cultural and psychological assumptions of inferiority of female gender and all activities and preoccupations associated with women. The assumed inferiority of female gender is the background of much of the received knowledge about women's everyday lives in patriarchy. Less-than attributions (i.e., that women are less intelligent, less objective, less competent, less supportive of other women) imbue our reasoning about women and relationships with women in ways that are remarkably intractable, as my illustrations below will attempt to show. Feminist epistemology should provide us with a systematic framework for reviewing assumptions of female inferiority as they recur in our thinking about men, women, society, art, culture, and truth on a daily basis. This kind of epistemology will not eliminate the suffering of human life; that is, feminism is not a salvation theology nor a complete explanation of women's or others' suffering. Feminist deconstruction of received culture should, however, provide assistance in formulating new methods of community, work, and relationship that are based on nonpatriarchal images and ideals—potentially on forms of shared existence, such as limitation, compassion, and mutuality.

Changing our thinking about inferiority-superiority and dominance-submission is a discipline of thought and action that requires a constant examination of assumptions and motivations. Is it possible first to change one's actions and then to change one's thoughts, motivations, or assumptions? Yes, indeed, but changed action does not necessitate reconceptualization. For example, a person may subscribe to the idea that doing dishes and sorting socks is an "inferior" activity. Having been influenced by feminism, and trusting its influence, the person may engage in these activities but continue to believe they are inferior, and may even feel angry about carrying them out. On the other hand, it is possible that these new activities will convert the person's thinking in an unexpected way—as, for example, experiencing the dishes and socks as worthy and repetitive structures of daily life. More likely, the decision to do something considered inferior is likely to result in sabotaged and dissipated actions, eventuating in feelings of helplessness: "I just can't make this work, no matter how much I want to."

Approaching the "inferiorizing" of women's work from a perspective of feminist deconstruction, I would examine and analyze the assumptions that determine the work is inferior. Typically we can conclude some particular work has been given lower status simply because it is done by women. Once the meaning of an activity is freed of its inferiorizing attributions, it can be reexamined in terms of an immediate life context— in terms of the skills, talents, and shared concerns of the people and the environments involved.

The reconstructive aspect of feminist epistemology is the articulation of a feminist knowledge system through new social contexts, new meanings, and new conversations about female work and identity. Two major belief systems stand in the way of women doing this directly at the moment, as Jean Lipman-Blumen (1983) has shown in her analysis of gender roles and power: 1) the belief that men control the knowledge necessary to direct our daily lives through the political and cultural forms of patriarchy (in which we are all engaged); and 2) the belief that men control the major resources on which we all depend.

Feminist analyses of resources, vitality, agency, and ideals connected to women and their activities must provide a persuasive counterposition to these beliefs. Indeed, we have begun to do this. Luce Irigaray (1985a, b) has provided us with some epistemological guidelines for reconstructing the understanding of female experience, especially for retrieving the meaning of female experience from the records and ideals we currently possess within patriarchy. Briefly, the method of Irigaray includes two steps: 1) analyze the gaps, the missing information, the unspoken meanings, irrationalities, and blind spots in the existing knowledge systems in order to "read" the text of female experience; and 2) use the method of original analysis to analyze the originator of the method in order to uncover his motivation and sympathies in constructing his system. The hidden position of the female and the feminine can be revealed through such analyses.

In my analyses of North American ideals and beliefs about female persons, I will use methods of Irigaray and guidelines offered by other feminists. Additionally, I will use the work of Rom Harré and some other philosophers, such as John MacMurray, who are not feminists but whose conceptual frameworks can be adapted to feminist deconstruction and reconstruction.

FEMALE PERSONS AND GENDERED SELVES

THE CENTRAL role of the social environment in providing the framework for being a person-among-persons has been traced by P. F. Strawson (1959), John MacMurray (1954), and Rom Harré (1984), among others. For my purposes, I will define "person" to be a primary, first-order experiential construct that refers to a mind-and-body unity, an embodied mind, or a spirited body. Persons are publicly visible and "endowed with all kinds of powers and capacities for public, meaningful action" as Harré said (1984, p. 26).

A "person" refers to a human being who is both a point of action (agency, intentionality, movement), and a point of view (cognition, mentality, perception). Through our relationships with other persons we (human beings) become persons. We acquire the meaning that defines us as knowers and doers, like other human persons. Through ongoing communication (linguistic and otherwise) with the world of persons and others, we articulate personality that is shared among ourselves. There is no knowledge or experience of being a person that is first learned alone and then attributed to others; in order to see ourselves as persons, we need the reflections, definitions, and perceptions of others. Personal experience is originally and continuously a shared existence.

A "self" is secondarily acquired, on the other hand, through commerce with a culture of persons. As a theoretical construct or belief about individual subjectivity, the concept of self takes on meanings of the culture in which we develop as persons. Beliefs about self are highly determinate of how persons relate to each other and to their environment. As Harré described it: "A person is a being who has learned a theory, in terms of which his or her experience is ordered. I believe that persons are characterized neither by their having a characteristic kind of experience nor by some specific genetic endowment. They can be identified neither phenomenologically nor biologically, but only by the character of their beliefs" (1984, p. 20).

Our ethnocentrism, as North Americans, frequently enters into our discussions about self-constructs of other cultures. We tend to believe that individuality, individual freedom, and self-reflectiveness are the truest, most valuable and least contestable aspects of self. In other words, we universalize the aspects of selfhood that suggest personal uniqueness and separateness. As a society (see Bellah 1985), we cultivate and sustain a morality of independent freedoms, self-reflective responsibility, and equity based on balancing individual claims.

Other societies, for example the Copper Eskimo (as recounted by Harré 1984), attribute characteristics of a collective self to persons. In such a society, there are no unique individuals. People share an identity as a group or tribe that is so profoundly collective that, as Harré said, if one person sneezes, most people sneeze. In such a collectivity, attributions of individual autonomy simply do not exist and no theory of independent individuality—no uniqueness, genius, independence, etc. as we know them—is fostered in the development of self.

In North American society, the concept of self includes an array of attributions that support an ideal of individual autonomy. We are a society that advocates and even hypervalues independence and uniqueness. Our selves are created by our coming to believe that we are independently motivated actors, makers and creators of our own lives. We do not live as participants within a cosmic or social order that sustains us—as we might have done in the Middle Ages of Europe—but rather we share the impression that we sustain our own individual order within a collectivity of other separate individuals. We are each responsible for enacting a morality and an ethic that are typically unsupported by convictions of a larger cosmic or social order.

How does female gender enter into our creation of independent selves and interact with the categories of "basic human rights" that provide a person with validity or legitimacy within the ongoing dialogue of personal life? Women regularly surrender the validity of their own truth in the face of challenges by men and by others perceived to be in power. Because they receive, support, and are supported in the construction of the female as inferior, North American women engage in building individual theories about their own inadequacy.

This activity is entirely unavoidable, as we all grow up within a patriarchal, androcentric social system in which our elders and our peers share deeply held beliefs that men control the knowledge necessary to direct our lives and that men control the major resources on which we all depend. Individual men are imagined to be geniuses, to have our best interests in mind, to be visionaries for the future, despite their dominance and devaluation of those whose lives they "direct." Consequently, all women in our society necessarily arrive at adulthood with feelings and significant beliefs about their own inferiority. These are not simply occasional or transitory beliefs; they are pervasive, inescapable ideas of being inadequate in regard to fundamental aspects of being a person. The typical framework of female inadequacy includes women's and girls' beliefs about inferiority of body, attractiveness, nurturance, strength, intelligence, and competence. These beliefs have been constructed as personal theories built from ongoing conversations about the identity characteristics of being male and female selves.

Individual women and girls unavoidably strive to validate theories of personal inferiority in a patriarchal society such as ours. Female persons surrender their personal authority for the validity of their own truth, beauty, and goodness; they replace this authority by personal theories of inadequacy and inferiority. Willingness to identify with reflections from patriarchal contexts of female inferiority is a fact of survival; we are socialized into negative self-concepts as female persons. We cannot refuse these reflections because they constitute the basis for our social participation in the world in a way that is "sane"—that is, consensually validated. As individual people, women and girls readily claim insufficiency or inadequacy and evaluate themselves (as persons) in terms of inferiorities perceived as bad and detrimental to self and others. These evaluations are attributed and sustained in ongoing conversations in which both the social contexts (i.e., verbal and nonverbal communications) and theoretical concepts for human health and welfare support the idea of female inadequacy to male standards for strength, independence, health, knowledge, objectivity, and so on. As female persons, we have been shaped by the belief that we lack something as persons. We witness our inability to fill the decision-making and status-holding positions of our societies, and the general devaluation of the work and culture we produce, and we inevitably conclude that something "is wrong with me."

DOUBLE-BIND OF FEMALE GENDER

WITHIN the context of patriarchal creations of female self, individual women must assume the validity of the concept of female person as inferior and collect personal data to prove they personally do fit the concept. Until women and girls are offered a feminist epistemology for examining and contradicting the received knowledge about female selves, they are necessarily in a double-bind regarding their status as females and adults within a patriarchal society—perhaps even most strenuously double-bound in a society like ours, which predicates goodness on personal freedom and individualism.

The creation of a concept of self (as subjective point of view and point of action) is a product of beliefs about subjectivity of individual experience in personal life. An individual's self is consequently constructed from the experiences of being a person-among-persons as these are evaluated and explained. ". . . [T]he semantics of the conceptual cluster around the general notion of the 'self' is to be understood as if the 'self' were a theoretical concept like those of the natural sciences, judged by its behavioral and material analogies . . ." (Harré, p. 25). Theories of the female self and her subjectivity are built so wholly around assumptions of female inadequacy (widely accepted in many literate societies) that we must wrestle with our basic concepts of being persons even to recognize the experiential difficulties generated by our theories.

In patriarchal society, we are constantly and everywhere subjected to tacit and explicit assumptions of male superiority. Male standards for health, mental health, leadership, culture, competence, judgment, relationship, and personal freedom constitute our recorded and received social reality, for the most part. Studies of North Americans' expectations of ideal women and men, conducted by Broverman et al. in 1970, and by Broverman et al. in 1972, are often cited as empirical evidence of the collective prejudices we share about gender identities. These studies show that we expect men to be stronger, more objective, more competent, and more independent than women—results that are obvious in daily life. Women are expected to be weaker, less competent, and more emotionally expressive and subjective than men. Perhaps more important, from the point of view of self-constructs, is the assumption that women are less competent and more passive than "healthy adults" when gender is not specified. This last finding from Broverman's research is a fine illustration of the double-bind of female adults. Ideals of personal responsibility and self-determination, which form the core of our democratic vision of a free adult agent, are directly in conflict with ideals for womanly behavior. If a woman behaves as a healthy adult, she will be criticized for being unwomanly; conversely, if she behaves as a feminine woman, she will be considered childlike or worse (e.g., mentally ill).

The double-bind of female authority is wholly unavoidable in a society that predicates the individual self on attributes and conditions of which the female is expected to have considerably "less than" an equal share with males. The categories that support the condition of being "free" in our highly individualized society—strength, judgment, knowledge, independence, and objectivity—are not expected to be fulfilled for individual women.

Many women oppose the labels of female inferiority in contemporary life in the United States. They openly fight feeling inadequate and identify themselves with strength, competence, and authority. Unfortunately, they cannot escape the double-bind of female gender until they examine the concepts on which they are enacting their strength, competence, and authority. Such women are frequently described (both by others and by themselves) as compensating or being "too masculine"—"too dominant." In many public situations such a woman experiences a great deal of distress when she is acting in an insistent or forceful manner, even when she is simply defending her own beliefs. As Harré (1984) pointed out, the legitimacy of being a person (the fundamental reality for one's existence) is limited by the "right" to occupy a space and time in the ongoing conversations of shared reality. This contingent right is closely related to consensual validation or intersubjectivity as "truth" or worth. Women who oppose female inferiority frequently find themselves in a mediated position; what they are saying or offering is being questioned simply because they assume a posture or manner of authority or competence. "Persons are embodied beings located not only in the array of persons but in physical space and time. The relation between the consequences of our joint location in both manifolds is mediated by the local moral order, particularly the unequal distribution of rights . . ." (Harré, p. 65). An authoritative woman may be physically present with others, but she may not have the right to occupy a position of contributor—analogous to the female secretary at a male board meeting. She will be seen, but she will not be heard. Because the personal existence of such an individual is threatened at such moments, she will necessarily get the impression that she is doing something wrong. Rather than lose her sanity (experience herself as a nonperson), she will tend to accept an explanation that she has not acted in her own best interest. Usually such an explanation will be constructed according to the rules of the female double-bind: she is too forceful, overly controlling, demanding, aggressive, rigid, compensating—in short, too masculine. Women who espouse female authority fall prey to evaluating themselves, both privately and publicly, in terms of their negative subjectivity. They see themselves, as others have reflected, as too emotional, too intellectual, and so on. Perhaps they even perceive their own personal psychology (family of origin patterns) as inherently problematic. Until a woman wholly understands how female gender is socially constructed to include her individual inferiority, she will be prone to proving and validating the patriarchal theory of inferior female self—whether or not she subscribes to the theory.

Women who do subscribe to the "less than" female categories and express themselves directly as more passive and less competent (than men and other women) are perhaps at greater risk. They may be perceived as valid persons under most conditions of their oppression, but they experience their personal validity as grounded in their childlikeness and inherent weakness. Many syndromes of mental "disorders" are descriptions of exaggerated femininity: depression, hysteria, phobia, dependent personality disorder, bulimia, anorexia, and some aspects of borderline psychotic conditions are but a few examples. When feminine-identified women experience life stresses and seek help, they are at risk for being labeled into mental illness categories. With a label such as "depression," an individual may waste most of her life's resources on unintentionally proving the theory of her helplessness.

NEW CATEGORIES FOR FEMALE PERSONS

IN THE following brief treatment of female authority, I attempt to reverse and exploit some of the received knowledge about female persons that contributes to the disabling ideas women commonly use in constructing individual female selves as inferior. Through a feminist epistemology, I would like to extricate concepts for personal being that are better aligned with women's experiences of themselves and are opposed to the androcentric constructions of female persons as "less than" male persons. I believe that women already operate by such assumptions and beliefs (largely unarticulated and unrecorded) that are both effacious and emergent in relationships with other women.

Three conceptual categories constitute my major focus in this paper: 1) personal freedom as *personal authority* (as distinct from illusions of independence, mental separatism, and individualism); 2) foundational experience as *dependence* (as distinct from self-reflective subjectivity, individual freedom, and social isolation); and 3) beautiful appearances as *personal power* (as distinct from narcissism, compensation, and selfishness).

These three categories of meaning are neither inclusive of all experiences that women bring to self-definition nor exclusive of masculinist influence in my analysis of them. I am using them as case studies of how I apply feminist epistemology in deconstruction and reconstruction of received meaning in my work in psychotherapy with women. By reversing received meaning, analyzing gaps and blindspots in our knowledge systems, and validating the "illegitimate" knowledge shared by women, we can extricate new meaning from our recorded cultural standards of patriarchy. Still, our methods may be androcentric and certainly require ongoing conversations and revisions through our using them in personal life.

Attributing intentionality and personal responsibility to one's self and others is critical to Western categories of personal freedom. In North American society, which bases the self on a concept of freedom of choice, we speak constantly about our duties and obligations to protect personal sovereignty. Women's experience of personal sovereignty—as intentionality and the knowledge that they act by free choice—is ambiguous at best, in terms of both their female gender identity and their location in social contexts. Because they are assumed to be less competent and less rational, they are also assumed to be less capable of self-determination; women are often unsurprised (naturally) to find that other women do not fill higher status and decision-making roles in our society. Furthermore, idealized passivity, lack of validation of female culture, and exclusion of women from the active life of community (women and children are supposed to "stay at home" or at least in the background), all contribute to inhibition of women's personal agency.

Although women routinely make decisions and cope with complex environmental data involved with relational and caregiving skills, they often assume that their decision-making activities are not "real" because they are dissociated from status and money. Then when we are offered theories about our "dependency" and our "need for protection," we tend to respond in one of two ways, concluding: 1) that we are *individually* less than adequate in decision-making skills and responsibility taking; or 2) that we would achieve the status of being "free" and "independent" if we were less inclined to acknowledge our needs for emotional contact or close relationship. Androcentric psychologies of separation-individuation tend to increase women's apprehensions about their relational needs *and* to undermine their experiences of personal agency. Because we females seek to validate the theory that we are inadequate to be adult persons, we automatically (as a social group) will locate ourselves in explanations about women's "dependency" in such a way that personal freedom and dependence are obscured in our conversations.

When women take the "command" to "be independent" as a resolution to feelings of low self-esteem and negative self-referencing, they become confused about their experiences of pleasure in relationships. Rather than give up cherished relationships, some women may undermine their motivations to be agents of their lives, and instead believe in a theory about their inferiority. This is a masculinist solution, as is the opposite route of living alone (or being literally "independent") as if social isolation were the path to personal freedom.

Living alone has little to do with personal agency, even though people can become more self-reliant under conditions of social isolation. Similarly, repressing one's own desire to express personal creativity and other resources—in order to "protect" one's relationships—does not lead to a useful and satisfying life. Ultimately, evaluations according to any mea-sure of masculinist independence-dependence configurations tend to re-sult in confusion about women's experiences of themselves, especially their decision-making and relational styles.

From women's experiences of their own lives, as illustrated, for example by Baruch, Barnett, and Rivers (1983), we can clarify a new orientation toward freedom that does not inhibit our desire for relationship, nor obscure our skill and intelligence in decision making. Freedom is personal authority—the ability to make claims to truth, beauty, and goodness based on one's own experience. Out of this authority people make deci-sions about their own lives and consider themselves within the contexts of others' lives. Female authority has been repressed and oppressed be-cause of the double-bind of female gender identity (see Young-Eisendrath and Wiedemann 1987, for a fuller discussion of this).

At this time in contemporary North American society, white males continue to dominate our knowledge systems and our decision-making groups although they are a clear minority in the midst of women and colored peoples. Attributing to white men a specialized knowledge and the dominant control of resources, we extend their authority beyond their numbers. As a feminist, I am aware that women have the necessary knowledge to master our social and natural environments and often do so in the absence of men—as for example in life-sustaining settings such as hospitals. I also know that women and others control major cultural resources—for example decoding of relational communications and mas-tery of domestic environments—on which white males depend and to which they have little access.

Feminist theologians help us spot new ideas and ideals for female authority. Mary Daly (1978) called our attention to the dominant-aggres-sive structure of patriarchal religious beliefs in a way that reveals an alternative of pleasure, affiliating, cooperating, and imagining with other women. Daly especially validated our pleasures and power in relational contexts as aspects of our own authority, on which we always and every-where draw in making our own choices. Naomi Goldenberg (1979) directed us to our own images and dreams to find configurations that support our experiences, our own categories of differentiation.

Along the same lines, I find myself opposing common androcentric dictates for success and power in patriarchy, although I am aware of how carefully one must proceed in this activity. When college women query, "Tell me the truth, isn't it really better to become a psychiatrist than a social worker if you want to make a difference in women's lives?" I must study the question carefully. I invite the questioner to enter with me into an analysis of her terms: what does she mean by "better" and how does she view her participation in a profession founded and shaped by men versus one founded and shaped by women? I am making an inquiry about the double-bind of her female authority, how she expresses it and how she manages it. In a patriarchal society, we need to protect our access to creative expression, personal power, integrity of our own beliefs and values, and our sovereignty over structuring time and space, as we enter into the world of "success." No false dichotomy of independence-dependence or selfish-selfless can help us orient ourselves to the complexity of the deconstruction of the foundation for our own truths.

As long as we confuse personal freedom with illusory independence, we will have no possibility of validating our experiences as agents and communicators. False talk about independence as separatism and individualism continues to confuse us in making choices based on our pleasure, mastery, and satisfaction.

Physical and emotional dependence is a primary condition of human life throughout the life cycle. In patriarchy we deny this condition and talk about ourselves as separate individuals. Our misleading fallacy of individualism—that we are uniquely separate beings housed in separate bodies—has led to endless confusion in our philosophies and politics. Every day I encounter people who idealize and promote cultural individualism in a way that supports phenomenology of mental and physical separatism. They confuse personal agency (the illusion of personal freedom) with the idea that we each live alone and make our own decisions. As organisms and persons, we never live alone. We must have a differentiated dependence on an elaborate environment of physical and social contexts in order to go on being.

Human existence is, in principle and obviously, a shared existence. We are individually vulnerable animals and part-persons. Personal being and the sense of self, as subjectivity, are elaborately dependent on relationships that provide contexts, reflections, and structures for all our activities from birth to death. Children learn how to be people, male and female persons, through interactions with other persons. There is no human activity that is first learned alone and then noted as corresponding to others' behaviors, yet we constantly speak as though there were such activities.

Women tend to repress their dependence less than men do, probably because women provide more nurturant care as dependable, as well as dependent, people. Our massive cultural and social denial of dependence in North American culture is a product of androcentric knowledge systems. Men repress their original dependence on a "big woman" and they oppose their identification with her. They fight female authority in all of its forms as it is reminiscent of the "big woman" of their childhood life context.

Many cultural by-products of men's repressed dependence confuse our analyses of human relationships. Remnants of the Cartesian epistemology of being—the belief that self-reflective thought brings subjective awareness into being—are with us still. These lead us to the absurd position of asking questions about how minds and bodies can get together and keep on going. Obviously, they were never separated, nor were minds separated from each other. When dependence is freed of its masculinist constraints through feminist methodologies and actions, we may find that much of our Western philosophical tradition since the Middle Ages seems useless and delusional. If an individual person is taken to be the unit of our study, the point of reflection, and/or the topic of conversation, then we are misled into conclusions that preclude the foundation of human experience, the shared existence of our being.

In her 1982 study of women's moral reasoning, Carol Gilligan discovered that women remember the contextual or relational reality as a foundation for moral principles. She noted that "... in all of the women's descriptions, identity is defined in a context of relationship and judged by a standard of responsibility and care. Similarly, morality is seen by these women as arising from the experience of connection . . ." (p. 160).

In order for women to validate their cherishing of relationship and their experiences of ongoing differentiated dependence, they must turn to female friends, and even then they may be loathe to call themselves "dependent." Calling oneself dependent has become tantamount to calling oneself a nonperson, a child, or a cripple. In order to share in the privilege of being an adult person and to have the right to contribute to the ongoing conversations of daily life, many women choose to see themselves as "independent" and/or to denigrate their dependence in patriarchal terms such as "over-controlling" and "needy." Naturally women become confused when they have no consensually validated terms for expressing their own dependence and their differentiation of dependent relationships throughout the life cycle.

A feminist analysis of communication practices, in both private (family) and public (communal) life, reveals that women control a valuable cultural resource that is frequently invalidated and referred to perjoratively as "feminine intuition." In mature and differentiated dependence, women accurately perceive the nonverbal and gestural communications of others in such a way as to anticipate others' words and actions. Within a masculinist knowledge system, they cannot legitimately refer to this situation, and sometimes they are hampered in using it as well. Intuition generates what feminists have called empathic regard and what I term "objective empathy" in order to differentiate it from projection, sympathy, approval seeking, and other forms of feeling undifferentiated from another in one's identity. Objective empathy, as we learn in psychotherapy practice, is the ability to put oneself in an other's perspective or point of view and to accurately infer the other's assumptions and feelings so as to anticipate the other's actions. Under conditions of such objective empathy, the perceiver is able to differentiate clearly between her own desires and feelings and the desires and feelings of the other. For example, it is possible for a thirty-five-year-old woman to infer accurately the frame of reference and assumptions of a two-year-old child without becoming like the child. The adult woman can anticipate the child's actions and even "speak the language" of the child. Putting oneself in another's place and constructing the meaning system of the other is a developmental achievement that appears to rely on blending what we commonly call *objectivity* and *subjectivity*.

Critical to claiming the valid authority of her intuition and the potential of her objective empathy, a female person must have articulated the authority of her female experience as distinct from the received knowledge of patriarchy, in which these forms of human experience are not recorded nor validated as truthful. To achieve this position a woman must free herself from the desire for approval by the authorities of patriarchy and/ or by its representatives in her immediate life context.

Undoing our rationalizations around internalized female inferiority in order to claim the personal power of our shared experiences as women is

a monumental task within patriarchal society. Cultural messages about our power must be unknotted and examined in terms of their gaps and blind spots. The hard knots of androcentric reasoning are most difficult to untie in regard to the assumption that women's preoccupations with beautiful appearances (of the body and the domestic environment) are compensations. Female narcissism has been interpreted variously (from the perspective of androcentric reasoning) as compensating for the missing penis, lower intelligence, less access to educational and economic achievement, and for unequal social power. Because women's concerns for beautiful appearances are so widely conceived as trivial and false, even women are reticent to speak among themselves about appearances. Indeed we often consider appearances to be façades or illusions—the products of patriarchal demands on us—although we have developed considerable skill and intelligence in creating them. We fail to notice that the knowledge and power of these skills belong to us. As Susan Brownmiller (1984) has pointed out, women's appearances—through skin, hair, clothes, etiquette, body shape and body movement—convey essential cultural and social messages. We communicate through our appearances, but we may not understand our messages—but then, again, we may understand them although we believe that they are not valid.

What remains unspoken, hidden, and repressed in our androcentric analyses of feminine narcissism? I believe it is the radical idea that a woman *is* her appearance. Within our patriarchal society, the personal power of woman is conveyed by her appearance. This power of appearance is the only socially condoned power openly afforded to all female persons in patriarchy. Women use the power, manipulate and trade in it, in a way similar to men's commerce in money. Implied in the statement "My, she has let herself go!" (as a criticism of a woman's appearance), is the patriarchal message that a woman is her appearance. It is a social fact that women are encouraged to compete for appearances and win material rewards for that competition; artifice is a social commodity of personal power among women in patriarchy. Women have become skillful and intelligent in using this power, but when they believe that it is merely compensatory, they are serving the purposes of patriarchy. Explanations that invalidate the serious social meaning of women's appearances bind women to approval seeking and put them under the control of a system that makes their daily concerns seem inferior.

When individual women develop beyond the received culture of patriarchy, they may be propelled into an existential conflict that I title "appearance versus reality." When a woman disavows the compensatory meaning of her appearance—that is, she assumes that she is "more than" an appearance—she necessarily remains caught in the androcentric knowledge system in which appearance is compensation for something more worthwhile. In her own search for authentic expressions of her self, she happens onto ways of appearing that are more comfortable or personally satisfying than her previous bound femininity. In her rebellious freedom, she makes judgments that reproduce patriarchy. She categorizes women in terms of their appearances, having achieved some personal resolution about her own appearance. Once again, she forces women to operate according to the patriarchal judgment that a woman *is* her appearance. The "new" feminist-seeming categories resonate with patriarchal contempt: women are judged as feminist versus nonfeminist, as bright versus dumb, as conformist versus liberated, on the basis of appearance.

Recognizing that beautiful appearances are social commodities of power, women can integrate their personal authority into a differentiated appearance and skilled beauty without reproducing patriarchy. Appearances provide access to personal power and drama; "dressing up" and wearing "high" heels can lend emphases of size and color to one's dramatic expression. Decorations, illusions, artifice, and personal esthetic contribute to the creative visions women express in their appearances. We can learn to appreciate the skills and intelligence we have developed in making beautiful appearances when we have freed our conceptual categories from reproducing the patriarchal dictate that a woman *is* her appearance, while not forgetting the social power of this dictate within a patriarchal society.

In reconstructing the meaning of female authority, my most serious aim is the rebonding of women and the integration of the female community. Competition for appearances has remained a patriarchal arena among women, which is often reproduced within feminist groups. As we pull apart the assumptions that lead us to denigrate each other, we continue to discover the powerful projection of our own authority onto male standards for truth, beauty, and goodness.

CONCLUSION

WE MUST REMEMBER that we are in a critical period for human survival, acutely aware of the dangers of annihilation that face our species. Those dangers arise directly from our repression of dependence, our desire for mastery and possession of the resources on which we depend. We have adapted to patriarchy principally through repressing our dependence and vulnerability as relatively weak animals. We have acquired enormous dominion over other life systems while we seem incapable of even imagining our existence as shared. Our species may go the way of many other life forms on our planet whose adaptation eventually led to extinction.

On the other hand, we are also certainly aware that we are not in control of our individual destinies. Our personal fate is individual extinction, having lived on a small planet, dependent on a relatively small star in a solar system that will eventually dissolve. The psychological condition of our lives as persons—of limited control and limitless dependence—is obscured by patriarchal social and cultural systems that idealize independence. A new model for human existence—grounded in ideals of personal authority and dependence, appreciative of differences and diverse beauty—may contribute to a new vision for personal being. By acknowledging the reality of our limitations and the meaning of human "freedom," we may ultimately understand ourselves to be, in essence, compassionate beings.

REFERENCES

Baruch, G., Barnett, R., and Rivers, C. (1983). *Life prints: New patterns of love and work for today's women.* New York: McGraw-Hill.

Bellah, R., et al. (1985). *Habits of the heart: Individuation and commitment in American life.* New York: Harper and Row.

Bordo, S. (1986). "The Cartesian masculinization of thought," *Signs* 11: 439–56.

Broverman, I. K., et al. (1970). "Sex-role stereotypes and clinical judgments of mental health." *Journal of Consulting and Clinical Psychology* 34: 1–7.

——, et al. (1972). "Sex-role stereotypes: A current appraisal." *Journal of Social Issues* 28: 59–78.

Brownmiller, S. (1984). *Femininity.* New York: Ballantine.

Daly, M. (1978). *Gyn/ecology: The metaethics of radical feminism.* Boston: Beacon Press.

Gilligan, C. (1982). *In a different voice: Psychological theory and women's development.* Cambridge: Harvard University Press.

Goldenberg, N. (1979). *Changing the gods: Feminism and the end of traditional religions.* Boston: Beacon Press.

Harré, R. (1984). *Personal being.* Cambridge: Harvard University Press.

Irigaray, L. (1985a). *Speculum of the other woman.* Ithaca: Cornell University Press.

——. (1985b). *This sex which is not one.* Ithaca: Cornell University Press.

Lipman-Blumen, J. (1983). *Gender roles and power.* Atlantic Highlands, N.J.: Humanities Press.

MacMurray, J. (1954). *Persons in relation.* New York: Faber and Faber.

Shotter, J. (1975). *Images of man in psychological research.* London: Methuen.

Strawson, P. F. (1959). *Individuals: An essay in descriptive metaphysics.* London: Methuen.

Young-Eisendrath, P., and Wiedemann, F. (1987). *Female authority: Empowering women through psychotherapy.* New York: Guilford Press.

ELEVEN

Women, History, and Practical Deliberation

Emily Grosholz

MANY philosophers will admit that the future is open and contingent and claim that past events have lapsed into the realm of necessity. Thus we deliberate and make choices about the future because it is still indeterminate, and our actions, informed by reason and desire, may bear upon it. But we do not deliberate about the past, because nothing can alter what has happened once it has happened. In this essay I will argue that on the contrary the human past is in many respects as much a social construction as the future, and that we do and must deliberate about it. Further, this insight should be central to any understanding of feminist historiography, whose purpose is to be both critical and hopeful.

If we accept the necessitarian claim about the past, then the historian's task appears to be faithful transcription of the unalterable, unambiguous, and necessary facts of human nature up to the present, "wie es eigentlich gewesen ist" ("how it really was.") If there are causal patterns in these facts, the historian will devise a correct theory that summarizes and explains the patterning.[1] Desire, choice, and practical reason are then beside the point; only theoretical reason directs this undertaking, and history has been assimilated into science.

Feminist historians adopt the same understanding of history whenever they denounce their predecessors as ideological and then claim to unmask all ideology so as to furnish the correct theory of the past, which explains a correct and complete description of the facts. Ideological theories are disproved by facts that have been distorted or suppressed; the correct theory will not distort, suppress, or contradict the facts, but will be uniformly confirmed by them. Usually, the kind of feminist who is looking for a correct theory of the past is methodologically sophisticated enough to admit that historical facts and theories are social constructions; indeed, this is the very insight she uses to unmask ideologies. Ideology masquerades as divine or biological necessity; but it is merely a human construction and so its claim to a special privilege (a special access to the truth) is illegitimate.

The question then arises, what legitimates the claim of feminist historical theory to special access to the truth? One reply is that at least feminist historical theory recognizes its own status as a construction, whereas ideological theories do not; one tries to build reflexivity and self-consciousness into the theory itself. But then the problem still remains, for why should theoretical reason choose one construction over another? Another reply is that, although the feminist historian reports on the constructions of other people, she is the one finally to get the facts straight, and to offer the only theory that explains them properly. But then what justifies her quasi-scientific certainty about facts and principles, which the ideologue also shares?

In what follows, I want to argue that practical deliberation, not scientific theory, is the right model for understanding what we are about when we engage in feminist historiography. A positive argument for this claim requires much more than the negative observation that a feminist historian can't consistently pretend to be a scientist. It requires extensive answers to the questions: Why are we feminists in the first place? And why are we historians?

Why are we feminists? Because we want to change social reality in accord with our perception of certain kinds of inequities; and part of this change is that women take a broader, more active role in the construction of social reality. We want to criticize the world as it stands, in accord with certain moral principles, and we want people (including ourselves) to act differently in the future.

I will begin by asserting that social reality is not given but is constructed in the process of practical deliberation; I hope that when the argument has been spelled out, this assertion will have proven its worth. Practical deliberation is a dialectical assessment of the moral significance of actions as we try to decide what to do next. It refines our understanding of moral principles as they are brought to bear on particular situations, and it clarifies without disambiguating the "essentially contested concepts" that define the meaning of actions in a process of attack and rebuttal (Gallie 1964, Chapter 8).

What a human action *is*—that is to say, what efficacy it will have, how it will bear on other events—is a function of what it means. If significance is worked out in practical deliberation, which is a social, conflictful, but cooperative assessment of action, then such deliberation determines the very being of human events. We construct social reality as we deliberate about it. Nor is this merely a matter of talk. If we want to get anything done, we must persuade other people to cooperate in the enterprise. True virtue must be effective, and efficacy depends on eloquence.

Persuasion is characteristically a long and difficult process, for on the really important issues—feminism is one of them—reasonable people can hold strongly incompatible views and moreover find it especially hard to acknowledge the strong points of the opposition. The "facts" cannot settle the issue, for if they could be agreed upon, the dispute would already have been settled. There are no relevant experts; everyone has opinions on such matters.[2] Feminism will not somehow suddenly win the day. Rather, a novel social reality is being constructed in societies in which feminism is an issue, through the various offensives and defenses that compose the debate even when there is no conclusive victory. The debate itself changes the social climate and therefore the conditions for action.

Once feminism is seen not as a correct theory, but as a long (indeed, endless) process of moral, practical deliberation, we can guard against false hopes and false despairs. It doesn't make sense to suppose that feminism will win its debate, generating a theory (even a highly reflexive one) from which we can deduce the true significance of events, or will simplify, or solve the issues. Rather, it will constantly engender disputes; it will not be argued out of existence by the other side; it will at best articulate and organize complexity; and it will change social reality in ways palatable to feminists (as well as other disputants).

The endlessness of deliberation does not, however, entail that our positions on the relevant issues are arbitrary, nor that the whole process is anarchical. Practical deliberation is highly structured because it is so severely constrained by the need to come to practical conclusions—that is, to act—and by the small number of moral stances a culture at any given time will accommodate. The concrete particulars of any situation in which we must act, social norms, and certain high-level principles constrain what we can choose, usually to a small finite number of choices.

The high-level principles are of special interest when they articulate the very conditions of deliberation, for these are principles often invoked by feminists to justify their perception of inequity. Simone de Beauvoir stated one such principle in *The Ethics of Ambiguity* when she said that it is wrong for one human being to block or put an artificial ceiling on the freedom of another (de Beauvoir 1962). My version is that it is wrong for people to be barred from entering the various processes of deliberation in which social reality is constructed. And it is wrong for deliberation to become murderous, for then deliberation ceases. Of course, even these high-level principles can and must be deliberated about, since their meaning lies partly in how they are applied, and the selection and application of principles is rarely unambiguous and straightforward. (It also lies in the way they transcend particular instances and relate them systematically.) How women (and men) enter these second-order deliberations furnishes the abstract principles with content, constrains and extends their application, and makes them practical. Pacific conflict, aggressive and cooperative, is the moral insight at the heart of the position I am urging.

Why are we historians? Because the past bears on the present, is alive in the present, and partly determines the conditions for action in the present, that is, how we construe the significance of events. Events have consequences, are effective and potent, due to the way in which they are meaningful. But events don't carry their meaningfulness on their faces, rather only as they stand in relation to other events. In particular, present events are meaningful only in relation to past events, and past events in relation not only to their past but also to events in what will become their future. Whitehead wrote, "Cut away the future, and the present collapses, emptied of its proper content"; he might have said the same thing about cutting away the past. These attributions of meaningfulness that involve the systematic relating of events, and the identifying of temporally and spatially diffused and discontinuous human actions as one action or event, are part of the social construction of reality. So we might expect that such attributions are "essentially contestable" and that our construal of past events, their significance, is generated through deliberation. And such deliberation is practical, since the past, revived in the activity of deliberation, is brought to bear on the present and determines the conditions of action for us. Feminists therefore also need to take a broader, more aggressive role in our deliberations about the past, a role that contests prior forms of historiography.

Two related kinds of *reductio ad absurdum* arguments show that the past is as much a contingent, debatable social construction as the present. Suppose, to hypothesize the opposite, that there is an Ideal Chronicle in which all events are recorded as they happen, in complete and accurate detail. Wouldn't such a chronicle put the squabbling historians out of business and bury the past where it belongs, in the vaults of necessity and exact description?

Suppose we allow that this chronicle is written in a language rich enough to include the ways in which historians normally pick out, characterize, and link events. This language contains a whole class of descriptions that characterize people and events in terms of their future vicissitudes as well as terms like 'causes,' 'anticipates,' 'begins,' 'precedes,' 'ends,' which no historian could forgo without lapsing into silence. But such descriptions and terms are not available to the eyewitness of events, who describes them at the edge of time on which they occur.[3] The description of an event changes with time because the event comes to stand in different relations to those that come after it; and the new relations in turn may point to novel ways of associating that event with contemporary and antecedent events or indeed to novel ways of construing the components of a spatio-temporally diffused event as one thing. Indeed, the historian's way of choosing beginnings and endings for her narratives, or for relating an event to its consequences, is her prime way of signaling the significance of the event, why she chose to write about it in the first place, and in what way it bears on the present. Allowing a sufficiently rich language for the Ideal Chronicle violates the original supposition about how the chronicle is to be written.

Yet, if we then insist that the chronicle be written in a language impoverished enough to meet the stringent conditions of its writing, we find that it is reduced to an account of matter in motion; the subject matter of history, people and the events they figure in, has dissolved. Then the chronicle is no longer about history, and we are only doing a version of descriptive physics (if indeed we are doing anything at all). If we want to do history, events must be related to their pasts and futures, must be construed as significant and therefore drawn into the circle of the essentially contestable. Then we are engaged in a process of deliberating about the past, and the past is alive in the present.

Once again, though history now appears as an endless process of deliberation, it is not therefore true that one can say anything at all about the past. This process, in which relations among events shift and are contested, exhibits an important kind of stability. We enter the debate only by locating ourselves with respect to previous historiography and the partly determinate, partly ambiguous physical record; the persuasive moves we can make in this context are severely constrained by them. We argue within a shapely but revisable structure, if we want to make our novel construals of history effective and practical.

At the beginning of *The Ethics of Ambiguity* Simone de Beauvoir gave a taxonomy of the ways in which people try to avoid the task of freedom, which is a way of explaining why people, though everywhere born free, so often end up in chains (de Beauvoir 1962, pp. 37–73). Her analysis both adopts Sartre's unfortunate way of analyzing people merely as individual agents in *Being and Nothingness,* and subverts it in an interesting way, because she concluded that all these evasions of freedom entail a self-isolation. "No existence," she said, "is validly fulfilled if it is limited to itself. It appeals to the existence of others" (de Beauvoir 1962, p. 67). This is the ambiguity of our condition.

I would like to review her taxonomy here, taking freedom in its social dimensions of access to deliberation and the practical activity of deliberation, and apply it to various ways in which feminist historiography can go astray. Then I will conclude with a few remarks about what the special practical and methodological import of feminist history might be.

The childish woman ignores history, and thus is simply unaware of how others construct her history, and so her present situation, for her. The childlike historian takes over the history others have written for her, reads and digests it, lives with it, takes it as one fact of life among others.

Once the historian has become reflective about her own activity as an historian, other more complex stances develop. The serious historian chooses to subordinate her constructive activity to values (that is, some particular construction of history) taken as absolute. She might well be a feminist, but she takes the meaning of history as fixed, scorns deliberation, and forgets that every goal is also a point of departure. Depending on her situation, she becomes a tyrant or a victim.

The nihilist historian turns her own seriousness back on herself and, finding no rapprochement between feminist history and its alternatives, plunges into a revolt against history itself. All construals of history are arbitrary and incommensurable. She can become an exoticist, an adventurer, or an esthete, trying to detach herself from the constraints of the social context in which she was educated and the demand to make history practical.

The passionate historian takes feminist history not as an object, but as an emanation of her subjectivity. She feels so obsessively the claims of her chosen subject that nothing exists outside of it or can modify her choice of it. She encloses herself in one self-limiting, self-justifying story.

The warnings we may draw from this taxonomy are manifold. We cannot afford to ignore history, nor to let others write our history for us. We cannot invent a novel historiography that refuses to engage what others have written before or in opposition to us. And we cannot escape into relativism; we must take sides, make moral discriminations about history, and try to render our judgments persuasive and therefore effective. They will be modified in deliberation, but only in the context of deliberation will they take on a genuine life of their own.

In some ways the past is a terrifying and disheartening spectacle for a feminist. Surveying it, we find the widespread assumptions that men are more valuable than women and that women are justifiably excluded from important spheres of deliberation, even though this indirectly results in their impoverishment and brutalization. What can we do with such a past? As we enter more and more into deliberation about it, in fact we do many things. We mourn the inequities, the oppression and victimization, and we rage against them. Our mourning unifies us and our rage makes us aggressive (but not murderous) in debate, and as we debate in this way, we must be claiming that it could have been otherwise. On what grounds do we base this claim? By revising the ways in which events stand in relation to other events, by approaching the written and physical record in novel ways. Thus we can associate violations of women in certain times and places with counterexemplary instances of more tolerant relations between the sexes in contemporary, antecedent, or precedent cultures; we can claim certain women as harbingers and forerunners; we can read the errors of the past as cautionary tales for the present.

In addition, the more we deliberate, the more we realize the ideal that informs our criticism and move away from the old conditions of terror and silence. The very fact that we are debating and writing history in contentious terms changes social reality: what problems arise on the agenda of practical deliberation and what kinds of solutions are proposed for them. If we change the significance of the past sufficiently, so that it no longer looks like a prison and ensnarement but a resource—still sad, still violent, but suggestive of how to avoid old defeats and to amplify earlier progress—then perhaps we can also move from mourning and rage to forgiveness. Forgiving is a slow and difficult process, not achieved by formal pronouncement but by our ratiocinative desire, desiderative reason, which chooses to forgive after a long course of deliberation. Thus, by mourning, condemning, praising, and forgiving the past, we take action with respect to it and give it a new configuration. Our deliberations have the power to change the meaning of past events, and so how they bear upon the present and the future.

The feminist revolution is different from all others in that we live with our opponents (men) and generally speaking we love them, and they love us. Thus, we have had to fashion a process of deliberation that includes our rage, sadness, and genuine opposition, and that nonetheless is not murderous. It is practically impossible for us to resort to that rupture of deliberation that brings peasant and aristocrat, black and white, easterner and westerner, to armed struggle, where each faction can repair to its separate station, culture, language, country, justifying hostilities by the claim that the other side is at best not really human, at worst diabolical. The grievances of women against men are as profound and terrible as those of any group against any other. Yet we know from experience, from love, that our opponent is all too human, only human, human as we are.[4]

So as feminists reconstruct our social reality and our history by making our claims persuasive in the matrix of practical deliberation, we are also creating for the world a paradigm of human activity that these days it desperately needs to learn. And that is a pacific conflict that never collapses into easy agreement nor sinks into murderousness, but remakes the world through the talkative action that ought to be the great achievement of humankind.

NOTES

1. Philosophers of science like Henri Poincaré have noted that any finite collection of empirical data underdetermines (and therefore fails to specify a unique) scientific theory. But, as I have argued (Grosholz 1986), the source of indeterminacy in history is located differently from that in physics.

2. My exposition of practical deliberation is strongly influenced by Garver 1984, which in turn is indebted to Schwab 1978.

3. This argument is borrowed from the Chapter "Narrative Sentences" in Danto 1965.

4. I refer the reader to Charny 1982 for an extended treatment of models of pacific conflict.

REFERENCES

Charny, I. (1982). *How can we commit the unthinkable? Genocide: The human cancer*. Boulder, Colo.: Westview.

Danto, (1965). *The analytical philosophy of history*. Cambridge: Cambridge University Press.

de Beauvoir, S. (1962). *The ethics of ambiguity*. Secaucus: Citadel.

Gallie, W. B. (1964). *Philosophy and the historical understanding*. New York: Schocken.

Garver, E. (1984). "The arts of the practical: Variations on a theme of prometheus." *Critical Inquiry* 14 (2): 165–82.

Grosholz, E. (1986). "Milosz and the moral authority of poetry." *The Hudson Review* 39 (2): 251–70.

Schwab, J. (1978). *Science, curriculum and liberal education*. I. Westbury and N. Wilkof (Eds.). Chicago: University of Chicago Press.

The author gratefully acknowledges the support of the National Endowment for the Humanities, which provided her fellowship at the National Humanities Center, where this essay was written.

TWELVE

Impasse in Feminist Thought?

J. G. Morawski

IN ACADEME, the culture of feminism is indeed a "hot" one. In fact, as a culture, feminist studies approach ideals of intellectual life that have been articulated during the twentieth century. There is an unending buffet of notable new texts to read, a large number of debates in need of resolution, endless displays of new data, and monthly debuts of sparkling new scholars. And then there are the myriad rediscoveries of neglected ideas and people—from the social science of Charlotte Perkins Gilman to the reading of social arrangements described by Woolf, de Beauvoir, and the Brontës.

In the culture of feminist studies, entertainment for the intelligentsia is stellar: the street theater of a (female) lecturer in drag, the magical denuding of canon (Marx, Freud), and even the local village struggles over hiring, tenuring, and sustaining academic programs. In terms taken from the sociology of knowledge, here is a knowledge structure in the making; here is a progressive period of "disciplinary utopia," marked by innovations in language, procedure rules, work practices, and hierarchies of power.[1]

It would seem that the culture of feminist thought is vigorous. Yet members of this society often act otherwise, and if nowhere else but at the edge of consciousness, many sense barriers, hard problems that threaten to impede future inquiry. As topics of discussion, these impediments typically receive comment near the end of seminars, just in time not to be examined in any detail. They similarly emerge in short paragraph caveats unobtrusively nestled in essays. I would like to identify five of these barriers (although not all work is plagued by all five) that recur in texts and conversations. They are presented as a preview to identifying a paradox that lies behind them. More importantly, this apparent paradox leads us to recall certain critical features of feminism that can dismantle the problems. This essay, then, ultimately concerns the possibilities of feminist deconstruction and reconstruction of some central ingredients in modern thought.

MANNED SPACE PROGRAM

LIKE Star Wars, the manned space program symbolizes the contemporary political climate of the United States. It is in this climate that feminists, especially those who have been around for the duration, mourn the recent losses in affirmative action programs, the ERA, attitudes toward abortion and reproductive rights, and a host of legislative reforms that negatively affect large numbers of American women.[2] The "new" conservatism is no longer considered a passing fad, and as symbolized in continuation of the manned space program, the cultural ideals are of manly heroism, rugged individualism, domination of nature, and territorial conquest. The girls go along mostly for the ride. Perhaps more than any other problem I will discuss, these symbols block feminist activities. Yet these barriers have existed longer than the new feminism and we must ask why we now see them as taller and feel a paralysis in seeing them.

EXPERIENCE

THE NEW wave of feminism originating in the 1960s had as a central mandate a reliance on women's experience. Personal experiences stand as the final test of theory and arbiter of truth. It had become evident that conventional theory, in social science as in literature, is male-centered and hence provides an inaccurate account of human affairs. Women's experience represented a more honest empiricism (and no small amount of liberal humanism). However, in following these premises, feminist scholarship risked the associated vices of essentialism (my reported experiences reflect the essence of my being a woman) and reductionism, typically taking the form of psychologism (my reported experiences are subjective, that is, simply reflect my psychological being).[3]

The two notable consequences of this reliance on experience, essentialism and psychologism, actually reproduce familiar barriers. In the privileging of "women's" experience and identity, it was possible to be seduced into embracing the very categories that sustain women's oppression. As Elaine Marks reminded us, it will "not allow us to do more than repeat our litany of woe, a repetition of clichés and stereotypes about victims and heroines."[4]

Second, taking only experiences (accounts of experiences) as working evidence teases us into mimetic psychological explanations that, at best, result in blaming the victims or exonerating the martyr. All too often psychological reductionism has lured us even further astray into the realm of psychoanalytic interpretation. It is the perfect twentieth-century thing to do. Here too lies the perpetuation of cultural categories that not only oppress women but work to invalidate women's rebellions against their oppression. While feminist psychoanalysis attempts to correct these phallocentric and patriarchal moves endemic to the field, it typically fails to comprehend the extent to which these prejudices are psychoanalysis itself. Thus, object-relations theories continue to recognize concepts of personal identity/individualism that, along with their visible ethnocentrism, reiterate male-centered fictions about a fixed and singular identity. The theories perpetuate categories of the biological family and stereotypical notions about the lives and experiences of infants and their caretakers.[5]

FANCY THEORY

ANOTHER set of purported ailments is a reaction to the development of dense and complex feminist theories. While some such complaints would seem to be made by those most committed to the recovery of experience without the biases of male-centered theory, they do not all come from that contingent. Some, like Barrie Thorne, see a new orthodoxy of "Feminist Theorists" who manage to rise to the top in a manned academia, primarily due to their mimicry of prestigious fancy theories rather than their commitments to political activism or pedagogy.[6] A related concern is the fancy Feminist Theorists' reproduction of orthodox, male-centered models. Such theories may serve to validate and sustain androcentric views more than the inventors of these unliberated theories realize. As with the use of psychoanalytic models, the risks of slipping into conventional presuppositions are high.

DISCIPLINE(S)

WHILE feminist work may be a current item within many domains of inquiry, the actual acceptance of this work is not secured. Especially in the social sciences, what passes as intriguing work may not have staying power. In practice, we are all too familiar with the story of the feminist scholar who is lauded for her ground-breaking project but rejected (from tenure or rehiring) because her research did not fit into the existing array of disciplinary interests. In such cases we are reminded that disciplines are constituted by procedural rules, by protocols for developing understanding of some phenomena and not others. The production of knowledge is thus rule-bounded, and questioning of the rules will be resisted.

Let me illustrate by turning to psychology, where we can see how a discipline defines its boundaries and uses discipline to maintain them. Despite a substantial current of feminist psychology over the last fifteen years, there has been little impact on the traditional methods, content, and theories.[7] Thus, the foremost textbook author in social psychology could write unabashedly in 1986 about the "necessarily sedentary" lives of all women prior to contraceptive technology and simply pronounce that feminist psychologists' explorations of "androgyny" are fundamentally mistaken.[8] In the very same spirit of boundaries, joint positions in women's studies and psychology cause severe schizophrenia in candidates who must partition themselves or be partitioned into their feminism and their psychology.

MIRED LANGUAGE

LANGUAGE has been a central subject of feminist analysis, from semiotic or textual feminism to elaboration of the meanings of women's language. It has become apparent that signifiers are not tied to some material signified, but shape the signified, and that writing and texts are themselves the product of how we "read" experiences. Feminists have examined the linguistic categories that break the world into false symmetries and dualisms that inevitably set into concrete categories of reality. And researchers have demonstrated how relations of power between men and women are expressed and maintained in conversations.[9]

Yet there are repeated instances where language becomes problematic. Even after critical deconstruction of some linguistic symbol, the analysis gets stuck. Even the successful critic of the essentialist language of cultural feminism herself becomes mired in the essence of mere linguistic categories like life/death and desire.[10] A similar miring affects the radical French feminist in her deconstruction of value-free science.[11] The feminist scientist who challenges the language of "objectivity" cannot help but return to that word when designing an alternative, feminist philosophy of science.[12] Attempts to distinguish "sex" and "gender" have a way of ultimately reconfirming the existence of meaningful natural difference. The feminist psychologists who renounce the linguistic dichotomy of masculine and feminine for the nondualistic personality prototype of "androgyny" in the process establish a privileged signifier, the new she-man and he-woman, who seems to value traditional masculine attributes while denigrating what is traditionally feminine.[13] To claim androgyny as a liberated signifier requires more than quantitative evidence and high-tech measurement instruments. Rather, it requires substantial changes in existing social arrangements. Such examples show that playing with language can result in played-out language; the traditional usage of language frequently wins.[14]

PARADOXES

I ENUMERATE these troubled issues en route to dismissing them. But such a dismissal project first requires an appreciation of a certain paradox surrounding the problems. Over the last several decades feminists have joined other all-purpose intellectual "subversives" in the rejection of theory as an ideological construction, a concoction made from a false realism combined with certain political or social interests.[15] Yet feminism has produced theory. The apparent paradox seems to dissolve with the realization that, in feminist discourse, our boundaries and theoretical commitments are self-consciously shaped and connected to our practical undertakings or struggles. One way to put it is that feminist theory is vision guided by experience (being) and experience corrected by vision. Theorizing is constituted self-consciously by engagement, by particular social relations, and by specific historical moments. Theories, then, are social phenomena produced in particular historical locations. Feminist ventures with theory are fundamentally different from those that have gone before. For feminists to talk of theory is not to speak of the same abstracting game as our forefathers understood. Certainly "grand," "general," "unified," or whatever expectations that generally are affixed to theory generally have no central place in these feminist ambitions.

Feminist work in the philosophy of science has elaborated several additional paradoxes apparent in developing feminist theory and epistemology. Sandra Harding has enumerated the different means by which feminism, an avowedly political or interested enterprise, can be employed to realize more objective science.[16] Elizabeth Fee has suggested how feminist perspectives can simultaneously claim that conventional science produces successful ways to understand and control objects in the world while paradoxically also being biased science. Fee sees this success as dependent upon and created through particular human relationships and advocates the development of multiple approaches that focus on these *relations of power*.[17] Donna Haraway has examined a related paradox whereby feminists realize that science is irreducibly ideological and masculine and yet remain committed to developing a successor science that is more accurate and coherent. This contradiction can be reconciled by seeing science as *politics*, by recognizing science as a *social process of making narratives* "where meanings are contested and stabilized for a time through the productive relations of knowledge and power."[18] Although these thinkers differ in the particulars of their solutions, they share a realization that the apparent epistemological paradoxes are fundamentally *social*, and that once recognized as such, they require resolution through the reconsideration and alteration of existing social relations of power.

TRANSFORMING EPISTEMOLOGIES

THE FIVE problems I described previously are no exception: they too ensue from socially constituted belief. In fact, we have participated in producing barriers to feminist work and have built them partially and paradoxically with the materials of our successes. This production has happened for complicated reasons, not the least of which is a premature sense of completion at having permeated the intellectual structures of power and the consequential tendency to take a comfortable place within those structures. However, my intent is not to dissect the reasons why we, as feminists, have engaged in such constructions, but simply to suggest how they might be undone. The new theorizing of feminism already has the capabilities to dismantle barriers that seem to plague our current conversations. Yet somehow these capabilities often get displaced or depreciated at critical moments. At such moments imaginative visions give way to all too familiar versions of reality—particularly to fabrications of an accessible (and controllable) empirical world along with a determinant and natural order—that are the basis of conventional epistemology.

It is precisely at these moments that the feminist theorist engages in a "philosophical seduction." As identified by Ruby Riemer, this philosophical seduction (of the daughter) is simply the adoption of masculine rules that are often alien to women's experience, rules that somehow contain "a promise of selfhood and inclusion in some philosophical community which, as women alone, they fully fail to achieve."[19] Although Riemer poses such seduction as typically occurring during an early stage in feminist political theorizing, there is nothing to prohibit it from happening at other times. Such seduction and its resultant epistemological slippage can be prevented by recollecting past lessons, particularly those learned during the last several decades. That is, masculine models, like patriarchy itself, are constituted and validated through social arrangements of power. They are warranted and sustained through the production of knowledge that continually affirms what counts as reality, truth, and progress and, consequently, what counts as experience, identity, desire, and "the good." Hence, both *epistemology* and *subjectivity* are given in these models, determined essentially through their underlying social relations. An unfortunately recurrent example of philosophical and ontological seduction is some feminists' recourse to psychoanalysis as the explanatory key to women's nature and subjugation. Yet adopting psychoanalytic models obscures even further the power relations that determine both psychological experience and theorizing about that experience.[20] Put simply, knowledge is constructed along with social power: having knowledge gives individuals social power, and individuals who hold certain social power can make claims to veridical knowledge.

These lessons continue, for they have entailed the realization of not just the local and socially situated nature of all knowledge, but also its plurality, dialectics, and tentativeness. Feminist work also has incorporated awareness of the reflexivity of knowledge. With such awareness, it is possible to attend to the importance of forgetting, denying, and deceiving—central processes that structure our intellectual efforts to interpret the world. Reflexivity occurs most obviously whenever humans are both observers (interpreters) and objects of observation (or interpretation). This simple act of turning back on oneself, however, has considerable implications. Initially self-conscious of their place as women in a predominately male intellectual world, feminist thinkers have been attentive to the workings and consequences of reflexivity. Paramount among these consequences is the prevalence of androcentrism in the canonical philosophical and social science paradigms. Feminist scholars have developed elaborate interpretive instruments for detecting and understanding how masculine self-images and desires permeate intellectual work. Thus, feminist philosophers have shown how the root concepts of individualism and human rights are androcentric and fail to encompass all humanity within their definitions.[21] Feminists studying science have uncovered ways in which masculine psychology has served as a framework for the development of what are taken as appropriate scientific methods and attitudes.[22] These analyses go even further in locating what has been re-pressed in these male-centered reflexive processes. For instance, Jane Flax has analyzed the male psychology of domination over or repression of others as it resurfaces in philosophical precepts, particularly in its proble-matizing of "others" and the relationships between basic constructs of mind and body, subject and object.[23] Feminist theorists have not ignored the reflexive properties of their own work; recent scholarship has been especially self-critical of its precepts, including some negligence concern-ing third-world women or women of color,[24] the tendency to compre-hend primarily psychological needs of middle-class professional women[25] or adoption of concepts of personhood that apply only to normally-abled women.[26]

Understanding the social production of knowledge, the attendant power relations, the seductive moments, and the reflexive processes are critical and necessary provisions to more complete transformations in epistemologies and theories. These understandings ground feminist opportunities to engage more fully in self-consciously normative and generative thinking. In other words, deconstructive practices enable reconstructive efforts. Feminist visions can be freed from fixed intellectual goals and expectations that they be warranted solely by their supposed "feasibility," "accountabil-ity," "efficiency," or "rationality."[27] Generative reconstruction allows for the possibility that our intellectual engagements can be based upon radi-cally different proof structures, ontologies, and technologies. In summary, our visions must be guided first by refusal to discipline and then by devising means to empower the disenfranchised and otherwise to experi-ment with new ways of seeing the world. Such work is predicated on revision and renewal.

It is with such strategies, worked out initially through feminist critiques of the structure of knowledge, that feminist thinking can be used to confront the troubling problems that we manufacture or allow to intrude into ongoing conversations. The current political climate must be met not with anxiety or retrenchment but by working through the dialectic of oppression to generate alternatives. Mired language and disciplinary boundaries require us to continue resistance and to redouble our interpre-tive cunning. Likewise, the construction of feminist theory needs reflexive self-consciousness and constant reminders of the force of knowledge structures. We must not forget why experience became a central focus of feminist analysis, yet we must simultaneously recall how experience itself is structured by the social relations and language of patriarchical culture. Feminist analysis of experience can account for these conditions while experimenting with even more imaginative and powerful interpretations.

INCLUDING FANTASY

THESE claims are hardly original, but they nevertheless risk the label of fantasy. In literature fantasy refers to the visionary, the speculative. In psychology it also refers to an inability to comprehend reality, the world-as-it-is. However, women are not always participatory subjects in this fixed world, much in the same way as Adrienne Harris has shown that woman cannot be subject in discourse on baseball: "To speak as woman about baseball is to be immediately entangled with baseball's ideological function and to be at odds with it."[28] She is its other, the fantasy side of male reality. Thus to women, fantasy may offer an entrance into her subjectivity. Above all, fantasy predicates transformation.

There are instances when the more pejorative sense of fantasy has a certain legitimacy. That is, women cannot just dream their way out of the political reality of sexist legislation or disciplinary rules. In these instances, other actions are necessary. This is where active resistance, political strategies, and even cunning refusal come in. We need to use the skills and strategies that enable us to pass through points of greatest resistance, to arrive at places where our refusal to participate in traditions and our visions of new worlds can be elaborated.

At the center of feminist thinking is imagination. Imagination enabled some women to speculate about different worlds, and it thus initiated the makings of a world where we now can work in academe, or at least at its periphery. Although rooted in a negative comprehension of the fixed boundaries of language, writing, and experience, feminist imagination is a positive venture. As illustrated by the rally at Greenham Common, feminist science fiction, and distopic fantasy, feminist imagination can be born from nightmares as well as majestic blueprints.[29] Such imagination permeates feminist work, from the study of the body as a situated place of inscription to the artful twistings of psychoanalysis and the logical demonstrations that the logic of science is sexed. Instead of being distracted by the snags of current conversations, we might recall past lessons. Then we can return without interruption to our imaginative work. Like "cyborg feminists,"[30] we can resist a singular identity, embrace the inventions of modern experience, and extend our destruction and reconstruction of consciousness.

NOTES

1. Warren Hagstrom uses the term *disciplinary utopia* to refer to that period of a developing discipline when its members speculate on the knowledge and practical achievements to come. For a review of recent thinking in the sociology of knowledge see Kuklick, H. (1938). "The sociology of knowledge: Retrospect and prospect." *Annual Review of Sociology* 9: 287–310; Shapin, S. (1982). "History of science and its sociological reconstruction." *History of Science* 20: 157–211. Analysis of knowledge structures is a common, although not always elaborated, feature of feminist scholarship.

2. For an example of such response to current politics see Fine, M. (1985). "Reflections of a feminist psychology of women: Paradoxes and prospects." *Psychology of Women Quarterly* 9: 167–83.

3. Haraway, D. (1985). "A manifesto for cyborgs: Science, technology, and socialist feminism in the 1980s." *Socialist Review* 15 (2): 65–107; Marks, E. (1985). "Feminism's wake." *Boundary Two* 14: 99–111.

4. Marks. "Feminism's wake." p. 105.

5. On the ethnocentrism of object-relations theories see Gewertz, D. (1984). "The Tchambuli views of persons: A critique of individualism in the works of Mead and Chodorow." *American Anthropologist* 86: 615–29.

6. Quoted from Sternhell, C. (1985). "Questions of difference: Three challenges to women's studies." *Ms* 14 (4): 83.

7. Brinton Lykes, M., and Stewart, A. J. (in press) "Evaluating the feminist challenge in psychology, 1963–1983." *Psychology of Women Quarterly;* Morawski, J. G. (1987). "Troubled quest for masculinity, femininity and androgeny." In P. Shaver (Ed.). *Annual Review of Personality and Social Psychology,* vol. 7. Beverly Hills: Sage.

8. Brown, R. (1986). *Social psychology: The second edition.* New York: Free Press.

I am indebted to the members of the Wesleyan Women's Studies Faculty Seminar, and to Robert Steele and Thomas Palley for their critical conversations.

9. A fine collection of such studies is McConnell-Ginet, S., Borker, R. and Furman, N. (Eds.). (1980). *Women and language in literature and society.* New York: Praeger.

10. Marks. "Feminism's wake."

11. Irigaray, L. (1985). "Is the subject of science sexed?" *Cultural Critique* 1: 73–88.

12. Keller, E. F. (1985). *Reflections on science and gender.* New Haven: Yale University Press.

13. Morawski. "Troubled Quest."

14. For a historical case study of the limitations of appropriating masculine language and imagery, see Smith-Rosenberg, C. (1985). *Disorderly conduct: Visions of gender in Victorian America.* New York: Knopf, especially pp. 245–96.

15. The expression of "all-purpose subversives" is Clifford Geertz's. For an account of these figures and their paradoxical see Skinner, Q. (Ed.). (1985). *The return of grand theory in the human sciences.* Cambridge: Cambridge University Press.

16. Harding, S. (1986). *The science question in feminism.* Ithaca: Cornell University Press.

17. Fee, E. (1986). "Critiques of modern science: The relationship of feminism to other radical epistemologies." In R. Bleier (Ed.). *Feminist approaches to science.* New York: Pergamon Press, pp. 42–56; Fee, E. (1983). "Women's nature and scientific objectivity." In M. Lowe and R. Hubbard (Eds.). *Woman's nature: Rationalization of inequality.* New York: Pergamon, pp. 9–28.

18. Haraway, D. (1986). "Primatology is politics by other means." In R. Bleier (Ed.). *Feminist approaches to science.* New York: Pergamon, pp. 77–118.

19. Riemer, R. (1986). "Political thought: A re-visioning." *Women and Politics* 6: 57–67.

20. In citing this example of discourse deconstruction and the avoidance of seduction it must be admitted that the feminist challenges to psychoanalysis yet remain a truly minority view. See Bart, P. (1984). "Review of Chodorow's *The reproduction of mothering.*" In J. Trebilcot (Ed.). *Mothering: Essays in feminist theory.* Totowa, N.J.: Rowman and Allanheld, pp. 147–52; Fee, E. (1985). "Critiques of modern science"; Lerman, H. (1986). *A mote in Freud's eye: From psychoanalysis to the psychology of women.* New York: Springer; Steele, R. (1985). "Paradigm lost: Psychoanalysis after Freud." In C. Buxton (Ed.). (1985). *Points of view in the modern history of psychology.* New York: Academic, pp. 221–58.

21. Among a number of works in this area are Jaggar, A. M. (1983). *Feminist politics and human nature.* Totowa, N.J.: Rowman and Allanheld; Scheman, N. (1983). "Individualism and the objects of psychology." In S. Harding and M. B. Hintikka (Eds.). *Discovering reality.* Dordrecht: Reidel, pp. 225–44.

22. There is now a substantial literature on the gender-bias of modern science. See Bleier, R. (1984). *Science and gender: A critique of biology and its theories on women.* New York: Pergamon; Keller, E. F. (1985). *Reflections on gender and*

science. New Haven: Yale University Press; Harding. *Science question in feminism;* Merchant, C. (1980). *The death of nature*. San Francisco: Harper and Row.

23. Flax, J. (1983). *Political philosophy and the patriarchal unconscious: A psychoanalytic perspective on epistemology and metaphysics*. In S. Harding and M. B. Hintikka (Eds.). *Discovering reality*. Dordrecht: Reidel, pp. 245–82.

24. For discussions on the need to restructure feminist perspectives to give voice to feminisms of women of color or third-world women see Haraway. "Manifesto for cyborgs"; Harding. *Science question in feminism*.

25. For just one case, that of psychological androgyny, where feminist conceptualizations may reflect desires primarily of a small class of women see Morawski. "Troubled quest for masculinity."

26. See Asch, A. (1986). "Uncertain futures: Review of B. K. Rotherman, *The tentative pregnancy*." *The Women's Review of Books* 4: 16–17.

27. For feminist criticism of conventional epistemology and social philosophy see Gould, C. G. (Ed.). (1984). *Beyond domination: New perspectives on women and philosophy*. Totowa, N.J.: Rowman and Allanheld; Harding, S., and Hintikka, M. B. (Eds.). (1983). *Discovering reality: Feminist perspectives on epistemology, metaphysics, methodology, and philosophy of science*. Dordrecht: Reidel; Jaggar. *Feminist politics*.

28. "Women, baseball, and words." *PsychCritique* (1985) 1: 35–54.

29. Atwood, M. (1986). *The handmaid's tale* and Elgin, S. H. (1984). *Native Tongue* exemplify recent fictional representations of ultimate patriarchal cultures. In their portrayals of women who live their lives as property, the authors explore women's refusal, denial, and revolt.

30. Haraway. "Manifesto for cyborgs."

Name Index

Subject Index